EXPL... RIDA

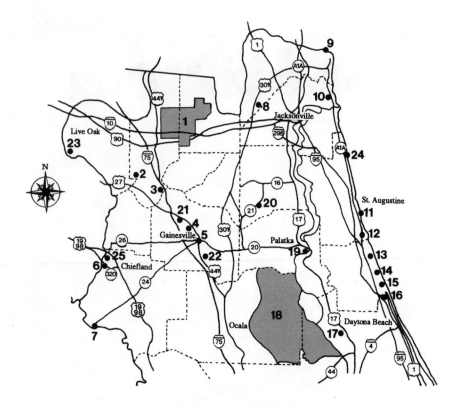

Exploring Wild North Florida

1. Osceola National Forest
2. Ichetucknee Springs State Park
3. O'Leno State Park
4. Devil's Millhopper State Geological Site
5. Gainesville's Nature Parks
6. Manatee Springs State Park
7. Lower Suwannee River and Cedar Keys National Wildlife Refuges
8. Cary State Forest
9. Fort Clinch State Park
10. Talbot Islands State Parks
11. Anastasia State Recreation Area
12. Faver-Dykes State Park
13. Washington Oaks State Gardens
14. Gamble Rogers Memorial State Recreation Area at Flagler Beach
15. Bulow Creek State Park
16. Tomoka State Park
17. Lake Woodruff National Wildlife Refuge
18. Ocala National Forest
19. Ravine State Gardens
20. Gold Head Branch State Park
21. San Felasco Hammock State Preserve
22. Paynes Prairie State Preserve
23. Peacock Springs State Recreation Area
24. Guana River State Park and Wildlife Management Area
25. Andrews Wildlife Management Area

Exploring Wild North Florida

GIL NELSON

PINEAPPLE PRESS
Sarasota, Florida

Dedicated to my mother
Mary Alyce Nelson
and to the memory of my father
Louis Athniel "Ike" Nelson

Library of Congress Cataloging-in-Publication Data

Nelson, Gil, 1949–
    Exploring wild north Florida / Gil Nelson.
        p.   cm.
    Includes bibliographical references and index.
    ISBN 1-56164-091-3 (sc : alk. paper)
    1. Natural history—Florida.   2. Natural areas—Florida—
Guidebooks.   I. Title.
QH105.F6N44   1995   95-22761
    508.759—dc20   CIP

Inquiries should be addressed to:
Pineapple Press, Inc.
PO Drawer 16008
Southside Station
Sarasota, Florida 34239

Composition by Octavo
Printed and bound by Quebecor/Fairfield, Fairfield, Pennsylvania

10 9 8 7 6 5 4 3 2 1

CONTENTS

VII. ADDITIONAL SITES AND INFORMATION 177

MAPS

ACKNOWLEDGMENTS

I would like to thank the many people who have offered their assistance to me throughout the writing of this book. Foremost among them are my wife, Brenda, and daughter, Hope. Each has been a consistent source of encouragement and I cherish their patience and love.

I would also like to thank Melissa Johnson, Hope Nelson, and Erin Yaw for allowing me to use the photograph of them hiking through the Osceola National Forest as the book's cover. Our time afield was especially enjoyable, and I appreciate their cooperation.

I would especially like to thank Dr. Walt Schmidt, Dr. Tom Scott, and Frank Rupert, all with the Florida Geological Survey, for their help in clarifying my understanding of Florida's geology. Their willingness to talk with me as well as to review and re-review parts of the manuscript is sincerely appreciated.

I owe a special thanks to Barbara Cook, Gail Fishman, Vic Heller, and Fritz Wettstein. All read and commented on parts of the manuscript. Barbara also helped with field work and provided information about Florida's three national forests, and Vic was a ready resource for information about Florida's wildlife management areas and native wildlife.

Others who assisted me with information and technical expertise about individual parks and natural areas include Randy Brown, Dana Bryan, Doug Carter, Bert Charest, Michael Evans, Susie Hallowell, Jeff King, Wendy Lechner, Ken Litzenberger, John O'Mera, Paul Perras, Leon Rhodes, Linda Tuffin, Matt Weinell, and R. West. I would like to thank all of these individuals as well as the many other rangers and staff at Florida's state parks, state and national forests, and natural preserves for the many helpful hints about the regions they serve and the parks they manage.

The line illustrations in this book were provided by Marvin and Lee Cook and their staff at Wilderness Graphics, Inc. in Tallahassee. Their willingness to assist me with this project is much appreciated. Working with them is always a pleasure. David Simms provided all of the maps. His easy manner contributed to an enjoyable working relationship, and his penchant for quality added considerably to the book.

I would also like to express appreciation to Su Jewell. Her outstanding book *Exploring Wild South Florida* provided the model after which this book is patterned and in many ways made the current book possible. I appreciated being able to share successes and challenges with her as this book, and her newest book, *Exploring Wild Central Florida,* progressed.

Last, but perhaps most importantly, I would like to thank June Cussen of Pineapple Press for offering me the opportunity to write this book. Her friendly style, cooperative spirit, commitment to quality, and excellent editing made writing this, as well as its companion volume, *Exploring Wild Northwest Florida,* an especially enjoyable adventure.

INTRODUCTION

Northern Florida (including that portion of the state that is often referred to as northeast Florida) is a magnificent and enchanted land. With topography that ranges from rolling hills and sandy ridges to swampy flatlands and boggy prairies, it is an area replete with opportunities for outdoor exploration. This region draws residents and visitors alike into a fascinating world that encourages the pursuit of nature study and outdoor recreation as a rewarding and encompassing hobby.

Exploring northern Florida can consume a lifetime. From the Atlantic Ocean on the east to the Suwannee River on the west, from the Georgia state line to the southernmost boundary of the sprawling Ocala National Forest, there are literally hundreds of locations that offer alluring glimpses of the Sunshine State's natural beauty. Many of these sites still reflect the way Florida may have appeared in more primitive times. Each has its own special attraction and can be revisited time and again with little fear of saturation.

The intense and recurring exploration of this relatively limited geographic area is the fundamental theme of this book. The more one visits Florida's natural areas, the more one learns. Each field trip offers something new. Every revisit allows one to look at familiar places in new ways. With each visit comes closer observation that reveals new discoveries, offers new insights about our natural ecological systems, and fosters a deeper understanding of our native environments. The more familiar we become with the intricacies of our special places, the more clearly we come to understand the interrelationships that make Florida special, and the more we come to appreciate the state as a dynamic, integrated whole rather than a collection of unrelated geographic entities.

I
OVERVIEW

HOW TO USE THIS BOOK

This book is a study guide to the natural bounty of north Florida. Its central purpose is to encourage readers to explore, to discover, to learn, and to develop a more comprehensive understanding and keener appreciation of this distinctive region.

Chapter 1 begins with important tips for exploring north Florida, then outlines the precautions one should take for ensuring enjoyment. Chapter 2 offers an overview of the region's landforms and topographic structure. Chapter 3 provides a conceptual framework for better understanding the region's several natural habitats. Chapter 4 introduces the reader to the native wildlife, with special emphasis on the more interesting species. Chapters 5 and 6 describe 25 major field sites that represent the best of north Florida's special places.

Chapter 7 includes an annotated list of 16 additional field sites that also provide nature discovery opportunities, as well as several lists of the more common plant and animal species normally found in north Florida habitats. These lists help readers focus on the species that are likely to be seen on a particular field trip or in a particular area. These lists will help you use your other field guides more effectively, while the discussions of the various field sites will help you fit your understanding of these species into a larger frame of reference and a more meaningful context.

The reference list at the end of the book contains a bibliography for further study. Many of the books and publications listed there will lead you to new discoveries about Florida's natural areas. Some of these books are commercial volumes and can be found in bookstores or ordered from their publishers.

Others are little-known government publications available only from the federal or state agencies that produced them, or in the government documents sections of local libraries.

Whether you are a longtime Floridian, a new resident to the state, or a short-term visitor, this book will enhance your study of the northern part of the state. Beginning and advanced amateurs alike will find its chapters broadening and its suggested field trips stimulating. It is hoped that you will find its pages rewarding reading and its content a ready reference to which you can return time and again.

PLANNING YOUR TRIP

Major Highways and Airports

Getting to north Florida is not particularly difficult. The area is crisscrossed by highways and served by several major airports.

For those driving to the state, three interstate highways provide the quickest access. I-95 parallels the eastern coast and provides passage to much of north Florida as well as to sites along the Atlantic Ocean. I-75 bisects the state east and west from Valdosta, Georgia, to Ocala, Florida, and offers the easiest path to the region's central locations. I-10 traverses the entire northern part of the state from Pensacola to Jacksonville and is a speedy approach from the west.

The interstate highways are the newest and most traveled of north Florida's major highways. Though they will get you to your destination quickly and with little confusion, they discourage a more leisurely, "stop-and-go" travel agenda, and they bypass much of what makes north Florida special. For explorers, the older roadways are by far the better choice.

US Highway 98/19 from Fanning Springs to Inglis provides access to the west coast areas. US 441 from the Florida–Georgia line through Lake City, Gainesville, and Ocala, and US 301 from just west of Jacksonville to Ocala are excellent routes that offer glimpses of what Gloria Jahoda has glorified as "the other Florida," those areas that are characterized by a slower-paced, more pastoral lifestyle. US 90 is also a good road. It parallels I-10 between the Suwannee River and Jacksonville but is much less congested than I-10 and more reminiscent of north Florida as it existed 30 years ago. For those visiting the east coast, US A1A extends from Fernandina Beach to Miami and is seldom far from the edge of the sea. It is a crowded thoroughfare along much of its extent south of Jacksonville but passes directly adjacent to several of the east coast's best state parks. Several other interior highways are also excellent for backroads travel, including Florida 100 from Lake City to Palatka, US 17 from Jacksonville to DeLand, Florida 21 from Starke to Ocala, US 129 from Jasper to Chiefland, Alternate US 27 from Chiefland to Ocala, and Florida 40 from Ocala to Daytona Beach.

Visitors arriving by air can choose from several airports, depending on which part of north Florida they plan to visit. Jacksonville is the destination for those who want to explore the upper northeastern coast and north central parts of the state. The Gainesville airport, though small, offers access to the central part of north Florida. Orlando International, though outside the coverage area of this book, is probably the best airport for exploring the southern part of the region, including the Ocala National Forest. All of these airports are serviced by several rental car companies. Since there are few organized tours and no mass transportation to most of the places described in the following chapters, a rental car is a must.

Weather

North Florida's weather is more variable than that of the state's more tropical regions. Though the average annual temperature across much of the region is in the upper 60s to low 70s, during a typical year the thermometer may fluctuate from winter lows in the mid-20s (at least in the northernmost sections) to the mid- to upper 90s, or even the low 100s, during June, July, August, and into September. Daily summertime temperatures average in the low 80s as they do throughout much of the state. Daily winter temperatures average in the 40s in the northernmost part of the region and somewhat higher the nearer you approach Ocala.

As might be expected, the southernmost regions of northern Florida, such as those areas near Ocala, have milder winter temperatures than do more northern areas. The latter areas may experience first frost near the beginning of November in average years, about one month earlier than for regions near Ocala. The more northern counties also have at least 25 more frost days in an average winter than do Marion and its nearby counties.

Because of the mitigating influences of the Gulf of Mexico and Atlantic Ocean, the temperatures along the coastlines are seldom quite as hot or cold as more inland locations. The lack of breeze throughout the inland parts of north Florida can make a midsummer's day a wilting experience. However, such days are often perfect for canoeing one of the region's spring-fed streams or meandering rivers.

Rainfall also fluctuates on an annual basis. The fall and early winter are typically the driest times of the year; late spring and summer the wettest. Annual rainfall varies radically from year to year but typically averages between 55 and 65 inches. The major rain events during summer are temporary but intense thunderstorms that most often occur in mid- to late afternoon and last less than an hour. Winter rain events are more often associated with a passing cold front and often last an entire day or evening.

Fishing Licenses

State saltwater fishing licenses are required, with the following exceptions: 1) an individual under 16 years of age, 2) an individual fishing from a charter boat that has a vessel saltwater fishing license, 3) a Florida resident 65 years of age or older, and 4) a Florida resident fishing in saltwater from land or from a structure fixed to the land. Residents may obtain a ten-day, one-year, five-year, or lifetime license, and nonresidents may obtain a three-day, seven-day, or one-year license. Licenses are also required for freshwater fishing. The "cane pole law" allows a person to fish without a license in the county of his or her residence, with a pole not equipped with a reel, and using live or natural bait (catch and size limits still apply). Licenses may be obtained from county tax collectors' offices or from bait and tackle shops.

The State Park System

The many state parks (including recreation areas, preserves, and reserves) are maintained to keep the lands in or restore them to their conditions when the first Europeans arrived. The historic sites preserve the cultural heritage. Fees are charged at most sites. People who plan to explore a number of parks, or who live near a park that they visit frequently, should consider buying an annual individual or family pass (available at any state park).

The parks are open from 8 A.M. to sunset every day of the year including holidays. The parks close at sundown, which means that the gate may close at an odd time. Parks with campgrounds generally allow check-ins after sunset. Primitive campsites have no facilities, and campers must pack out their trash. Pets are permitted only in designated areas and must be kept on a 6-foot (maximum) hand-held leash. Pets are not allowed in swimming, camping, beach, or concession areas. Guide dogs for the disabled are welcomed in all areas. Horses (where permitted) must have proof of a recent negative Coggins test.

The National Wildlife Refuge and National Forest System

The National Wildlife Refuge system is composed of over 500 refuges across the country. Many, such as the ones included in this book, were established to protect habitat for migratory birds, such as waterfowl. Unlike national parks and national forests, refuges are created solely for protecting natural resources. Only compatible activities are permitted. This is why some refuges offer few interpretive activities or public amenities. Many have educational facilities, such as a visitor center. Some offer guided tours. None of Florida's refuges permit camping. When you visit a refuge, come prepared with drinking water and anything else you may need. Pets may or may not be permitted (see separate entry or call the refuge to confirm).

The national forest system was originally established to provide renewable timber resources. However, through the years the U.S. Forest Service has expanded its objectives to include a multi-use approach to managing the lands under its control. Hunting, fishing, camping, hiking, backpacking, and wildlife observation are encouraged in most national forests (including those in Florida), and a number of national forests provide protection for national wilderness areas and areas of special historical, geological, or natural significance.

Purchasers of a federal Duck stamp (available at post offices and refuges; currently $15) are allowed free admission to all national wildlife refuges. Duck stamps are good for one year from July 1 to June 30, and nonhunters may purchase one. The funds from the stamps are used to buy habitat for more refuges.

Purchasers of a Golden Eagle pass (currently $25), good for one year from the date of purchase, are allowed free admission to any federal fee area. This includes all national parks, monuments, seashores, historic sites, and national wildlife refuges anywhere in the United States. Handicapped individuals may obtain a free Golden Access pass (good for free admission to any federal fee area). Senior citizens may obtain a Golden Age pass for a modest one-time fee, good for free admission to any federal fee area. All passes may be obtained at any federal fee area.

Maps

Several maps are useful for getting around in northern Florida. The most comprehensive and compact is the state's official road map, which may be obtained by addressing a request to the Florida Department of Commerce, Collins Building, Tallahassee, FL 32304.

In addition to the official road map, the Florida Department of Transportation also produces detailed black-and-white maps for each of Florida's 67 counties. These may be obtained by writing the department at 605 Suwannee St., Mail Station 12, Tallahassee, FL 32399-0415. There is a small fee for each map but they are well worth the expenditure.

DeLorme Publishing Company produces the *Florida Atlas and Gazetteer*. It is an oversized softcover booklet but has color maps and is an excellent reference. For information, write to DeLorme Publishing Co., P.O. Box 298, Freeport, Maine 04032.

Finally, many of the larger federal installations, such as the national forests, produce very good maps. Information about these maps is given with the descriptions of the areas.

LOCAL PRECAUTIONS

Snakes

There are six species of poisonous snakes in Florida, five of which are found in the northern part of the state. Of these, only three are widespread or commonly encountered.

The Florida cottonmouth is the most likely poisonous snake to be found in the wetlands. Older cottonmouths are typically dark in color and their bodies often appear encircled by even darker bands; younger snakes are much lighter and may appear patterned with regular, bronze-colored splotches or bands. Like most pit vipers, the cottonmouth has a narrow neck and relatively large, triangular head. The sides of the head appear flattened, and each shows a wide black stripe running from the back of the head nearly to the nose. These wide black swabs often appear outlined below by a thin white line. Taken together, these latter characteristics provide an excellent field mark.

The eastern diamondback and dusky pygmy rattlesnakes are the more common poisonous upland species. The common name of the diamondback derives from the distinctive diamond-shaped markings along the center of its grayish back. The pygmy rattler gets its name from its small size; it seldom exceeds about 20 inches in length. The diamondback has an exceptionally large head and conspicuous "neck," and its tail is tipped with dark rattles. It is more often found in dry areas than the cottonmouth, and is most common in pine–palmetto flatwoods near the edges of the wet areas. The pygmy is common in a variety of habitats and is noted for its disagreeable disposition. It will strike with little provocation and often lies coiled along the top of fallen logs or under the edge of native vegetation.

Florida's third rattlesnake is much less common than the previous two. Restricted primarily to the counties of the extreme

Cottonmouth

north central parts of the state, the timber rattlesnake, which is also sometimes called the canebrake rattlesnake, is found only in Hamilton, Baker, Suwannee, Columbia, Union, Bradford, and Alachua counties, with an outlying population in Levy County. Its most distinctive field marks are the black zigzag bands along its back.

The eastern coral snake is the most colorful of our poisonous species. It is adorned with yellow, red, and black bands, and is easily confused with the scarlet kingsnake. The adages, "if the nose is black, its bad for Jack" and "red touch yellow, kill a fellow; red touch black, good for Jack" will help you remember two of the key distinguishing features between these species. The nose of the coral snake is black and its bright red and yellow bands are adjacent to one another, while the nose of the king snake is red and its red and yellow bands are separated by wide black bands. The coral snake has the most potent venom of any of Florida's poisonous snakes, but it is not as often encountered as the rattlesnakes or cottonmouth. In addition, it is not a pit viper and does not strike in the same way as these other species. Small coral snakes have relatively small mouths and must chew on their victims to inject their venom, though larger coral snakes can inflict serious bites without chewing. Most bites on humans are confined to areas between the victim's fingers or toes. The combination of arresting beauty and deadly venom make the coral snake a creature to be admired, but never accosted.

Much has been made of the potential of snakebites, and most of us have an unrealistic and unsupported fear of these reptiles. None of Florida's snakes are particularly aggressive, and none lie in wait for human intruders. The number of snakebites in Florida is quite few when compared to the number of people who visit the state's woodlands each year. You are much more likely to have an automobile accident on the way to your field site than a snakebite after you arrive. Nevertheless, it pays to be observant and to refrain from handling snakes if you are not sure of their identity. If you are bitten, it is important to remain calm, clean the affected area thoroughly, and seek competent medical help immediately.

Alligators

Whether because of their massive bodies or imposing appearance, alligators are one of those unfortunate animals that have developed a somewhat bad reputation. Like their reptilian relatives, the cottonmouth and eastern diamondback rattlesnake, they are often seen as sinister animals with an evil propensity for willingly and maliciously attacking unsuspecting humans. Also like their reptilian relatives, much of this fearsome reputation is factually unfounded and finds its basis mostly in a combination of myth and misunderstanding.

To be sure, alligators are powerful and effective predators with little desire, and perhaps even less ability, to discriminate among their targets. Their powerful jaws and seemingly indestructible digestive tracts have no trouble crunching and metabolizing full-grown deer, hogs, goats, dogs, and even the largest of hard-shelled turtles. Observing a ten foot bull gator noisily ingesting a turtle—bones, shell, and all—is an awesome and inspiring demonstration of primitive power.

While most of a gator's natural predation goes unnoticed, those events that include human victims always create a stir of activity and apprehension in those of us who frequent the wetlands. However, since 1948, when the Florida Game and Fresh Water Fish Commission began keeping records, there have been fewer than 175 alligator attacks on human targets. No more than

15 of these altercations have been fatal, and it is suspected that at least six of these 15 attacks may have been directed toward victims who were already dead. Even with an estimated population of over one million alligators in Florida, the probability of attack, even among avid outdoorspeople, is extremely low. The average Floridian is much more likely to fall victim to a bee sting, automobile accident, or household tragedy than to an alligator.

This is not to suggest that alligators are completely without threat. Nor is it to suggest that one should be unwary when in their company or lack vigilance when in their habitat. Gators will attack if provoked, particularly if the disturbed animal is a nesting female or a mother with newly hatched young. It is foolish to swim in waters where gators are known to occur or let children or pets venture too close to the edges of lakes where alligators live. It is also unwise to encourage an alligator's association with humans by feeding or molesting it. The most troublesome gators are those that have become accustomed to humans or have learned to associate humans with food. Alligators are, after all, wild animals that should be respected as such and left entirely to their own instincts and devices.

Insects and Ticks

Most of north Florida's insects are more appropriately considered nuisances than actual dangers. Mosquitoes, biting flies, no-see-ums, or chiggers have the potential to make a woodland outing tedious, but seldom impossible. For those susceptible to such critters, it may be wise to have a supply of repellant handy. It should be noted, however, that the use of commercial repellant is not guaranteed safe and has been associated with illness or even death in some instances. It should probably be used sparingly. Some outdoorspeople recommend nonrepellant products such as Avon's "Skin-So-Soft" and have used them with at least moderate success. Alternatively, wearing long sleeves and long pants, and taping the leg openings to the tops of boots, sometimes also proves effective.

There are at least two types of insects that should be carefully avoided. The first type includes the wasps and hornets. A number of these flying insects have excruciatingly painful stings and can cause severe, or even deadly, reactions in those who are allergic to their poison. Many wasps are difficult to see due to their cryptic nests which are often well hidden among dense foliage. Canoeists who like to poke their canoes into the woodsy edges of slow-flowing creeks should be especially careful to check overhanging limbs before disturbing them. It is also probably wise to carry a supply of over-the-counter or prescription antihistamine in your first-aid kit.

The second troublesome insect is the fire ant. Fire ants are nonnative species that build sandy mounds up to one foot tall. They are easily provoked by unwary intruders and react quickly to disturbance. Their stings lend credence to their name, and the welts they inflict can stay with the victim for several days or weeks. Fire ant mounds are easily seen if one is observant. However, since many amateur naturalists spend a considerable amount of time looking ahead, or up, or through a pair of binoculars, the mounds are also easy to stumble onto accidentally. Suffice it to say that care should be taken when walking in any disturbed sandy site.

In addition to insects, north Florida's woodlands are noted for a number of tick species. While all of the species are known to attach themselves to humans and can cause an irritating sore if not quickly found and removed, only the deer tick has the potential for real danger. This tiny relative of the spider isn't much larger than the head of a pin. Hence, it is difficult to find on the body. The deer tick is associated with lyme disease which has been reported in north Florida. The best strategy for prevention of tick bites is to be observant while on an outing and then to take careful stock of oneself upon returning home. Ticks like places where clothes fit tightly, such as around the waist. They also seem to be drawn to underarms, the groin area, and the edges of the hairline at the back of the neck.

Poisonous Plants

North Florida has only three plants that are likely to cause serious irritation on contact. These include poison ivy, poison oak, and poison sumac. The first two of these are by far the most common and are so nearly similar that the average observer does not distinguish them. Both are weakly erect shrubs or, more commonly, climbing vines that have compound leaves with three leaflets. The leaflets of both species are lobed on at least one side, though leaves of poison oak seem to display this feature more consistently. These plants are easy to identify because there are no other common woody vines that have alternate, compound leaves and only three leaflets.

Poison sumac is a seldom-encountered plant of swamps, bogs, bays, and wet woodlands. It has compound leaves with seven to 15 leaflets and reddish to tan twigs.

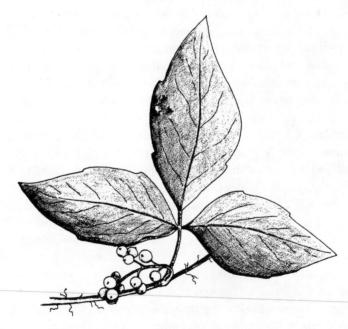

Poison Ivy

II
ORIGINS OF NORTH FLORIDA'S LANDSCAPE

Of all there is to learn about northern Florida's natural history, few things are more fascinating or intriguing than the Pleistocene origins of its geology and topography. A drive through the region's countryside leaves the impression that powerful forces have been at work in shaping its land. Gently rolling hills to the north give way to pine-studded flatlands and sandy inland dunes to the south. The large upland lakes and deep, rich soils of the Central and Northern Highlands are replaced near the coasts by a land dotted with swamps, springs, sinkholes, and scrubby coastal woods. Numerous rivers and streams thread their way through the landscape, dividing the geography into a series of natural drainage basins. Understanding the evolution of these landforms provides the underpinning for a full appreciation of the north Florida landscape as it exists today. Our floral communities, native habitats, and general ecology are all inextricably tied to and explained by the history of our land.

The story of the processes that have shaped Florida's topography necessarily begins with the history of a rising and falling sea. Several times during the last 1.6 million years, much of what is now the Florida mainland was sea bottom. As the earth alternately cooled and warmed, reacting to major climatic changes, the seas advanced and retreated in response. Massive glaciers expanded during the cooling periods, creeping down the continents, absorbing all available water, and forcing the shoreline far out into what is today the Gulf of Mexico. During the warming periods the great ice sheets melted and the glaciers released their water to the rising sea, squeezing the Florida peninsula into a narrow finger of sandy dunes that are still visible in such places as the Ocala National Forest's 200,000-acre Big Scrub region.

Four major glaciations and three corresponding interglacial periods dominated Florida during the ice ages (see Figure 2-1). Geologists say that a rise in sea level occurred during each of these interglacial intervals. During at least the Yarmouth period, and perhaps during the other two interglacials as well, the influx of water raised the sea far above its current level. Each of these seas left a mosaic of shorelines and eroding marine terraces for present-day scientists to unravel and interpret.

One accepted interpretation of these complex geological events recognizes 60 to 100 feet as the maximum extent to which the ice age seas encroached on present-day Florida real estate. The most convincing evidence for this comes from the extent and persistence of a landform known as the Cody Escarpment, a sudden drop in elevation that outlines much of northern Florida. In northern Florida this scarp follows a meandering line that begins along the upper reaches of the Suwannee River and traces the boundary of the Northern Highlands geologic province. Recognized by geologists as the most continuous topographic feature in the state, this escarpment extends across much of north Florida, passing through Tallahassee and Gainesville and turning northward just before reaching Palatka. In places there is as much as 50 feet of relief from the crest of the scarp to its toe.

Each of the seas that followed the Okefenokee Sea were successively lower in elevation. None left a mark as clear as the Cody Scarp, and none are as easy to recognize in the landscape. Their identification and description is a task for geologists who study topographic maps, fossils, sedimentology, and geologic structure.

By the time of the Wisconsin glaciation, only 20,000 years ago, the sea had dropped to at least 300 feet (some say more than 400 feet) below today's level. This low stand of the sea pushed the shoreline well seaward of its current position. With the retreat of

PLEISTOCENE	Upper	Wisconsin Glacial
		Sangamon Interglacial
		Illinoian Glacial
	Middle	Yarmouth Interglacial
		Kansan Glacial
	Lower	Aftonian Interglacial
		Nebraska Glacial

Figure 2.1.

the glaciers, the water again returned, drowning both river valleys and freshwater springs, some of which still remain well beyond the present coastline. Our present sea level was attained about 3,000 years ago and has since remained relatively stable, though there is now documented evidence that it is once again on a slow but seemingly constant rise. As a result of these past events, north Florida today is composed of a fascinating assortment of topographic features that offer outstanding opportunities for exploration. Figure 2-2 illustrates these landforms.

The Northern Highlands constitute the dominant geologic subdivision in northern Florida. Extending from the edge of the Withlacoochee River on the west, to the outskirts of Duval County on the east, this topographic high is bordered on the

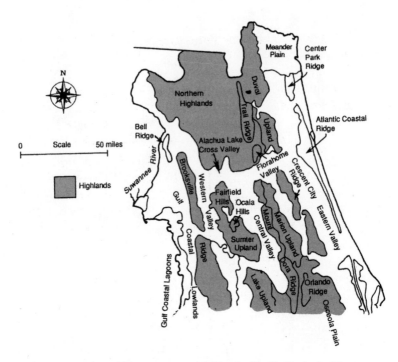

Figure 2.2. Adapted from maps provided by the Florida Geological Survey.

north by the massive Okefenokee Swamp, and is composed in its center of deep sands noted for supporting a vast pine-studded forest interrupted only by outstanding examples of swamps and forested wetlands.

On their southern edge the Northern Highlands give way to an interesting collection of sandy ridges known collectively as the Central Highlands. Although some maps suggest that these latter highlands constitute an uninterrupted landform stretching almost to Lake Okeechobee, in actuality they are composed mostly of a collection of discontinuous uplands that are now separated by a variety of lowlands, lakes, and valleys. Beginning with the Trail Ridge and Duval Upland on the western boundary of Duval County, both of which are sub-units of the Northern Highlands, a variety of similar landforms extend southward and throughout the heart of much of the central peninsula.

Of that portion of the Central Highlands included in the geographic area covered by this book, perhaps no area is more interesting or accessible than the large, sandy areas that make up much of the Ocala National Forest. Known to geologists as the Mount Dora Ridge and Marion Uplands, the pine-studded eastern portions of this sprawling federal installation are one of the most persistent remnants of the massive sand dunes that were built by ancient ocean waves during a higher stand of the sea, and that once served as an even narrower buffer between the Atlantic Ocean and Gulf of Mexico. The sand scrub country that is so common to this region today endures as an important historical reminder of our changing landforms as well as of the power of the earth's geologic processes.

East and west of the Central Highlands lie two strands of reclaimed sea bottom referred to respectively as the Gulf Coastal Lowlands and Atlantic Coastal Lowlands. The first of these units is generally clothed with flat, limestone-studded woodlands that are characteristic examples of north Florida's coastal hardwood hammock community. The gently sloping plain on which these woodlands subsist extends far out into the Gulf of Mexico, reducing wave action along the shoreline and allowing a vast expanse of tidal marsh to dominate the landscape.

The Atlantic Coastal Lowlands, on the other hand, take on a somewhat different character from their western counterpart. The western part of these lowlands is commonly referred to as the Eastern Valley, a narrow strip of relatively flat terrain that extends the length of the peninsula and is sandwiched between the ridges of the Central Highlands on the west and the aging inland dunes that make up the Atlantic Coastal Ridge on the east. Unlike the quiet Gulf waters of the upper west coast, the Atlantic Ocean is a powerhouse of energy that has long served as the primary sculptor of east coast beaches. The inland dunes that make up the Atlantic Coastal Ridge and that now stand a few miles landward of the current shoreline were the product of this ocean during yet another stand of the rising and falling sea.

It is generally agreed today that the intervening flatlands that now make up the Eastern Valley were once the floor of a shallow inland lagoon. That this lagoon existed is evidenced largely by the current position and drainage pattern of east Florida's St. Johns River and its constituent chain of lakes. Touted as the longest river in the state as well as one of the largest northward-flowing rivers in North America, it flows nearly 300 miles from its headwaters in Indian River County to Jacksonville. It drains over 8,000 square miles but falls in elevation less than 30 feet, or an average of about 0.1 ft. per mile, throughout its length. In northern Florida, the St. Johns is relatively wide, influenced by tidal influx, and largely estuarine in nature. In many ways it is a relict of the past, the final physical link between the powerful Atlantic currents and the quiet shallow waters of a bygone salt-water bay.

Throughout its extent northern Florida is unique. It offers abundance in its natural places, in its flora, and in its fauna. In many ways this abundance derives from, is dependent upon, and is explained by its present landforms and its more recent geologic past. An understanding of this past aids our exploration of this region and provides us with an organizational context into which we can fit our discoveries.

III
HABITATS AND
NATURAL
COMMUNITIES

The natural communities that make up Florida's landscape are as varied and interesting as the topography and geologic substructure that support them. At least 81 natural communities have been identified for Florida, all of which are subsumed within about 20 major ecosystems. All are readily identifiable in the field through a basic understanding of Florida's native plants. Learning the similarities, differences, and unique features of these several communities provides an important organizational scheme for exploring the state's natural endowments and for better understanding what makes its wildlands special.

A number of Florida's natural communities are found in the northern part of the state. While a detailed treatise of these systems and subsystems is beyond the scope of this book, the following paragraphs will help readers recognize the major communities they are likely to encounter in their explorations, and better appreciate what they may find in them.

SALTMARSHES

Both coasts of northern Florida are blessed with large stretches of protected saltmarsh. Long viewed only as mosquito hatcheries and waste places, saltmarsh communities are now recognized as important marine-life nursery areas and are heralded for their biological productivity. Currently protected by legislation, an accumulation of knowledge, and a generous amount of luck, many of north Florida's saltmarshes have either avoided or survived the ditching, draining, burning, and filling that have plagued similar regions along much of the eastern seaboard. Left to their natural devices and sheltered from the encroachment of advancing urbanization, they are both testimony to our growing conservation of natural things and fascinating areas in which to wander and explore.

To the uninitiated, the saltmarsh appears to be a monotonous, forbidding territory consisting of little variation. In some ways this is an accurate assessment. The several plant communities of the marsh are typically limited in species diversity and often cover large, unbroken expanses. But beneath the low canopy of each of these communities lies a veritable wilderness. Tiny nematode worms and herbivorous crustaceans consume both the juices and tissue of the living marsh grass. Snails graze on the abundant benthic algae. Bivalves consume the detritus suspended in the tidal influx. Together, these organisms constitute the lowest tier of an extensive food web that supports a surprising variety of reptiles, mammals, and birds.

Saltmarsh communities occur along both of north Florida's coasts. Although similar in the plant and animal species they support, east- and west-coast marshes differ in their structure and proximity to open water.

The west coast of Florida contains some of the finest examples of irregularly flooded saltmarsh to be found anywhere in the world. Composed chiefly of black needlerush (*Juncus roemerianus*) and several species of *Spartina*, the largest area of Gulf coastal marsh stretches nearly continuously from just north of Tampa all the way to the mouth of the Ochlockonee River.

One of the most striking features of the largest expanses of Gulf-coast marshes is their proximity to open water. Whereas east-coast marshes are normally found in protected bays, lagoons, and estuaries, those from the Ochlockonee River southward lie immediately adjacent to the open Gulf.

This phenomenon is accounted for by the region's topographic structure. The northern quadrant of the Gulf of Mexico is characterized by a relatively wide, gently sloping bottom cov-

Typical *Juncus* Saltmarsh

ered by an immense area of shallow water. With deep water lying well offshore and the area sheltered by the curvature of the coast, wave activity between Cedar Key and Alligator Point is reduced. In addition, the region contains few rivers large enough to provide significant quantities of sediment to the coastal shelf. With little sandy material from which to build islands and in a near-zero wave energy zone, beach and barrier development is discouraged in favor of the marsh. The coastal portions of the Lower Suwannee River and Cedar Keys National Wildlife Refuges, and the Waccasassa Bay State Preserve are good examples of these Gulf coastal saltmarshes.

In contrast to the Big Bend area of Florida's northern Gulf Coast, the east coast of Florida lies along a high-energy shoreline. Deep water lies only a few miles offshore, and large, powerful Atlantic waves beat against open beach. The force of these waves continually shapes and reshapes the coastal barrier strip, discouraging the development of permanent plant communities.

The landward side of east-coast barriers is separated from the mainland by brackish lagoons that are variously referred to as lagoons, rivers, lakes, bays, and sounds. Relatively shallow in depth and protected from heavy waves by the land masses of the barrier strip, these lagoons are often bordered by wide swaths of saltmarsh. They are similar to Gulf-coast marshes in plant zonation and species diversity. The striking difference lies in the dominance of smooth cordgrass (*Spartina alterniflora*). In most east-coast marshes *Spartina alterniflora* constitutes the largest portion of the marsh, extending from the watery edges of the lagoons nearly all the way to the sand flats and uplands. Since east-coast barrier lagoons always contain standing water and are replenished regularly by the salty Atlantic tides, growth of smooth cordgrass is favored over less salt-tolerant species.

ESTUARIES AND INSHORE MARINE ENVIRONMENTS

With more than 1,200 miles of saltwater shores and over two-thirds of its boundary bordering the Gulf of Mexico or Atlantic Ocean, it is not surprising that inshore marine environments constitute an important Florida resource. Shallow lagoons, salty bays, and brackish estuaries punctuate the coastline throughout the state and are counted among some of the world's most productive ecosystems.

Estuaries are essentially brackish environments that exist in the narrow zone where fresh water mixes with salt. Generally found near the mouths of major rivers, their salinity levels range dramatically throughout the year; this contributes to their importance as a primary nursery ground for a variety of sea life.

Besides being extremely productive, estuaries are also extremely fragile. Perhaps more than any other natural community, they find their success in the ecological, biological, and geological interdependence they share with surrounding habitats. They rely on coastal barriers to protect them from the onslaught of ocean waves, and on rivers for freshwater input. The fringing saltmarshes trap nutrients and reduce erosion that might otherwise cloud the salty currents; seagrass beds spread across the murky bottom, providing cover to a host of developing organisms. In various ways, the health of Florida's near-shore coastal environments is directly tied to the health of their supporting habitats.

BARRIERS, BEACHES AND DUNES

Florida's extraordinary coastline has long held a fascination for tourists and amateur naturalists alike. Its coarse quartz sand, deep blue waters, and variety of crabs, snails, insects, and other near-shore marine inhabitants make it an outstanding habitat in which to explore nature. Breaking waves run up on wide, sandy beaches against a backdrop of mountainous sand dunes topped with a smattering of sea oats and ground-hugging morning glory. Atop and just behind the dunes lies an intriguing habitat that supports a limited but interesting array of plants and animals. Unlike the saltmarsh regions discussed above, the seaward side of northeast Florida's sandy shoreline is distinguished by greater depth, stronger currents, increased quantities of sand, and higher wave energy. All of these features contribute to the formation of a magnificent coastal strip.

A cursory look at almost any state map will reveal the Atlantic shore as a long narrow strip of land separated from the mainland by a near-continuous string of saltwater inlets and lagoons, with deep water lying just offshore. Coupled with strong winds and swift currents, these deep waters produce large waves that dramatically shape and reshape the northeastern coast's massive dunes.

The most obvious coastal feature that fringes the northeast Florida coastline is its enchanting barrier islands. Completely surrounded by water and lined along their seaward faces by typical strands of Atlantic coastal dunes, they offer some of Florida's most magnificent scenery. Compared with most landforms, Florida's islands have had a surprisingly short lifespan. Whereas much of geological history is measured in terms of epochs and eras, the history of our coastal barriers is measured only in centuries. Originating within the last 6,000 years, these landforms are the result of a combination of complex processes, some of which are still not well understood.

The short geologic history of most barrier beaches suggests

Sea Oats

that they are one of the world's most restless landforms. Their tendency to appear, disappear, or relocate—often changing dramatically even within the span of a single human lifetime—is legendary. Composed chiefly of shifting sands and subjected to the powerful forces of wind and water, they are anything but permanent. Those who have built cottages, and even entire cities, on our islands—especially along the eastern seaboard—only to watch the foundations wash away with time, can certainly testify to their transience.

Although much of Florida's coastal zone has succumbed to the destructive forces of residential and commercial development, it is still possible to find at least a few preserved examples of this once much more extensive habitat. On the east coast, Fort Clinch State Park, Big and Little Talbot Island State Parks, Anastasia State Recreation Area, Matanzas Inlet, and Flagler Beach State Recreation Area are important examples.

SAND PINE SCRUB

Sand pine scrub is a xeric, or exceedingly dry, sandy community with a rather sparse understory of shrubby, evergreen oaks and an overstory of its namesake tree: sand pine. During the late Pleistocene, when conditions were drier, scrub may have dominated much of the Florida peninsula. Today, the largest expanses are generally restricted to three locations in Florida.

By far the most impressive of these regions is the Big Scrub that makes up much of the Ocala National Forest in Clay and Putnam counties. The other two locations include a narrow strip along the panhandle coast from about Franklin County to the Alabama state line, and the scrub areas of the lower central peninsula.

A surprising variety of wildlife inhabits scrub country, a few species of which are considered threatened or endangered. More than half of the scrub's wildlife inhabitants are narrowly endemic to its specialized conditions and are seldom seen outside the scrub. These highly restricted species include such Florida specialties as the Florida mouse, the Florida scrub jay, and the Florida scrub lizard. Other animals, such as the gopher tortoise, black bear, bobcat, white-tailed deer, and a variety of songbirds visit the scrub regularly at varying times of the year and use it for foraging or nesting.

TEMPERATE HARDWOOD FORESTS

The temperate hardwood forest community finds the southern extent of its range along the wooded hillsides of Florida's uplands, underscoring the state's location at the overlap between temperate and tropical climatic zones. Temperate

Hardwood Hammock

forests are widely known to the north of the state and are considered the climax forest community for most of eastern North America. As might be expected, most of Florida's examples are confined chiefly to the northern parts of the state. Unlike in cooler climes, where temperate forests often stretch for thousands of uninterrupted acres, most examples of this community in Florida are found in localized pockets, commonly referred to as hammocks.

The meaning of the term hammock is somewhat elusive; the word is generally applied to any area that is characterized by a diverse collection of both deciduous and evergreen hardwood trees. In south Florida parlance, *hammock* refers to the distinctive collections of tropical trees that dot the state's southern tip. In north Florida it denotes any one of several assemblages of primarily temperate hardwood species that typically occur in mixed stands and that may be found in a variety of soil situations.

As might be expected, not all north Florida hammocks are alike. Some are xeric in nature and are located on dry, sandy sites along the coastal strand or within ancient inland dune fields. Others occur in mesic uplands where the soil is rich and moist.

Still others are hydric and are confined to areas with poorly drained soils and high water tables, such as along the Suwannee River or bordering the area's major spring runs, or within the state's wooded coastal wetlands. The woodlands along the Ichetucknee River are prime examples of those found along spring runs; Gulf Hammock near Cedar Key in Levy County and much of the area contained within the Lower Suwannee National Wildlife Refuge are good examples of coastal wetland hammocks.

Florida's temperate hardwood hammocks are best known for their diversity of broad-leaved trees and intriguing collection of herbaceous wildflowers. Southern magnolia, American beech, yellow poplar, spruce pine, American basswood, and several species of oaks, elms, and hickories make up the overstory in the more upland hammocks, while sweetbay, sweetgum, loblolly bay, ironwood, sabal palm, diamond leaf oak, and loblolly pine are more representative of the lowlands.

FLATWOODS AND BAY SWAMPS

Northern Florida's pine flatwoods offer exhilarating opportunities to explore some of the state's most primitive and pristine lands. Wide expanses of pine-studded flatlands are broken by twisted tangles of titi swamps and richly luxuriant forests. The sounds of one or more of Florida's numerous species of frogs and toads often echo through the stillness. Woodpeckers hammer out their mating drum rolls on the resonant boles of hollow trees, and Florida black bears hole up in the dense swamps, seldom making their presence known by more than tracks left in the mud, or territorial scratch marks left on tree trunks. All of these combine to form a mysterious land visited by only a few adventurous souls who know the quietness and beauty of this extraordinary ecosystem.

Venturing into Florida's flatwoods–bay swamp ecosystem is an experience that no amateur naturalist should forego. Yet it is also a place one should not go unprepared. Trails are few and the thickets dense. Shallow pools of standing water often block the way. Wading is the standard mode of locomotion. But the wildlife is abundant and the plant communities intriguing. Opportunities for discovery are limitless.

Much of Florida is covered by pine flatwoods. Found on the mostly level, remnant sea bottom associated with the Oke-fenokee Sea (see Chapter 2), the most spectacular examples in north Florida occur in the lowlands just south of the Okefenokee Swamp and along the St. Johns River in the Eastern Valley (see p. 17). In these areas there is a rather thick layer of fine sand over-lying the limestone. This sand retards the downward percolation of surface water, and the relatively flat terrain discourages the development of major drainage systems. Because of these factors, the ground within the flatwoods is often wet and soggy.

The characteristic appearance and vegetation make the flatwoods an easy vegetational unit to recognize. The overstory typically consists of slash pine, longleaf pine, or a mixture of the two. Sometimes, particularly in portions of the Osceola National Forest, pond pine will also be dominant or included in the overstory. The shrubby understory is composed primarily of saw palmetto but often includes gallberry, dangleberry, fetterbush, staggerbush, sweet pepperbush, and tarflower.

Although a panoramic view of a well-developed flatwoods gives the impression that it is all pines and palmetto, a closer inspection reveals numerous additional species. One of the most interesting and dominant plants in the ground cover is wiregrass. Wiregrass leaves are narrow, wiry, about two feet long, and grow in dense, spreading bunches. On undisturbed sites, the bushy clumps grow so close together that they nearly cover the ground.

Due to low elevation and a water table that is very near the surface, swamplands are an often-seen subunit of the flatwoods habitat. Often called bay swamps or bay galls after the typical tree species found in their overstory, swamps typically comprise thickets that are too small or too scattered to show on general-ized vegetation maps. These communities frequently contain standing water and occupy shallow depressions.

Although several types of swamp communities inhabit

northern Florida, the tendency for types to intergrade, or for one type to be contained within another, make precise characterization of some swamps difficult. Titi swamps occur across the entire northern portion of the state and are normally dominated most often by swamp cyrilla. Often there is no overstory associated with titi regions. In some instances, however, scattered pond and/or slash pines are present. Common shrub associates in both communities include the large sweet gallberry, fetterbushes and staggerbushes, and a variety of thorny smilax vines.

RIVERS, STREAMS AND LAKES

Florida's surface water systems offer some of the state's most attractive recreational enticements. From large alluvial rivers and clear, spring-fed runs, to deeply tannin-stained backwater sloughs or attractive cypress-ringed lakes, all are important components of our natural environment.

Three main types of rivers are found in northern Florida. Each can be distinguished by the color of its water and the type of land it drains.

Alluvial streams are those that receive the majority of their water from the surface runoff that originates in the silty-clayey soils of the uplands. Such rivers typically appear turbid or muddy due to the high concentration of suspended particulates and organic detritus. Blackwater streams are found in sandy lowlands where fine-grained soils retard the downward percolation of precipitation. Such sands are often saturated with water that is only slowly released from belowground into the channels of nearby rivers. Blackwater rivers are usually free of suspended particles due to the filtering action of the sand, but are a rich reddish black in color from the high content of organic tannins that have been leached from decaying vegetation. Most have attractive sandy bottoms. The St. Marys in the Osceola National Forest and the Santa Fe are good examples.

Spring runs are clear, flowing streams that originate at the headwaters of Florida's best-known natural feature. Typically cool in summer and warm in winter, spring runs display a relatively stable temperature range throughout the year and are especially attractive to an assortment of plants and wildlife. Important native plants include wild rice, arrowheads, spatterdock, and tape-grass; native wildlife species include the Suwannee cooter, American alligator, brown and red-belly watersnakes, and a variety of fishes and insects. The best-known winter inhabitant is the West Indian manatee, which spends the cooler months of the year near the warmer headwaters of large springs that are accessible from the ocean. Our best-known spring-fed streams include the Ichetucknee in the north central part of the state, and the Juniper, Alexander, and Silver Springs runs in or near the Ocala National Forest.

In many ways Florida is as well known for its lakes as for its rivers. And even though the majority of its nearly 8,000 lakes are located outside the regions discussed in this book, there are still enough in north Florida to keep lake explorers busy. Most of Florida's natural lakes result from the solution of subsurface limestone. Solution lakes are usually circular in outline, conical in cross-section, and are situated in locations where the limestone is buried under a relatively thick overburden. Many contain dark, tannin-stained water and are variously ringed or studded with cypress trees. In most cases they are directly connected to the subsurface drainage system, including neighboring lakes, and have no visible outflow at the surface.

Florida's lakes are complete ecosystems that support a variety of life through a complex set of biological processes. Green plants produce food through photosynthesis and provide an energy source for an assortment of zooplankton, insects, fishes, turtles, and birds. Organic waste is decomposed and recycled by bottom-dwelling bacteria. Some animals, such as frogs and ducks, use lakes temporarily for breeding or foraging; others make bodies of standing water the primary habitat in which they carry on all of life's processes. At every level, the denizens of our lakes interact in a dynamic, self-sustaining, but ever-changing system that insures the health of the lakes themselves, as well as the health of our lakes' inhabitants.

RIVER SWAMPS AND FLOODPLAIN FORESTS

Florida's largest rivers create their own unique and fascinating wetlands. Although similar in appearance to the bay swamps and hydric hammocks discussed above, they differ in the source of their water. Bay swamps and hydric hammocks are recharged with surface water runoff from the surrounding land. River swamps and floodplain woodlands, on the other hand, are periodically inundated from the overflow of their associated alluvial stream. As a result, the soil of the floodplain and bottomlands is

River Swamp

31

silty, very rich in nutrients, and supports a large assemblage of trees and vines and an impressive collection of wildlife species.

Water oak, overcup oak, diamond-leaf oak, water hickory, sugarberry, several species of ash, and river birch are among the more commonly seen trees. Common wildlife includes several species of salamanders and snakes as well as the wild turkey, southern flying squirrel, great-horned owl, eastern screech owl, barred owl, pileated woodpecker, gray fox, bobcat, and white-tailed deer.

WET PRAIRIES

Three major areas of wet grasslands appear in northern Florida, one at Paynes Prairie State Preserve (see p. 146), one in the southwestern corner of the Apalachicola National Forest in the Florida Big Bend, and the other along Florida Highway 87 in the western panhandle. All are classified as part of the wet prairie ecological community and are exceedingly interesting habitats that support a wide variety of amphibious and reptilian wildlife as well as a fascinating assortment of low-growing herbaceous plants. Only the first of these is encompassed in the territory covered by this book.

Wet prairies are boggy, treeless areas that support a huge assemblage of plant species. Sedges, rushes, and herbs abound in the moist to wet soils. Sundews, marsh pinks, black-eyed susan, white-topped sedge, spatterdock, cattail, spikerush, beakrush, meadow beauty, tickseed, and wax myrtle are some of the more common species.

In addition to their diverse and fascinating plant populations, wet prairies are also well known as important habitats for frogs and snakes. The little grass frog, southern chorus frog, Florida cricket frog, southern black racer, eastern cottonmouth, and yellow rat snake all thrive in this wetland habitat. Paynes Prairie, in particular, has long been known for its abundant snake population, though the number of snakes there today is somewhat reduced from the historically high levels of only a few years ago.

SINKS AND SPRINGS

Sinkholes are natural features found across much of Florida. They are common in regions underlain by limestone and form in response to the movement of underground water. Sinks serve as the earth's drainage spouts, collecting surface runoff as they recharge the underground aquifer that holds most of the state's potable water.

In one type of sinkhole a solution cavity forms within the earth as water dissolves the underlying limestone. Eventually, the cavity becomes so large that the cover material is no longer supported. The cover collapses into the cavity, leaving the water below visible from the surface. The walls of these cover-collapse sinkholes are sometimes lined with exposed limestone.

Another type of sinkhole results from cover subsidence through solution rather than cover collapse. Although less dramatic in origin, such sinkholes also involve the solution of limestone. In solution sinkholes, however, it is the surface water rather than the ground water that is the culprit. Most often, such sinkholes occur where the limestone is at or very near the surface. Rainwater percolating downward through the thin veneer of soil erodes and dissolves the surface of the limestone before it passes through the subsurface cracks that carry it deeper into the ground. As the limestone surface dissolves, the soil above gradually sinks, forming a depression that collects increasing amounts of runoff. The more runoff that is collected, the more the limestone is eroded, and the further the area subsides. Sometimes the runoff brings impermeable clays and sands that effectively seal off the sinkhole from further interaction with the ground water, forming a lake. Most sinkholes in the major portions of Putnam, Flagler, Marion, and Lake counties are of the cover-collapse type. Solution sinkholes are most common in parts of the panhandle.

If sinkholes are the earth's drains, then springs are its faucets. While sinks recharge the underground water supply, springs act as flowing wells, responding to the tremendous artesian pressure of underground water storage systems and discharging excess liquid to the surface. In total, Florida's springs produce about 8 billion gallons of water a day, a staggering figure that rivals the daily amount of water that is artificially pumped in Florida for human use.

North Florida is one of the best locations in the United States for spring lovers. Nearly half of the 300 or so of Florida's springs occur in the area covered by this book, including at least a dozen of the 27 that are classified as first magnitude. Such places as Alexander, Juniper, Ichetucknee, and Silver Springs, many of which are protected by public property, are legendary landmarks.

IV
EXPLORING NORTH FLORIDA'S WILDLIFE

For the amateur naturalist whose passion is wildlife, northern Florida offers a varied assortment of faunal inhabitants that represent almost every level on the evolutionary scale. Stationing oneself in the predawn stillness of a woodland thicket, sitting quietly along the edges of a gurgling stream, or walking gently along a primitive trail can yield an abundance of observation opportunities.

REPTILES AND AMPHIBIANS

For the amateur herpetologist, few places can match the abundance and diversity of northern Florida. Nearly all of its habitats offer a variety of reptiles and amphibians to discover and identify.

Snakes

Over 50 species of snakes live in that portion of Florida that lies north of Ocala and east of the Suwannee River. With the exception of the five poisonous species highlighted in Chapter 1, all are essentially harmless, though some will bite. All are also important components of our native communities.

The most commonly seen of our native snakes include the black racer, red rat or corn snake, gray rat or oak snake, yellow rat or chicken snake, eastern hognose snake, and the banded and brown watersnakes.

Few things are more delightful than a glimpse of the season's first black racer. They are found in many habitats but are most often seen in open areas, along roadways and highways, and in generally brushy sites near water. They begin moving in early spring and are often seen darting across roads and rural highways.

The rat snakes, too, are found in a wide variety of habitats but are particularly partial to old buildings and trash piles. The red and yellow rat snakes are brightly colored and very attractive. The gray rat is less colorful, but is quite docile and easily handled.

As their names suggest, the watersnakes are generally restricted to rivers, swamps, lakes, ponds, and sinkholes and are often seen stretched out on fallen logs. They are typically drab in color, have a temperamental demeanor, and will bite if accosted. They are often misidentified as cottonmouths, though they are easily differentiated by lacking the distinctive dark swab that is obvious along either side of the cottonmouth's head.

The eastern hognose is the most docile of Florida's snakes. When disturbed or threatened it will often put on quite a show by flattening its neck and head to resemble a cobra, and by making a variety of swaying and menacing gyrations. However, if touched it usually turns on its back and feigns death. If turned right side up, it will immediately turn upside down again.

Alligators

Florida's most distinctive reptile is, undoubtedly, the American alligator. Found in a variety of wetlands throughout the state, this prehistoric creature is considered by some to be the most magnificent example of Florida's native fauna, and is certainly an animal that few of us tire of seeing.

There is little question that the lowly alligator is Florida's most primitive link with the ancient earth. They, along with a variety of other now-extinct crocodilians, ancient birds, and thunderous dinosaurs, date from the Mesozoic Era, or about 230 million years ago. They are at least a hundred times more ancient than we humans, and constitute one of our closest connections to prehistoric life.

American Alligator

Much of the alligator's evolutionary success can be attributed to its position at the top of the food chain. Its large body, intimidating jaws, and powerful tail make it the Sunshine State's most respected predator, and it is virtually without natural enemies in adulthood. The only decline in the alligator's population came earlier in this century when it became the target of humans, the only predators that have ever caused it harm. Before being placed on the nation's list of threatened wildlife, its population declined significantly. However, with its newfound regulated status its numbers have recovered rapidly, offering further evidence of its natural staying power.

Although fearsome at maturity, the gator is not without enemies during other phases of its life cycle. Young gators, in particular, are not so insulated from danger as are adults. While still enclosed in their hard, leathery eggs, they provide choice morsels for raccoons, bears, opossums, and skunks, and as hatchlings they have little defense against predation. Less than ten inches long when born, young gators are extremely vulnerable to small animals as well as large wading birds such as the great blue heron. The latter is known to relish young gators and is especially adept at forcing them head first down its long, sinuous neck.

Alligator nests are composed of large, conspicuous mounds of decaying vegetation. They are typically constructed in late June or early July and can be up to about three feet high and several feet wide. The female lays up to 50 eggs in the center of the mound and depends on the heat generated by natural oxidation to incubate the growing embryos. The three-inch-long eggs hatch in about 70 days, and the hatchlings are carried from their darkened birth chamber in their mother's mouth. Young gators remain together for at least a year and spend much of the winter in a den with their other siblings.

Young gators are quite good at sounding an alarm when danger approaches. On a recent outing I examined a number of gator holes for signs of new hatches. At one location I found a number of young, yellow-striped hatchlings sprawled along the edge of a small, muddy puddle. As I walked past the lethargic colony I began to hear a high-pitched croak reminiscent of a muffled bark. Almost immediately, the head of an adult alligator surfaced in the middle of the tiny basin as if to warn me that I had ventured too close for the mother's comfort.

Much has been made about the size of an average alligator. It is common to hear uninitiated observers report gators that exceed 12 feet in length. In reality, such sizes are not common. While the longest American alligator on record measured more than 19 feet, gators longer than about 10 feet are not easy to find today and are not often seen by the normal outdoorsperson. The length of the average female does not exceed 9 feet; the length of the average male is usually less than 11 feet. There must be something about an alligator's form or general demeanor that makes it loom much larger in the imagination than in reality.

Frogs and Toads

Learning to identify our native frogs and toads is often more easily done by sound than by sight. More than 30 species are represented in northern Florida, all of which have distinctive and easily identifiable voices. Hardly a month of the year passes without hearing the distinctive call of at least one of these secretive critters. From the barking tree frog's houndlike chatter or the bullfrog's deep resonant drone, to the chuckling and clattering of the southern leopard frog or the high-pitched squeak of the familiar spring peeper, few things make north Florida evenings more delightful or more distinctive than the sounds of our frogs

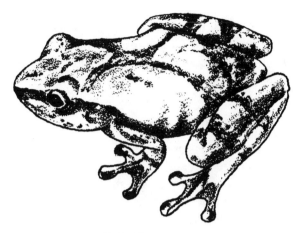

Spring Peeper

and toads. A complete accounting of those species native to the northern part of the state is included with the wildlife checklists in Chapter 7.

BIRDS

Birdwatching has become a popular recreational pursuit for a wide range of nature enthusiasts. Increasing numbers of us spend at least some of our weekends visiting wildlife refuges, state parks, and other birdwatching hot spots, discovering the enjoyment that invariably comes with learning to identify our native birds.

Well over 300 species of birds visit northern Florida on a regular basis. Some of these are residents and may be observed at almost any time of year. Others are with us for only one season. Those that stay with us during the summer constitute our local breeding populations and normally spend their winters farther south. Conversely, those that overwinter usually have breeding grounds farther to the north.

A large number of birds pass through north Florida only during their migration to or from their wintering grounds. Of these, some appear during both spring and fall; others appear during only one of these seasons. While space does not allow a complete coverage of all of these species, a brief overview of some of the more common orders of birds will prove helpful, particularly if you are a beginning birdwatcher.

Herons, Egrets, and Ibises

The herons and egrets are probably the best known of Florida's marsh-loving birds. Heralded for their beauty and grace, they are most commonly associated with shallow waters at the edges of the wetlands. With heads outstretched and bodies erect, they are often seen standing motionless, gazing into the water in search of an unsuspecting frog or fish.

There are 12 members of the heron family in the continental United States. All of them can be seen at various times of the year within the confines of Florida.

Perhaps the most familiar of these splendid birds is the great blue heron. The great blue is a large bird with a slate blue body, white face, and a conspicuous black stripe above its eye. A seven-foot wingspan easily makes it the largest of our native herons. When startled, the great blue ordinarily takes flight, uttering a harsh croaking call as if to emphasize its displeasure at being disturbed.

Another of our conspicuous large waders is the great egret. Only slightly smaller than the great blue, it is all white with a striking yellow bill and black legs. It is normally found wading slowly in shallow waters along the edges of marshes and ponds and can sometimes be seen stirring the water with its feet in an attempt to startle its prey into movement.

More than one highway motorist has been amused at the sight of a cattle egret standing atop the back of a dairy cow in a roadside pasture. One of Florida's most prolific small herons, the cattle egret was a rare sight in the state until the early 1950s. Since then, it has rapidly expanded its range and is now a common resident in all parts of Florida. Its preference for dry, open, grassy feeding areas distinguishes it from our other heron species and probably helps account for its rapid expansion.

The little snowy egret is one of the most beautiful of our

Great Blue Heron

wading birds. Taken together, its dazzling white feathers and straight black bill distinguish it from all other members of its family. When in summer dress, it displays graceful plumes that curve upward from its head, neck, and back and form a strikingly beautiful array. The snowy's most unique feature, however, is the color of its feet. Referred to as the egret with the golden slippers, its bright yellow feet contrast sharply with its jet black legs.

The night-herons and bitterns are the most secretive members of the heron family. As their name implies, night-herons feed primarily during the evening and early morning hours, preferring to spend the daylight hours roosting quietly in the branches of trees. Bitterns, on the other hand, feed by day but typically stay hidden deep in the marsh. They seem to favor the protection of dense stands of cattail and only rarely venture into open view.

North Florida also plays host to two members of the ibis family. Unlike the herons, ibises have long, down-curved bills and fly with their necks outstretched. They are most often seen crouching in the marshes, actively foraging for fish, crabs, cray-fish, snails, and an assortment of aquatic insects.

The most commonly seen member of this family is the white ibis. In adult plumage it is all white with black wingtips and bright pink legs and bill. It is equally at home in both fresh and brackish water and is often seen flying in "V" formations, reminiscent of the Canada goose.

The glossy ibis is one of north Florida's least abundant long-legged waders. Although fairly common in the southern part of the state, it has only recently begun expanding its range northward. When observed closely, the breeding plumage of the glossy ibis is exquisitely beautiful. Its deep chestnut color is highlighted with tinges of glossy green and purple. At a distance or in poor light, however, the bird appears almost all black.

Ducks and Geese

Nothing conjures up a more pleasing vision of the coming winter than the sight of waterfowl winging southward on their fall migration. Long lines of high-flying ducks silhouetted against a wintry sky often recall pleasing fragments of our fondest childhood memories. The beginning of a new school year; the first cold front; crisp, cool mornings; and the colorful change of seasons are all associated with the spectacular migration of our ducks and geese.

Over 20 different species of ducks and one species of goose frequent north Florida in winter. As early as September, migrants begin arriving from their northern breeding grounds. Blue-winged teal, northern pintail, American widgeon, and northern shoveler are among the first to appear. These are followed in rapid succession by canvasback, gadwall, redhead,

American black duck, green-winged teal, common goldeneye, bufflehead, and three species of mergansers. By the onset of December, nearly all have reached their winter homes.

Learning to identify these cold-weather visitors is not as difficult as learning the identities of our smaller songbirds. Whereas songbirds normally stay hidden in the brush, or dart secretively among the branches of trees, the ducks and geese often stay easily visible in wide open spaces. Many spend their days diving and dabbling in shallow freshwater ponds, or in near-shore coastal waters. This relatively sedentary feeding behavior allows extended observation of their habits and plumage.

Male ducks are easiest to recognize. Their bright colors and characteristic patterns make them conspicuous denizens of the marshlands. Each seems to have its own distinctive feature. The green head of the mallard, the white forehead of the American widgeon, the spoon-shaped bill of the northern shoveler, the large white crescent on the face of the blue-winged teal—all are distinctive field marks.

Identifying female ducks is more of a challenge. Usually attired in much drabber colors than the males, the females of different species often appear quite similar. Body shape, bill length, overall size, and the color of the wing patch are often the only characteristics available for distinguishing one female from another.

One of the most exciting duck-watching activities is following the gradual preparation for the spring migration and breeding season. Throughout the winter, the plumage of the males becomes more colorful with each passing week. By late January the birds enter a stage of migratory restlessness and courtship activity that foreshadows the coming of spring. Small groups of males band together in cavorting flight and aerial acrobatics in hopes of attracting a mate. Other males engage in ritualized postures, movements, and vocalizations that advertise their availability to interested hens. In some species, potential mates form bonds even before they migrate. These pairs can frequently be seen swimming together for several weeks prior to leaving on their northward flight.

Shorebirds, Gulls, and Terns

Birdwatchers distinguish three general types of coastal birds. Although representatives of each group are seen on north Florida shores, the collective name shorebirds is usually applied only to representatives of the plovers, oystercatchers, stilts, avocets, and sandpipers. More than 30 species of these birds visit north Florida's coastal areas or inland ponds. While a few stay hidden in the brush and are difficult to find or see, a larger number are quite visible among our dunes or along our beaches.

The sandpipers are by far the largest group of shorebirds found in north Florida. Ranging in stature from the sparrow-sized least sandpiper to the much larger willet, they are frequently seen on muddy or sandy beaches jabbing their bills into the soggy soil in search of insects.

Plovers are also birds of the open beach. More compact in appearance than sandpipers, they typically have short necks, short bills, round heads, and large eyes. They appear eternally hurried and race across the sand from point to point, stopping only briefly to search for food.

The American oystercatcher is one of Florida's largest and most distinctive shorebirds. Listed as a threatened species, it is the only member of its family in the state and is one of our easier shorebirds to identify. An adult oystercatcher is about the size of a small crow. It has a jet black head, a dark brown back, and a large bright orange bill which it uses to pry open oyster shells and other mollusks.

To the uninitiated beachgoer, all large white birds often fall into the catchall category "sea gull." Such classification, however, is not technically correct. There are actually several species of gulls as well as a number of the usually smaller and more streamlined terns.

Gulls are typically wide-winged birds with stout, often hooked, bills and squared or rounded tails. Several species of gulls frequent north Florida. Our three most common include the ring-billed, herring, and laughing gulls. While laughing gulls normally prefer to remain within just a few miles of the coastline, herring and ring-billed gulls regularly venture farther inland and are often observed during winter frequenting shopping center parking lots, large neighborhood lakes, and sanitary landfills.

Terns differ from gulls in having pointed wings and bills and sharply forked tails. They are typically seen diving head first into the water after prey. As many as ten species of terns visit north Florida at various times of the year. Four species—the Caspian tern, royal tern, sandwich tern, and black skimmer—are listed as species of special concern by the Florida Committee on Rare and Endangered Plants and Animals. The smaller and more dainty least tern is considered threatened.

Raptors

The hawks, eagles, owls, falcons, ospreys, and kites are the predators of the air. Their keen eyesight, sharp talons, and pinpoint attacks make them some of the bird world's most feared aggressors. Entire rafts of ducks take flight when a bald eagle or red-tailed hawk circles, and songbirds dart for cover at the approach of a Cooper's or sharp-shinned hawk. Their form alone seems to incite a kind of frantic terror in their prey.

Red-tailed and red-shouldered hawks are probably the most common of north Florida's resident birds of prey. Though they differ in several respects and are relatively easy to distinguish, many beginning birders have difficulty telling them apart. The red-tailed hawk is the larger of the two and often soars high in the sky. The combination of dark belly band, white chest, and rufous-red tail easily sets it apart. Both of these species are often seen perched atop dead snags or in the trees along highways and interstates. This vantage gives them a good view of road shoulders, and their sharp eyes can easily pick out snakes and rodents that might otherwise be hidden in the roadside grass.

North Florida's falcons include the peregrine, merlin, and American kestrel. The peregrine and merlin are by far the least common of the three. They visit in winter from about September to May and are most often seen along the coast, particularly during migration.

The peregrine was once common to most of the world's continents and was widely used for falconry. With the introduction of the pesticide DDT in the early 1950s, its population decreased dramatically. Reintroduction efforts, pesticide regulations, and close attention have stemmed the loss; its population is now increasing and the species will likely be proposed for delisting in the near future. Until then, the bird is still listed as an endangered species and is uncommon enough to make seeing it a birder's delight.

The bald eagle is another of our more special raptors. Once a common nesting species throughout Florida, it, too, suffered dramatic losses as a result of DDT, particularly to the north of Florida, and even disappeared from many locations in the southern United States. Florida's population is slowly recovering, and the bird is much more commonly seen today than it was 30 years ago. Ocala National Forest and the floodplain of the St. Johns River are good locations for spotting the bird in the northern part of the state.

Many beginning observers confuse the bald eagle with the osprey, another coastal raptor. Both show white on their heads, but only the mature eagle has an all-white head; the osprey's head always shows a brownish stripe through the eye. The osprey also shows an all-white underside which is never true of the bald eagle. Even very young eagles show only splotches of white on their bellies before taking on their dark, adult plumage.

The osprey has historically been called the fish hawk by locals because of its efficiency as an airborne angler. It is not unusual to see a foraging osprey hovering excitedly over the shallow waters of a saltwater bay, then diving feet first into a school of fish. More times than not the bird is rewarded handsomely; it is common to see an osprey perched atop a dead snag or power pole devouring a large mullet or some other saltwater species.

MAMMALS

North Florida's terrestrial and freshwater mammals are not as great in number as its reptiles, amphibians, and birds. Only 50 to 60 species of native or established exotics are known to be present in the region. While some of these, such as the raccoon and white-tailed deer, are common and often seen, others, such as the several species of rodents, stay well hidden and are seldom encountered. At least a few deserve special mention.

River Otter

The river otter is one of the state's most delightful creatures. Its torpedo-shaped body and webbed toes are perfectly adapted to an aquatic lifestyle and its dark brown to black, closely cropped fur gives it an exceptionally sleek appearance. Otters are found in an assortment of aquatic habitats from lakes, ponds, and impoundments to alluvial and blackwater streams. They are most like the mink in general appearance and the two animals are quite closely related.

River otters are inquisitive and intelligent animals that seem genuinely interested in humans. They have been known to follow canoeists or swim along lake edges adjacent to hikers, intermittently poking their heads above the surface as if to stay abreast of the whereabouts of their intruders. Although they spend much of their time in the water, they also come ashore regularly and are often quite playful. Groups of otters will sometimes wet down a muddy bank, then use it as a sliding board, letting their body weight plunge them repeatedly into the water. Chancing unnoticed upon a group of otters at play is a rare but engaging adventure.

Florida Black Bear

The Florida black bear is one of Florida's largest but most seldom seen land mammals. In historical times it was probably quite common in the denser woodlands throughout Florida and southern Georgia. Today, however, its population is much smaller. Its large, black form is unmistakable and needs no description.

Florida bears are not pugnacious animals. Although most are powerful enough to inflict considerable damage, there are no recorded reports of bear attacks on humans in the state.

Florida Black Bear

The Florida black bear is a passive and highly secretive omnivore that avoids human contact whenever possible. Although classified a carnivore and known to occasionally feed on feral hogs, it is also fond of a variety of berries, young insects, and honey, including the fruit of the saw palmetto and the tender growing bud of the sabal, or cabbage, palm. It is essentially nocturnal and is most likely to be seen in the early evening, or in the hour just before sunrise. Most sightings occur near the Ocala National Forest, probably due to the unfortunate juxtaposition of an area with increasing urbanization to an area with an increasing number of bears. The relatively fewer sightings in the Osceola National Forests probably stem from this area's more remote location.

There are between 1,000 and 1,500 bears in Florida, and the northern part of the state harbors some of the species' largest and most successful populations. The swamps, bays, and dense woods of the Ocala and Osceola National Forests, as well as the bottomlands of the St. Johns River, are some of its better-known haunts.

There is evidence that the Ocala population, in particular, is expanding in number, a phenomenon that will likely continue given the Florida Game and Fresh Water Fish Commission's 1993 decision to prohibit hunting of the species. Even so, most populations are still considered threatened, and all populations are protected by virtue of their non-game status.

Florida Panther and Bobcat

Only two members of the Felidae, or cat family, are reported from north Florida's wildlands: the Florida panther and the bobcat. The Florida panther is the state's rarest mammal. Although often reported in northern Florida by amateur observers, most wildlife management professionals suspect that these reports are either misidentifications or sightings of captive released animals. It is generally agreed that the northern part of the state currently supports no naturally occurring panther populations. In recent years the Florida Game and Fresh Water Fish Commission has conducted reintroduction experiments as part of a comprehensive program to restore the animal as part of the region's wildlife.

Unlike the panther, the diminutive bobcat is common in a variety of north Florida habitats. Adults are two to three times larger than a large house cat and are easily distinguished from the latter by their short, stubby tail, triangular ears, and black spots on a reddish or gray background. Although common, they are not as easily seen as their abundance might suggest. Bobcats often move under cover of darkness, making them difficult to observe. Even when they hunt in the daytime, which they also commonly do, they are secretive and avoid crossing paths with humans. They are quite territorial and tend to inhabit the same general location for long periods of time if a stable food source is present. Finding a bobcat's foraging area usually insures greater success of regular sightings.

Bats

Florida is home to 16 species of bats, all but one of which occur in the northern part of the state. The southeastern bat, eastern pipistrelle, and yellow, red, hoary, and Seminole bats are among the most common.

Florida's bats are the butterflies of the night. They typically appear at dusk, seemingly from nowhere, and dart through the air, often too erratically for human eyes to follow. Their jerky, staccato flight is unmistakable and results from their method of gathering food. As they approach a flying insect, they cup their wings below them and literally scoop the unsuspecting prey into their open mouths. The entire process takes only a second or two, but is long enough to cause a noticeable pause in their flight pattern.

Bats are generally believed to live only in caves. Although this is essentially true for a handful of Florida's rarer bats, most spend their days hanging upside down from the ceiling of an old building or from the limb of a tree or shrub.

Finding a sleeping bat during the day is not impossible but not easy. They usually close themselves up tightly and often do not resemble an animal of any type. As a result, they often go unnoticed. They are also not easily aroused from their slumber when found, and ordinarily do not respond to anything less than the most severe intrusion.

West Indian Manatee

The West Indian manatee is one of the Sunshine State's best known and most loved animals. Its large, lethargic form is unlike that of any other of our marine mammals, and its exceedingly gentle nature sets it apart from nearly all of Florida's wild creatures.

Manatees are most often seen in winter when they congregate in warm coastal waters, around the headwaters of the larger springs, or near the mouths of the larger rivers. They are sensitive to cold and tend to seek warmer waters when seawater tem-

Manatee

peratures begin to drop. Although much of their range falls out-side of north Florida, they are sometimes seen on the west coast in the Suwannee River and near Manatee Springs, and on the east coast in the Tomoka River near Tomoka State Park.

Manatees are strictly herbivorous and have no natural ene-mies. They are sometimes referred to as sea cows because they graze on underwater vegetation and are absolutely harmless and defenseless. There are about 2,000 manatees in the state today, but their future is uncertain. Many show the telltale scars of collisions with motor boats; it is estimated that between 35 and 50 of the nearly 150 that are likely to die annually will do so as a result of accidents with motor boats. Although the state has taken a series of steps to protect the animal by enforcing speed zones in its most often-used haunts, accidents still happen too frequently, and there is grave concern about the creature's ability to survive in the long term.

BUTTERFLIES

Watching and identifying butterflies is fast becoming a popular interest for many of north Florida's amateur naturalists. A variety of these delicate winged creatures migrate through various parts of Florida each fall and spring and provide the basis for an intriguing pastime. Although particularly evident along the coastal strand, an equal number of butterflies also frequent more inland locations.

North Florida's most commonly seen species include the black, eastern tiger, spicebush, and zebra swallowtails, as well as the monarch, queen, viceroy, gulf fritillary, painted lady, long-winged zebra, and orange and cloudless sulphurs. Most are attracted to one of several native plants including lantana and saltbush, as well as several species of milkweed and beggar-ticks.

V
NATURAL AREAS—
FEDERAL LANDS

LAKE WOODRUFF
NATIONAL WILDLIFE REFUGE

Lake Woodruff National Wildlife Refuge is one of those places that when you arrive, you still have a long way to go. Although there is an easily accessible and extremely enjoyable public use area within about a mile of a paved highway, most of the refuge is accessible only by water and requires a certain degree of commitment and skill to explore thoroughly.

This refuge is a 19,545-acre natural area located in the heart of one of the most rapidly developing areas of the state. It was established in 1964 to provide managed habitat for wading birds, migrating and wintering waterfowl, as well as to prevent the further loss of wetlands in central Florida. Lake Woodruff preserves a variety of habitats including 11,700 acres of freshwater marsh, 5,400 acres of hardwood swamps, 1,200 acres of uplands, and 1,000 acres of lakes, streams, and canals. There are also 445 acres of humanmade impoundments that lie at the heart of the public use area, one of the refuge's favored attractions.

Location, Mailing Address and Phone

Turn west on Retta St. off US 17 in DeLeon Springs, then left onto Grand Ave. (CR 4053). The refuge headquarters is located on the west side of Grand Ave.; turn west on Mud Lake Rd. just south of the headquarters to reach the public use area.

Facilities and Activities

Birding, hiking, fishing, nature study, canoeing.

Hiking and Nature Trails

Lake Woodruff's designated public use area is its most often visited facility. Several miles of walking trails pass through or adjacent to a number of central Florida habitats as well as the
refuge's three managed freshwater impoundments. A number of
these walking paths run along the tops of the dike roads that
hem in the pools, while others are along developed nature trails
that pass through hammock and pineland woods. Wildlife can
be abundant here, particularly during the winter, and there are
many opportunities for close observation of a number of
Florida's native species.

The longest walk begins at the entrance to the public use area,
then follows the dike road to Jones Island and on to Pontoon
Landing on the shores of Spring Garden Run. This is a 6-mile
round trip that leads walkers through pine and oak woods as
well as along the edges of the impoundments. The trip is well
worth the walk.

Two shorter walks lead off to the south of the public use area.
The Live Oak Nature Trail leaves the south side of the parking lot
and follows through a dry woodland before circling back to the
start. The Hammock Nature Trail leads to the south at the intersection of Pools 1 and 3, is slightly longer than the Live Oak Trail,
and leads through a scenic hammock.

Boating and Canoeing

For those who have a powerboat, canoe, or sea kayak, the more
remote areas of Lake Woodruff can also be important attractions. There is a landing and canoe rental concession at DeLeon
Springs State Recreation Area (a state-owned park just north of
the wildlife refuge) that allows the best access to the water.

Putting in at the state recreation area and then following the
spring run allows a variety of paddling excursions of varying
lengths. Just after leaving the state park, the south side of the
run opens into the mouth of shallow Spring Garden Lake. It is
possible to paddle into the lake but advisable to remain near

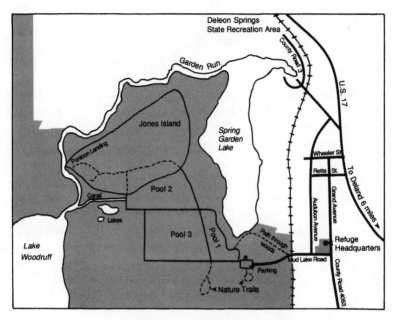

Lake Woodruff National Wildlife Refuge

the edges where the water is less encumbered with aquatic vegetation.

For longer paddles, Spring Garden Run also leads to Lake Woodruff, then on to Lake Dexter through the Tick Island Run which exits Lake Woodruff at its northwestern extent. Tick Island, which lies to the south of the run, is noted for the huge congregations of both black and turkey vultures which roost on the island during winter. Observing their late afternoon arrival in the fading light of a cool winter's day is an impressive experience.

Boat access is about the only way to visit the refuge's two wilderness areas. Dexter Island, the larger of the two, is located adjacent to Lake Dexter and is accessible via the Tick Island Canal. St. Francis Island is located along the St. Johns River on the southern end of the refuge and is most easily accessible from the landing on Florida 44. You can paddle around three sides of St. Francis Island by turning south onto the St. Francis Dead River, but must retrace your route to the St. Johns since the St. Francis dead-ends.

Birding

Birdwatching is one of the most popular activities at Lake Woodruff. At least 212 birds have been recorded on refuge lands, including a number of uncommon species. Black-necked stilt, bobolink, snow geese, black-billed cuckoo, Leconte's sparrow, pine siskin, and snail kite are among the rarely seen visitors, while long-legged waders, wintering waterfowl, osprey, kingfisher, both species of vulture, and several species of hawk are among the most plentiful. As many as 2,000 white ibis, 500 glossy ibis, 350 great blue heron, 300 great egret, 2,000 little blue heron, and 400 snowy egret have been recorded on the refuge in the fall, many of which are easily seen in the impoundments at the public use area. Wintering waterfowl include several thousand ring-necked duck and American coot as well as smaller populations of blue- and green-winged teal, hooded mergansers, and about 15 other species.

In addition to wetland birds, the refuge also provides habitat to a variety of land birds. At least 300 osprey use the refuge during summer and more than 200 red-shouldered hawks winter here. Bald eagles nest on the refuge and as many as 29 species of warblers pass through the refuge during migration, a few of which stay to nest.

Other Wildlife

Birding is not the only outlet for wildlife watchers at Lake Woodruff. A variety of other game and nongame species make their homes here. A small population of seldom-seen Florida black bear use Tick Island and the swamp adjacent to Harry's Creek, as do a sizable population of white-tailed deer and feral hogs. River otter are often seen in the impoundments at the public use area, and raccoon and bobcats are sometimes seen on the dike roads. Alligators are plentiful year-round and are best seen in quantity in summer and on warm winter days. Manatee use the refuge and its adjacent waters during early summer;

Osprey

power boaters should be mindful of these slow-moving creatures and observe idle speed when boating within the refuge.

Best Time of Year

Fall, winter, and spring are best for birding; alligators may be present any time of year; spring, summer, and fall are best for wildflowers.

Pets

Not allowed.

LOWER SUWANNEE RIVER AND CEDAR KEYS NATIONAL WILDLIFE REFUGES

The Lower Suwannee River and Cedar Keys National Wildlife Refuges are actually two distinct U.S. Fish and Wildlife Service stations, both of which are managed under the same administrative unit. The Cedar Keys refuge, which is the older and smaller of the two, was established in 1929 when President Hoover set aside Snake, Deadman's, and North Keys as refuges for colonially nesting wading birds. Since then, a number of other locations have been added to this important preserve; parts of at least 16 islands are now included within the refuge's boundaries.

The Lower Suwannee National Wildlife Refuge, which is larger and much more accessible than the Cedar Keys Refuge, was established in 1979. Lower Suwannee's express purpose is to protect and preserve the fragile ecosystems that characterize the mouth of the Suwannee River, as well as 26 miles of adjacent tidal saltmarsh and wet coastal islands.

Location, Mailing Address and Phone

Lower Suwannee National Wildlife Refuge is located along Florida's west coast from a few miles southwest of Cross City southward nearly to Cedar Key; Cedar Keys National Wildlife Refuge is a collection of islands that surround the town of Cedar Key. The headquarters for both of these refuges is in Levy County just west of CR 347, about 13 miles south of Chiefland; the entrance is marked.

Refuge Manager, Lower Suwannee and Cedar Keys National Wildlife Refuges, Rt. 1, Box 1193C, Chiefland, FL 32626; (904) 493-0238.

Facilities and Activities

Hiking, bicycling, nature trails, wildlife observation, birding, canoeing, sea kayaking, boating, botanizing, scenic drive.

It is worth making the headquarters your first stop. There are refuge maps, bird lists, general information brochures, and helpful people here.

Lower Suwannee National Wildlife Refuge

Loop Road

One of the best ways to see the Lower Suwannee Refuge is by driving, bicycling, or walking the 9-mile loop road that begins at Gate 1 and bisects the refuge east and west before returning to the highway at Gate 9. The roadway, itself, is hardpacked clay and easily driveable by most vehicles. It is also an outstanding bicycling route, particularly in cooler weather. A number of spur routes turn off the main loop and provide access to some of the refuge's more remote locations.

The system of roadways associated with the Loop Road passes through or adjacent to each of the refuge's major habitats and provides an outstanding opportunity for wildlife observation. White-tailed deer, river otter, wild turkey, and a variety of raptors are abundant and easily seen, and it is not uncommon to hear a number of Florida's frog species calling from the wetlands just off the road's main course. The refuge's expansive bird list, which also includes the Cedar Keys National Wildlife Refuge, encompasses at least 250 species, a large number of which are wintering species, or migrants which pass through the refuge during spring or fall. Over 40 species of gulls, terns, and shorebirds regularly use refuge habitats, as well as about 35 warblers. The Florida scrub jay, one of the state's specialties, is an uncommon resident here.

Wildflower enthusiasts, too, will enjoy the Loop Road. During spring, in particular, an amazing variety of herbaceous and woody plants clothe the refuge in varying shades of blue, pink, lavender, orange, and yellow. The easiest place to look for wildflowers is along the roadside; moist to wet areas generally display the greater abundance. For those who prefer getting away from their vehicle and traipsing through native vegetation, the flatwoods are also outstanding wildflower locations. Such species as colic root, tickseed, beggar tick, yellow-eyed grass, fetterbush, buttonbush, smilax, blazing star, and a variety of sedges, rushes, and grasses dominate at varying times of the year.

Hiking and Nature Trails

Lower Suwannee has three designated nature trails, each of which provides a short but interesting walk in distinctive terrain. The northernmost path is the river trail, a 0.3 mile jaunt through hydric hammock and floodplain woodlands to the edge of the Suwannee River. The final segment of the trail passes atop an elevated boardwalk that terminates at a widened platform with a view of one of the Sunshine State's more historic and notable streams. Barred owl, wood duck, and a variety of water snakes are common here, and birding can be productive. Cypress, sweetgum, red maple, and ironwood are some of the more common trees in the overstory.

The other two trails are located near the end of Levy CR 326, near the refuge's southern border. The Dennis Creek Loop begins at a designated parking lot just past the end of the pavement; the Shell Mound Trail begins just a few feet beyond the parking lot.

Dennis Loop is a 1-mile walk that leads adjacent to, then across a narrow expanse of sand flats and needlerush marsh. Snowy egrets and a variety of other long-legged waders regularly feed here, and a sizable colony of fiddler crabs inhabit the wet sand. The large-clawed males are sometimes seen positioned next to their burrows, waving their huge appendages relentlessly in an attempt to attract a mate. In addition to the fiddlers, the sand flats also support an interesting plant community consisting of saltwort, glasswort, saltgrass, and sea lavender. The succulent leaves or stems of the first two of these species were likely used by the area's early Indians as a source of salt in their diets. Beyond the marsh the trail passes through a sand scrub island that overlooks the open waters of Dennis Creek before circling back toward the parking lot. An observation point on the creek provides an opportunity to enjoy the scenery.

The 0.3-mile Shell Mound Trail is as much of historical and archaeological interest as of natural interest. This area served intermittently as an Indian village from about 2500 B.C. to 1000

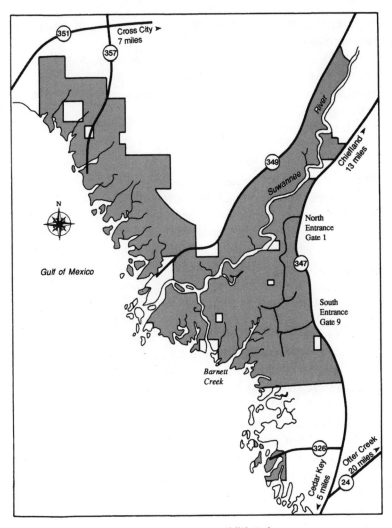

Lower Suwannee River Wildlife Refuge

A.D. and was probably inhabited by the forerunners of the Timu-cuans, one of Florida's largest aboriginal tribes. The five-acre, 28-foot-high shell mound that occupies the site today is the largest prehistoric shell mound on the central Gulf Coast and is testimony to the industriousness of these early Floridians, and to their fondness for seafood. The footpath leads up and over the largest part of the mound and provides a magnificent vista of the nearby coastal landscape.

In addition to the designated trails, there are many woods roads that turn off the Loop Road but are closed to vehicles. It is possible to walk these narrow trails to access some of the more remote areas. All of these roads are easy to follow and provide good opportunities to view wildlife.

Boating, Canoeing, and Sea Kayaking

There are a number of places to launch boats on this refuge, and a number of places that are best reached by water. The northernmost landing is at Shired Island, several miles north of the mouth of the Suwannee. The landing is located at the terminus of CR 357 which is reached by driving approximately 7 miles west from Cross City on CR 351. The coastline at this location is dominated for several miles by needlerush saltmarsh that is penetrated by a number of named creeks. Paddling or boating northward or southward along the shoreline leads to a number of good places from which to explore the marsh. As with all saltmarsh excursions, paddlers should be particularly mindful of their route. It is easy to become confused in the labyrinth of criss-crossing waterways. In addition, tidal changes sometimes obliterate or alter landmarks, or leave boaters stranded for several hours without navigable water.

There are two good put-in points off the Loop Road, both of which provide access to Barnett Creek. The first of these is located on Barnett Creek Road about 0.8 mile from its intersection with the main loop. A small area of open water and a tiny stream on the south side of the road mark the spot. There is no developed landing here and water levels are dependent upon tides. It is important to check local tide tables to insure that there will be enough water to return safely to the landing. This is another area where it is easy to become confused, so proceed with caution.

The other access to Barnett Creek is at the end of an unmarked road that turns off the Loop Road about 1.4 miles south of Barnett Creek Road. This latter landing is suitable for canoes, sea kayaks, and small power boats. It should be noted that neither of these latter sites is marked on refuge maps and neither is maintained as an official landing site.

The southernmost landing on the refuge is located beyond the Shell Mound Trail, at the end of CR 326. This landing provides access to Dennis Creek as well as to several nearby islands and a large expanse of coastal marsh. Powerboats also use this landing to access the open Gulf.

As might be expected, the Suwannee River is one of this refuge's major attractions. Approximately 25 river miles are bordered by refuge lands, and there are several landings which are suitable for motorboats. Two of the closest public ramps include one at Fowlers Bluff, on Levy CR 347 about 1.5 miles north of the refuge headquarters, and another at Suwannee Store Marina, in the town of Suwannee. Other landings include Yellow Jacket Camp, located on Dixie CR 349 at the refuge's northern border, and Munden Creek Camp about 2 miles north of Suwannee.

Most of the lower river is influenced by the encroachment of saltwater tides but supports outstanding hydric woodlands and wetlands. Cypress and bottomland hardwood swamps dominate upriver while the lower river grades first into forests of stunted trees, then into wide expanses of open saltmarsh. The gentle transition to coastal marshes is one of the west Florida coast's more attractive ecotones.

Birding and wildlife observation is also good along the river. Bald eagles are often seen in winter, and swallow-tailed kites are regularly seen in summer. Osprey are abundant all year. It is not uncommon to see manatees during the warmer months, especially near the Gulf of Mexico. Turtles and alligators round out the more commonly seen species.

Cedar Keys National Wildlife Refuge

Cedar Keys National Wildlife Refuge is accessible only by boat. One easy access to the northernmost islands is from the landing at the end of CR 326, described above. Another access is from landings in or near the city of Cedar Key. Public use is limited at this refuge; too much human interference would likely disrupt these heavily used and important colonial bird nesting grounds.

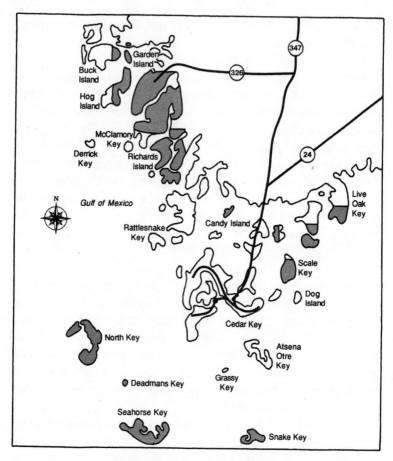

Cedar Keys National Wildlife Refuge

The interiors of all the islands are closed to the public, and all of Seahorse Key, including a 300-foot buffer surrounding it, is closed from March 1 to June 30 of each year. About 50,000 herons, egrets, ibises, pelicans, and double-crested cormorants nest here annually, down from a peak of over 200,000 less than three decades ago. The goings and comings of the parent birds make quite a spectacle during late spring and early summer.

A surprising variety of coastal plants inhabit these islands, including large patches of yucca and yaupon, as well as wild olive, red bay, red cedar, saw palmetto, and prickly pear cactus.

Saltmarshes are common in the low areas of the larger islands, and this is about the northernmost point on the Gulf coast to find mature populations of black mangrove.

A paddling excursion to the islands can be an enjoyable outing or a challenging adventure. Most of the islands are surrounded by shallow waters that can turn into extensive mud flats when the tide is out. In fall and winter the strong north winds associated with fast-moving cold fronts can push the waters far out into the Gulf, leaving much of the area around the islands completely visible, even at high tide. It is important to check tide tables and weather conditions carefully before embarking on an exploration of this refuge.

Best Time of Year

Any time of year has something to offer. Spring and fall are best for migrating birds; winter is best for a sea kayaking exploration of the saltmarsh; spring, summer, and fall are good for wildflowers and wildlife observation.

Pets

Pets are prohibited in any part of the Cedar Keys National Wildlife Refuge. Pets are allowed at Lower Suwannee River but must be leashed and under the owner's control at all times.

OCALA NATIONAL FOREST

The Ocala National Forest is the oldest national forest east of the Mississippi River and the southernmost in the continental United States. It was established in 1908, just 18 years after the birth of the national forest system, and currently contains a little over 383,000 acres, about double its original size. In recent years it has become one of the state's most popular recreation areas and hosts approximately two million visitors annually.

The 200,000-acre Big Scrub is one of the Ocala's main attractions. Described by Marjorie Kinnan Rawlings as "a vast dry

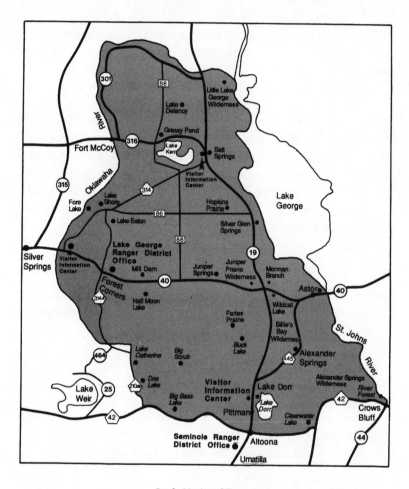

Ocala National Forest

rectangular plateau, bounded on three sides by two rivers," this sandy upland is a singular ecosystem, as unique as anything Florida has to offer. It is dominated by vast stands of sand pine— the largest sand pine forest in the world—with a shrub layer of both Chapman and myrtle oak, as well as several other sand scrub specialties including scrub palmetto, silk bay, scrub holly, and Florida rosemary. In many parts of the forest the pines look like gigantic toothpicks that have been jabbed into the ground at random. Some lean one direction, others another, as if all have been pushed this way and that by some powerful but unseen force. The sugar-white quartz sands that undergird this fascinating scene were laid down eons ago, when the Florida peninsula was only a narrow strip of land dividing the Atlantic Ocean from the Gulf of Mexico (see p. 17). In some places the sand is still dry and shifting, reminiscent of its seaside origins; in other places it seems as hard-packed as a roadway.

In addition to the expansive regions of scrub, the Ocala National Forest also contains a number of other native habitats that offer outstanding opportunities for exploration. There are dry, wet, and moist hammocks with diverse collections of hardwood trees, characteristic pine flatwoods dominated by slash and longleaf pine, freshwater bays densely vegetated with red maple, blackgum, and loblolly bay, beautiful wet and dry prairies carpeted with colorful wildflowers, and enchanting spring runs bordered by lush woodlands.

Besides its alluring terrestrial habitats, the Ocala also includes literally hundreds of ponds and a large number of freshwater springs. Famed Silver Springs, the world's largest, is located just west of the forest's boundary, and two of the state's first-magnitude springs—Alexander and Silver Glen—are contained within the Ocala's extensive holdings. At least 20 small springs are scattered along the Oklawaha River alone.

Plant lovers will find plenty to keep them busy in this national forest. The varied habitats and unique conditions in much of the forest support an expansive and diverse flora. In addition to the scrub specialties mentioned above, the forest also contains the southernmost population of Atlantic white cedar, an uncommon tree in northern Florida that is found in widely separated populations across the southeastern United States. Vinewicky, a climbing member of the heath family, grows in conjunction with the white cedar and uses the latter plant as support. Other interesting species include the tarflower and yellow anise. The latter is endemic to Florida and occurs naturally only in and near the Forest.

Location, Mailing Address and Phone

Ocala National Forest is located just east of Ocala. SR 40 crosses the forest from west to east; SR 19 crosses it from north to south. There are two ranger districts.

Seminole Ranger District, 40929 Highway 19, Umatilla, FL 32784; (904) 669-3153.

Lake George Ranger District, 17147 State Highway 40 E., Silver Springs, FL 34488; (904) 625-2520.

Facilities and Activities

Hiking, backpacking, horseback riding, birding, fishing, botanizing, canoeing, camping, bicycling, swimming, fishing, wildlife observation, nature trails, hunting, boating.

Visitor Centers

There are three visitor centers. The Ocala Visitor Center is located on SR 40, near the forest's western boundary. The Salt Springs Visitor Center is located across from Salt Springs on SR 19. The Pitman Visitor Center is along SR 19, near the southern boundary. All three provide brochures, maps, and campground information.

Camping and Recreation Areas

There are over 50 designated camping areas in the Ocala National Forest. Thirty are considered primitive and contain few accoutrements but are accessible by vehicle. About 20 are developed and offer a range of facilities from boating and fishing to nature trails and swimming areas. The most popular recreation areas in the Lake George District include Juniper Springs, Silver Glen Springs, Salt Springs, Mill Dam, and Fore Lake; the most popular in the Seminole District include Alexander Springs, Clearwater Lake, and Lake Dorr. All of these are fee areas that include both tent and trailer sites. For backpackers and backwoods explorers who require no amenities, it is permissible to camp almost anywhere in the forest, except during hunting season.

Juniper Springs

On SR 40, about four miles west of its intersection with SR 19.

Juniper Springs is the largest and most visited of the forest's campgrounds. It is situated adjacent to a charming spring that issues about 20 million gallons of water a day into beautiful Juniper Springs Run, one of the forest's designated canoe trails. The spring is enclosed by a concrete wall and has the appearance of a swimming pool. There is also an excellent interpretive nature trail here, as well as access to the Florida National Scenic Trail.

Juniper Creek is navigable from just below the swimming area. It is said to be one of the state's clearest waterways and is currently being recommended for National Wild and Scenic River status. It is a designated canoe trail that passes through the Juniper Prairie Wilderness for most of its route and is accessible only by canoe or by foot. It begins as a narrow, twisting stream with densely vegetated banks and a magnificent canopy; sabal palm, live oak, cypress, and blackgum border the tiny corridor. About two miles downstream it begins to broaden significantly and eventually becomes several hundred feet wide. The entire canoe trail is about 7 miles long and takes about four hours, longer if you like to take your time. Canoes may be rented at Juniper Springs Recreation Area, and a shuttle service is available to ferry paddlers back to the Recreation Area.

Salt Springs

On SR 19, a little more than 8 miles south of the forest's northern boundary.

The Salt Springs Recreation Area offers camping, fishing, picnicking, hiking, swimming, and canoeing, as well as a fascinating study in earth processes. Though located in nearly the center of the peninsula, away from any visible source of ocean currents, the springs that bubble up here issue about 52 million gallons of salty water per day into the 4-mile run that empties into Lake George. Salt Springs' water contains about six parts per thousand (ppt) of mineral matter, a considerable quantity given that full-strength seawater contains only about 35 ppt. Most of this unusually high content is attributed to the spring's origin. Beginning much deeper in the earth than many of the area's springs, it passes through the salty deposits of an ancient sea before finally emerging as a terrestrial watercourse.

Salt Springs Run is 4 miles long and empties into Lake George at its mouth. It is generally clear and its edges harbor an assortment of birds and wildlife, including the manatee. It is an attractive canoeing stream that is easily accessible from the landing at the recreation area. Since there are no landings between the spring and the lake, paddlers will have to make this a round-trip.

Mill Dam

On SR 40, about 2 miles east of the Lake George Ranger Station and 0.25 miles north on Forest Rd. 79.

Mill Dam is a day-use area situated on a small lake. There are fewer than 21 tables and grills located in a grove of live oaks as well as a shelter, swimming area, and boat ramp. Boating and fishing are the major recreational uses.

Fore Lake

Just off CR 314, a few miles north of SR 40.

This area contains scenic campsites near a small lake. Swimming, boating, and picnicking are also available.

Alexander Springs

On CR 445, several miles north of its intersection with SR 19.

This recreation area offers camping, swimming, canoeing, canoe rental, and a 1-mile nature trail. Its central feature is Alexander Springs, one of Florida's 27 first-magnitude springs. Many visitors come here to swim or snorkel or scuba dive in the spring, or to paddle the spring run that trails away to the southeast. Alexander Springs produces over 76 million gallons of water a day and has long been one of the area's main attractions. The Alexander Springs Recreation Area lies on the southern edge of Billies Bay Wilderness, and the Florida National Scenic Trail is accessible nearby.

Alexander Springs Creek is another of the forest's popular

canoeing streams. It is a 7-mile paddle from the spring to a national forest landing on Forest Road 539, much of which is wide and slow-flowing and choked with aquatic vegetation. Many paddlers rent canoes at the recreation area and make a round-trip by paddling downriver for a few miles, then turning back against the gentle current. Just below the landing on Forest Road 539, the river narrows and turns into the Alexander Springs Wilderness Area, then leads for several more miles to Shell Landing before continuing on to the St. Johns (see Alexander Springs Wilderness, below).

Silver Glen Springs

Off SR 19, seven miles north of SR 40.

Silver Glen is a very popular swimming and day-use area. The picnic area is located in a scenic oak hammock and includes grills and tables. Most people come here to swim or snorkel in the clear spring.

Clearwater Lake

On SR 42, several miles east of SR 19, on the southern edge of the forest.

Clearwater Lake lies just west of the southern trailhead of the Ocala section of the Florida National Scenic Trail. It includes a nature trail and a small, attractive camping area. The lake is suitable for swimming, fishing, and canoeing.

Lake Dorr

On SR 19, just north of SR 42, near the forest's southern boundary.

Lake Dorr is a relatively large lake. Its associated recreation area includes facilities for camping, picnicking, swimming, boating, fishing, and canoeing.

Hiking, Backpacking, and Horseback Riding

The Ocala National Forest has special significance to the evolution of the Florida National Scenic Trail. The initial development of this visionary footpath began here in 1966, and at least part of the trail's current corridor still passes along its original route.

Today, nearly 70 miles of the trail wind through the forest, passing through or adjacent to nearly all of the forest's major habitats.

The trail's southern terminus is located on Florida 42, near the Clearwater Lake Recreation Area, several miles east of SR 19. The northern terminus is near the spillway at Rodman Dam. Throughout its extent, this part of the Florida Trail offers mostly off-road hiking through easy terrain. Numerous lakes, streams, and hardwood hammocks offer scenic camping and resting spots, and the numerous periodic road crossings offer easy access as well as the availability of many short day hikes.

For horseback riding enthusiasts, the Ocala One-Hundred-Mile Horse Trail provides an outstanding way to see the forest. The 40-mile Flatwoods Trail loops through scenic pine flatwoods; the 40-mile Prairie Trail follows along grassy prairies and sand pine scrub; the 20-mile Baptist Lake Trail makes a round trip to Baptist Lake. All three trails begin just off SR 19, about 2 miles north of Altoona near the forest's southern border.

Canoeing

The Ocala National Forest's numerous rivers, lakes, and scenic spring runs offer many miles of canoeing and sea kayaking opportunities. Intrepid explorers can spend many years searching out all of the suitable places for practicing their pastime. For those with less time, a number of easily found areas provide quick access to some of the forest's more popular locations. In addition to the Alexander, Juniper, and Salt Springs Runs (all of which are described above), the Oklawaha River also provides enticing paddling opportunities.

The Oklawaha is a northward-flowing river that begins in a series of lakes well south of the National Forest. It follows along the forest's eastern edge for more than 40 miles before turning east through Lake Oklawaha and eventually emptying into the St. Johns River. It is a well-known symbol among environmentalists and its protection has had a tumultuous and somewhat unsuccessful history. It is the site of the now defunct Cross Florida Barge Canal, an ill-fated project that was eventually stopped by former President Richard Nixon, but not before large portions of the river were dredged and channelized. Nevertheless, at least some of the river's course still passes through scenic hardwood wetlands and offers interesting paddling.

The 20 miles of the Oklawaha that stretch between SR 40 and Florida 316 include some of the river's most attractive scenery. There is a landing at both of these highways, as well as at Gores Landing, a public campground and boat landing located about halfway between 40 and 316. The latter site offers the opportunity to divide this trip into two 10-mile segments.

Wilderness and Scenic Areas

Four designated national wilderness areas are scattered throughout the Ocala National Forest, two of which are fairly easily accessible by foot or canoe. For those who enjoy out-of-the-way locations with little access, both make outstanding destinations.

Juniper Prairie Wilderness

Just north of Juniper Springs Recreation Area, bordered on the south by SR 40.

Juniper Prairie is a 13,260-acre mosaic of wet and dry prairies interspersed with scenic woodlands. Over 100 small lakes dot the area, and the Florida National Scenic Trail and Juniper Creek Canoe Trail pass through its interior. Beginning at Juniper Springs Recreation Area and walking the trail northward for 5.4 miles leads to Hidden Pond, a small lake in the middle of the wilderness. A small grove of trees overlooking the lake makes an outstanding campsite for a short overnight round-trip backpacking excursion. Continuing northward for another 5.6 miles leads through Pat's Island, an interesting island of longleaf pine and oak scrub, then past the wilderness area's northern border to Hopkin's Prairie. This latter site offers a 22-mile round-trip from Juniper Springs. Since it is not within the wilderness area, water, sanitary facilities, and a developed campground are available at Hopkin's Prairie.

Alexander Springs Wilderness

Located in the forest's southeast corner and accessible by turning north onto Forest Rd. 540-3 from SR 42.

Alexander Springs Wilderness includes 7,700 acres that abut the western edge of Lake Woodruff National Wildlife Refuge (see p. 53). It is most easily accessed by the Alexander Springs Creek canoe trail, described above. The easternmost part of this wilderness is dominated by marsh, lakes, and marshy streams. It is possible to paddle to the St. Johns River, then into Lake Woodruff from the wilderness. It should be noted that there are no access points within this region and the routes are not always clear. If you plan an extended excursion, it is probably wise to mark your way with engineer's tape, then collect it on your return. Camping is not permitted within the boundaries of Lake Woodruff National Wildlife Refuge.

Billies Bay Wilderness

Along the northern edge of Alexander Springs Recreation Area, off SR 445.

This 3,120-acre wilderness is mostly wetland and contains no trails. During much of the year it is extremely wet and requires wading to explore thoroughly. A short stretch of the Florida National Scenic Trail skirts the area's southwestern edge for about 1 mile but does not enter the wilderness. Several small creeks cross Billies Bay but are not suitable for canoeing.

Little Lake George Wilderness

Between Little Lake George and SR 19 at the forest's extreme northeast corner.

Like Billies Bay and Alexander Springs, this 2,500-acre wilderness is mostly wetland and has little easy access. It is situated just south of the confluence of the Oklawaha and St. Johns Rivers on the western edge of Little Lake George and is dominated by swamps and marshes. This wilderness may be reached on foot (there are no trails) or by boat from the St. Johns River.

Morman Branch

Just north of Forest Rd. 71 which turns east off SR 19 a little over a mile south of the Juniper Wayside. Forest Rd. 71 contains deep sands and is not passable by two-wheel-drive vehicles. It is better to walk the road to the culvert that crosses Morman Branch.

This is a beautiful, trailless area that borders the southern edge of Juniper Creek. It contains magnificent woodlands that include Atlantic white cedar, yellow anise, and vine-wicky, all of which are counted among the forest's more special plants. It is possible to enter the area along a fire lane that turns northward off 71 just east of the culvert over Morman Branch, or by following along the branch from the road. During high water this area can be difficult to traverse, but dry weather offers outstanding exploration opportunities. It should be noted that some places within this area contain a quicksandlike substrate. Using a walking staff and testing the ground in front of you will help insure that you do not become mired in such places. Carrying a compass is also important since there are no marked paths.

Wildlife Observation

An abundance of wildlife find refuge in this national forest, including an assortment of mammals, reptiles, amphibians, and birds. Some of these species are widespread and easily seen while others are generally restricted to one or two specific habitats.

About 50 mammals are known to inhabit this forest. The largest include the white-tailed deer and Florida black bear, both of which are found in sizeable populations and inhabit or visit a number of the forest's habitats. Smaller mammals include the raccoon, striped skunk, river otter, wild boar, gray fox, eastern cottontail, opossum, bobcat, gray squirrel, fox squirrel, flying squirrel, cotton mouse, wood rat, and golden mouse. Most of these animals, with the exception of the river otter, are found in a variety of the Forest's habitats. The otter is restricted to wet areas with sufficient water to support its typically aquatic lifestyle.

Scrub Jay

At least 35 amphibians and 66 reptiles inhabit the Ocala National Forest. A surprising number of these species live in scrub and sandhill communities, including the southern toad, oak toad, pinewoods tree frog, barking tree frog, Florida scrub lizard, and Florida gopher frog. The latter is a hard-to-find specialty that typically inhabits gopher tortoise burrows along with a number of other species, not the least of which is the endangered eastern indigo snake.

As might be expected, an even larger number of amphibians are found in the forest's wetland areas. Frogs and toads, the most commonly encountered species in this habitat, include the pig frog, bullfrog, river frog, and bronze frog, as well as several species of tree frogs; most are easily recognized by their distinctive calls. Other aquatic amphibians include the two-toed amphiuma (sometimes called congo eel), and a variety of sala-

Red-cockaded Woodpecker

manders, newts, and sirens, all of which are secretive creatures that are usually found only through diligent searching.

More than 200 bird species live in or visit the Ocala during various times of year. Many are typical of northern Florida and are included in the list in Chapter 7. At least a few are specialties that bear mention. The raucous, blue and brown, crestless Florida scrub jay is a common resident in oak scrub areas and is easily seen in its habitat. This bird, which is a subspecies of the western scrub jay, is endemic to Florida and is highly restricted to its preferred habitat. The longleaf pine islands scattered throughout the Big Scrub also support several red-cockaded woodpecker colonies, as well as resident populations of brown-headed nuthatch and Bachman's sparrow.

Best Time of Year

There is something to do here year-round. Summers are typically hot and insects can be bothersome. However, the numerous swimming areas and canoeing streams make the forest well used, even in the hottest months. Winter is usually mild and is a good time to make extended hiking or backpacking excursions. The springs in the Ocala remain a constant 72 degrees year-round. Many visitors swim even during the winter months.

Pets

Allowed.

OSCEOLA NATIONAL FOREST

The Osceola National Forest is one of those places at which few people think about stopping. It is out of the way, not well known, and visited mostly by nearby residents who have learned to appreciate its interior. When racing along on Interstate 10, as most drivers do, the signs that announce the Osceola's boundaries merely whiz by, offering no hint of how to access the forest's offerings, or even what those offerings are. It is difficult to imagine so many acres of outstanding natural areas that remain so rarely visited by enthusiastic naturalists—particularly in a state as populous as Florida.

This 197,242-acre holding is the smallest but most rapidly growing of Florida's three national forests. It was dedicated by President Herbert Hoover in 1931, though its original 157,000 acres had been purchased for timber production in 1924. It is forested mainly with pine flatwoods but also includes large areas of prime hardwood swamps and wetlands. As with most national forests, the Osceola is serviced by an extensive labyrinth of graded roads, as well as a handful of highways.

Location, Mailing Address and Phone

Northeast of Lake City; reached off either US 90 or CR 250.
USDA Forest Service, Osceola Ranger District, P.O. Box 70, Olustee, FL 32072; (904) 752-2577.

Facilities and Activities

Camping, picnicking, swimming, hiking, bicycling, fishing, canoeing, botanizing, wildlife observation, wilderness area.

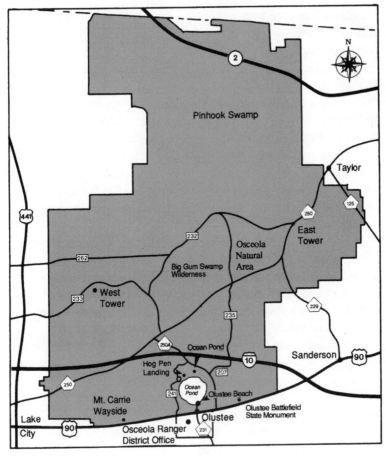

Osceola National Forest

The Osceola offers a variety of outdoor recreation and nature study opportunities. The ranger station, which is located on US 90 approximately 10 miles east of Lake City, should be your first stop. Maps and information are available here as well as a small book rack with several publications that focus on the area's history, wildlife, and plants.

Camping and Picnicking

Olustee Beach is the forest's most popular picnic and recreation area. It is a fee area that is located on Ocean Pond, a nearly circular 1,760-acre freshwater lake that lies just north of US 90 and east of the ranger station. A directional sign on the highway marks the way to the site.

Olustee Beach includes a roped-off swimming area, an expansive, grassy lawn that contains numerous picnic tables, a small fishing dock that overlooks the lake, and a short nature trail. The trail leads along an old logging tram then follows a boardwalk across a low woodland to the edge of the lake. The trail offers an interesting introduction to the Osceola's natural bounty.

There is a boat landing off the main road to Olustee Beach that provides access to the lake. Canoeing or sea kayaking along the lake's edges is enjoyable but sometimes subjects paddlers to strong winds and waves.

The Osceola's only developed campground lies on the northern shore of Ocean Pond, directly across the lake from the picnic area. There are about 50 campsites here, many of which face the water. The campground is located under a high canopy of pines and hardwoods and includes a boat launch, swimming area, and centrally located restrooms. Ocean Pond campground is a national forest fee area and is a popular weekend recreation site.

Canoeing

In addition to the open (and sometimes rough) waters of Ocean Pond, the Middle Prong St. Marys River can also be a good paddling stream, provided that there is enough water. As with the upper reaches of many small rivers, the stretch of the St. Marys that lies near its source is highly dependent on rainfall, as well as on the ground and surface water that is present in the forest.

When water is sufficient, it is possible to launch a canoe into the small pond at the SR 250 bridge, then follow the narrow, twisting, waterway to SR 125, SR 122, or past the boundaries of the forest to the landing on SR 127. The trip to 127 is about 10 miles in length, with the first 4 miles or so flowing totally within the forest.

This trip can be quite demanding and should probably not be attempted by inexperienced canoeists. When the water is low, there can be many downed trees and other obstructions

Ocean Pond

blocking the way; at almost any water level there are at least a few impediments to easy paddling. After leaving the forest the river widens, becomes more channelized, and the banks become more defined. It is probably wise to inquire at the ranger station before attempting this trip.

Hiking

The Osceola section of the Florida National Scenic Trail stretches for 22 miles across the Osceola National Forest. Beginning at the roadside parking lot adjacent to Olustee Battlefield State Historic Site on the southeastern side of the forest, this well-known pathway cuts diagonally across the forest and exits near US 441. The trail passes through typical north–central Florida woodlands for most of its route and offers several very scenic stretches.

For those with limited time, the first 6 miles provide the best sampler of what this forest has to offer. Beginning at US 90, the trail leads through bay swamps and flatwoods for nearly the entire route. Black gum, red maple, loblolly bay, and cypress are the more common trees and a variety of shrubby blueberries,

81

dangleberries, and staggerbushes line much of the route. The ground cover includes many species of showy wildflowers that change with the season, making the trail take on different aspects throughout the year.

At mile 5.6 the trail intersects the paved access road to Ocean Pond campground, which makes a good termination point. However, the short stretch just beyond the campground road is worth the extra few minutes it takes to explore it. A boardwalk traverses a cypress pond then passes through a pine flat with mature loblolly bay. About 0.5 mile beyond the boardwalk the trail empties onto Forest Road 241, then connects with SR 250 before crossing I-10 and continuing to a primitive campsite near Turkey Run. The stretch that contains the boardwalk makes an interesting nature trail for those who prefer shorter walks.

Big Gum Swamp Wilderness

There are several large swampy areas within the confines of the Osceola National Forest that preserve outstanding habitat and a variety of north–central Florida wildlife. The largest of these is Big Gum Swamp Wilderness, a 13,660-acre national wilderness area situated near the middle of the forest. Big Gum is surrounded by several improved forest service roads and is easy to circumnavigate.

Gaining access to Big Gum's fascinating interior is not always as easy as locating its boundaries. No blazed foot trails or marked access routes penetrate the huge swamp, and there is a dearth of information about how one should go about choosing a way in. The official U.S. Forest Service map shows only the general outline of the few trails through the area, none of which are officially marked on the encircling roadways. However, for intrepid explorers who do not mind getting their feet (or sometimes even their entire lower torsos!) wet, and who are comfortable with map and compass, venturing into Big Gum is a rewarding adventure.

The trails shown on the official U.S. Forest Service map are actually a handful of antiquated logging trams that are usually discernible once you find them. The remains of these old roads, which were probably constructed in the 1930s, make acceptable though sometimes obscure walking paths, and usually lead at least as far as the edges of the swamp's wettest portions. At least one crosses the entire wilderness from east to west. It is probably wise when walking these old roadways to carry a roll of engineer's tape to mark your path. Sometimes the routes diverge or intersect in places not shown on the map, or pass through dense tangles that challenge even the most competent outdoorspeople.

One of the easiest paths into Gum Swamp is an old roadway that turns off Forest Road 232 just north of its intersection with Forest Road 272. The turn-off is conspicuous and relatively easy to find. Those who follow this trail should probably do so with the aid of the Big Gum Swamp topographic map published by the U.S. Geological Survey or, at minimum, the U.S. Forest Service Osceola National Forest map. The pathway is relatively easy to follow but divides periodically at places not shown on the Osceola map. The first unmarked turn-off is at a Y-shaped intersection less than 1 mile from the trail's entry point. The left fork leads ahead for some distance, then terminates in a scenic woodland. The right fork leads into a particularly scenic hammock, and then deeper into the swamp. The edges of the roadway and hammock are crowded with an interesting variety of plants including sweetgum, hickory, ironwood, cypress, loblolly bay, southern magnolia, and some large specimens of slash pine. Black bear, white-tailed deer, and bobcat are known to frequent the area.

Near the hammock the trail is crossed by a second old roadway. Turning left (east) at this intersection takes hikers into the deeper parts of the swamp and eventually leads all the way across the wilderness area to Forest Road 235. The route is shown on the Osceola National Forest map.

Osceola Research Natural Area

Just east of Big Gum Swamp Wilderness, across Forest Road 235, lies another interesting, though trailless, area. The Osceola Research Natural Area is a 373-acre parcel that is bounded on the south by Middle Prong St. Marys River and on the north by a small, two-lane woods road that skirts the natural area's outer edge.

The best place to enter the natural area is just north of the bridge that marks its southern boundary. There is an area of open woodlands on the eastern side of the road that allows easy passage. This area supports some particularly large and attractive loblolly bay, several clumps of upright saw palmetto that have taken on treelike proportions, a variety of fetterbushes and staggerbushes, and a shallow cypress pond that lies in the perpetual shade of the lush forest canopy. Wandering around in this natural area can sometimes be challenging due to the large areas of dense shrubbery, but the reward is well worth the visit.

Pinhook Swamp

The Pinhook Swamp is among the Osceola National Forest's newest wild areas. Its 1989 purchase was another of those important acquisitions shepherded by The Nature Conservancy, then turned over to the public trust for continued management and preservation.

The importance of protecting the Pinhook cannot be overestimated. The forest, shrub, and marsh communities that it preserves constitute a natural corridor between the huge and well-known Okefenokee Swamp that lies to the Pinhook's north and the pristine wetlands of Big Gum Swamp and the greater Osceola National Forest to the south. The vast mosaic of wetland systems that make up these preserved natural areas also contribute to the cleanliness and conservation of both the Suwannee and St. Marys River watersheds.

The Pinhook also supports a wide array of wildlife. River otter, bobcat, Florida black bear, and white-tailed deer are the better known and most likely seen species. However, there are also substantial populations of southern mink, muskrat, and southeastern weasel. The Pinhook's open areas also support one of the few north Florida breeding populations of sandhill crane, a large, long-legged grayish bird that is reminiscent of the extremely endangered whooping crane. The lands contained within the Pinhook Swamp provide an important wildlife corridor for these and other native species.

Botanizing

There are several natural habitats represented in the Osceola, all of which provide outstanding outlets for plant hunting. The four major vegetative assemblages found in the forest are pine-palmetto flatwoods, cypress swamps, creek swamps, and bay swamps. All provide opportunities for learning to identify north Florida's native plants.

The flatwoods community, which is typically dominated by slash pine, longleaf pine, or pond pine, is the most extensive cover type and accounts for about 70 percent of the forest's landscape. Though such shrubs as the gallberries, blueberries, and

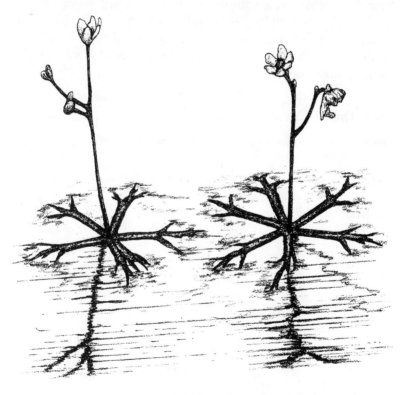

Bladderwort

fetterbushes are the most conspicuous flatwoods species, there is also a variety of herbaceous plants that includes wiregrass, panic grass, bracken fern, deer tongue, climbing butterfly pea, meadow beauties, fleabane, hat pins, sundew, sabatia, violets, and a large number of less common species.

The swamp communities cover much less of the forest's territory than the flatwoods, but are no less botanically interesting. Pond cypress, bald cypress, blackgum, sweetbay, red maple, water tupelo, and loblolly bay are the dominant trees, and Virginia willow, sweet pepperbush, buttonbush, fetterbush, swamp candleberry, wax myrtle, myrtle-leaved holly, yaupon, and large sweet gallberry make up the most conspicuous shrubs. The deep waters that regularly inundate the Osceola's swamplands restrict the number of plants that are found in the swamp's deepest portions. Nevertheless, a number of vines and low-growing herbs are typically present in the ground cover, including smilax, hat pins, arrowhead, sundew, pitcher plant, lizard's tail, bladderwort, cinnamon fern, marsh pennywort, and several species of sedges and rushes.

Best Time of Year

There is something of interest at any time of year.

Pets

Allowed on a leash.

VI
NATURAL AREAS—
STATE AND LOCAL
LANDS

ANDREWS WILDLIFE MANAGEMENT AREA

If you are looking for mature woodlands with record-sized trees, Andrews Wildlife Management Area is a must-see location. Four Florida state champion trees are found here, as well as one of the best remaining examples of a north Florida hardwood hammock. Stretching for nearly 4,000 acres along the lower reaches of the Suwannee River, this wildlife management area (WMA) is noted for its abundant wildlife, old growth forests, and many miles of walking trails.

The mature hammock woodlands that clothe the Andrews area are one of its major attractions. Multi-aged forests of hickory, live oak, bluff oak, maple, and sweetgum tower above an overstory of eastern hophornbeam, American holly, ironwood, horse sugar, devil's walking stick, and red bay. The deep shade of the high, dense canopy effectively eliminates most ground cover vegetation, leaving a nearly open, parklike forest at the hammock's lowest level. In some places the shrub vegetation is so thin that it is possible to strike out in almost any direction, with only a compass as a guide.

Andrews WMA was acquired by the state in 1985 as a joint project of the Florida Game and Fresh Water Fish Commission and the Suwannee River Water Management District, with assistance from The Nature Conservancy. Funds for the purchase came from the Save Our Rivers (SOR) and Conservation and

Recreation Lands (CARL) programs, two of Florida's most important land acquisition initiatives. The tract is currently managed by the Game and Fresh Water Fish Commission. Limited hunting is allowed by special permit, but the primary management objective is preservation and protection of an important natural remnant.

Much of this area's beauty and natural condition stems from the stewardship provided by its previous owners. For 40 years the Andrews family, for whom the tract is named, managed the property primarily for outdoor recreation and with an eye toward its restoration and conservation. The land has been altered little since the early 1950s, and today is the largest remaining contiguous hardwood forest along the Suwannee River.

Location, Mailing Address and Phone

From the Suwannee River bridge in Fanning Springs, drive south on US 19 for 3 miles to CR 211 (look for the directional sign on the highway), then west on 211 for 1 mile to the entrance.

Florida Game and Fresh Water Fish Commission, 620 S. Meridian St., Tallahassee, FL 32399-1600; (904) 488-3831.

Facilities and Activities

Hiking, bicycling, birding, botanizing, fishing, hunting, wildlife observation.

Trails

The best way to explore this area is by bicycling or driving the roadways, or hiking along the extensive system of backwoods paths. There are six designated nature trails, each of which was established to lead to one of the record trees, and a number of old roadways that are now closed to vehicular traffic but offer outstanding walking and peddling opportunities.

Three of the most interesting walks offer several miles of hiking and allow extended exploration of the northern, central, and southern parts of the area. All are easy to find and easy to follow.

The northern route begins at the entrance to the Basswood Trail, which can be reached by turning north onto Fanning Road, then following it to the point past which further vehicular traffic is restricted. Just past the gate, the Basswood Trail leads off to the left at an obvious sign. It is only a short walk to the trail's intersection with Andrews Road, an old, narrow woods road that leads along a scenic floodplain swamp. It is possible to walk either north or south from the intersection and to take one of several circular routes back to the starting point. The large basswood that this trail was built to access, which was formerly on the National Big Tree Registry, is now dead. Only the remains of its lower trunk are left standing.

The Buckeye and Turkey Track trails are accessed off the central portions of Fanning Road and form a relatively short, circular route that leads to the river on the west and nearly to the boundary of the WMA on the east. Either of these trails may also be used to access other paths for extended walking.

Continuing south on Fanning Road to its intersection with Randall Road and Dick Slough Road leads to a parking area adjacent to a locked gate. Beyond the gate is the extension of Fanning Road, an outstanding walking path and the access route to many of the walking opportunities available in the southern part of the WMA. Just beyond the gate, the Persimmon Trail leads off to the east at a marked sign. A short way down the path is Florida's champion persimmon tree, 90 feet tall with a circumference of 60 inches and a crown spread of 39 feet. Its dark, blocky bark alone is enough to suggest this tree's advanced maturity.

Beyond the Persimmon Trail, Fanning Road leads to an intersection with Winged Elm Road. Turning east leads along a relatively short, circular route back to Randall Road and the starting point. Turning west leads to the Bluff Oak Trail or to the end of Dick Slough Road. There is an abundance of bluff oak along much of this trail, including Florida's champion. The latter's 101-inch circumference, 105-foot height, and 78-foot crown spread are impressive dimensions.

The Florida Maple Trail is most easily found from the north

side of Dick Slough Road. The champion tree is just north of the roadway and is marked by a sign. This tree is 85 feet tall, 82 inches in circumference, and has a crown spread of 51 feet. Beyond the tree, the trail continues into a very scenic stretch of hammock woodlands before leading on to Fanning Road.

For those who prefer driving to walking, the main roads are generally well maintained and driveable by most vehicles. However, periods of extensive rainfall can create muddy areas along some routes and make them impassable by anything less than four-wheel-drive vehicles.

The entrance road (River Road) leads directly to the river and to a suitable place to launch a canoe or to leave a vehicle for an extended walk along Andrews Road. Andrews Road leads both northward and southward along the edges of the river and connects with several other of the WMA's walking routes. (It should be noted that there is no suitable landing for trailered boats along the river.)

Wildlife Observation

All of Andrew's walking paths and driving routes provide many opportunities for seeing wildlife. White-tailed deer, wild turkey, feral hogs, gray and southern flying squirrels, bobcat, and a variety of birds, including pileated woodpeckers, barred and screech owls, warblers, vireos, orioles, cuckoos, and titmice are commonly seen.

Several small clearings are scattered along or just off the trails and roadways. These are planted with grasses and grains and are designed to provide edge habitat and food resources to attract a variety of wildlife. Gopher tortoises are common in some of these clearings as evidenced by the sandy mounds that cover the openings to their burrows.

Two of these clearings, one large and one small, have wildlife observation towers located nearby. Both of these vantage points are covered, completely enclosed, and provide a screen that keeps observers out of view of the animals. Patient, quiet observers often see white-tailed deer and wild turkey from these platforms.

Best Time of Year

Wildlife is abundant year-round. Cool winter days may be better for extended walks. Most trees here are deciduous; identifying them is easiest during late spring, summer, and early fall. Migrating birds are most prevalent during April and October. The area is open only during daylight hours and is closed to the general public, except permitted hunters, during hunting seasons. In general, hunts are conducted on Friday, Saturday, and Sunday during October and November and portions of January, March, and April.

Pets

Allowed.

ANASTASIA STATE RECREATION AREA

The first thing you notice is the shape of the oak trees—flat topped, twisted trunks all leaning in unison, almost as if some giant horticulturist had attempted to create an entire landscape of oversized bonsai. Its not that this is such an unusual sight along the Atlantic coast. In seaside parks from Fernandina Beach to Miami, much of Florida's shoreline vegetation shows the telltale signs of having been sculpted by the centuries-old onslaught of salty winds. Its just that the trees at Anastasia are so striking, and so obvious.

Anastasia Island is unlike most other Florida east coast barriers. Instead of being constructed solely of loose quartz sands, its beaches are underlain by coquina limestone that was deposited during the Pleistocene Epoch. Coquina outcrops have long been a defining character of the island and continue to play a role in diminishing the effects of wave-induced erosion.

Coquina also has a long cultural history in the area. Old St. Augustine, touted as the oldest town in the continental United States, was essentially constructed of the porous rock. Fort Marion, the old city gate, and many of the older houses in the historical district bear evidence to the limestone's use and longevity.

Anastasia State Park, which is located across the river from St. Augustine, has a lot to offer, particularly for birders, but is not without its problems. It is one of those parks that forms an oasis in the midst of burgeoning development. Its nearly 1,900 acres are sandwiched between a busy highway and the Atlantic Ocean, and its weekend use in summer can be intense. As with other coastal parks, there has been some vandalism and abuse here by unenlightened visitors, but park staff have taken a proactive approach to insuring the park's protection. Patrons are encouraged to be observant and to report potential violations to the rangers.

Location, Mailing Address and Phone

Take SR 16 east to St. Augustine, then south on A1A to the park entrance.

Anastasia State Recreation Area, 1340-A A1A South, St. Augustine, FL 32048; (904) 461-2033 or (904) 461-2000.

Facilities and Activities

Camping, bicycling, swimming, wind surfing, sea kayaking, canoeing, birding, botanizing, nature trail.

After leaving the ranger station, the main access road cuts directly through the center of the park. Dense tangles of coastal scrub line the road's western edge; a narrow saltwater lagoon bounds the east.

There is a picnic and concession area not far past the entrance station. The concession rents canoes, sea kayaks, and wind surfboards. Private craft can be launched here, too. Paddling the edges of the lagoon as well as its marshy southern tip can be an interesting adventure.

The end of the paved road terminates at a beachside parking lot with a boardwalk across the dunes. Adjacent to the boardwalk is an automobile entrance to the beach. This is one of the few state parks that still allows vehicular access to bathing beaches; it is a traditional use that the park service has found it difficult to eliminate.

There is also a nice picnic area at the road's end. Open-air and covered tables are available and the salt-pruned oaks at the site make it particularly attractive. The dense thicket behind the picnic area has several openings, and the surrounding woods are perfect for exploration. Don't be surprised if rabbits join you for lunch here; the picnic area seems to be a favored haunt for these bushy-tailed mammals.

For wildflower and native plant enthusiasts, a walk across the boardwalk to the beach is worthwhile. Typical plants on the dune face and in the back-dune meadow include the colorful blanket flower as well as a healthy population of sea oats, seaside elder, and at least two species of morning glory.

Bicycling

Anastasia is a great place for peddling. A sidewalk parallels the road for its entire length and makes an excellent trail. If you are camping, you can use the sidewalk before the park opens for the day. Then you won't have to share the gentle onshore breezes and rich salty air that wafts across the dune ridge in early morning.

The campground access road and campground loop roads are also good for peddling. All are hardsurfaced and provide easy riding for almost any kind of bike.

Camping

Just before the main road reaches the beachside parking lot, a roadway turns off to the west and leads to one of the Florida park system's finest campgrounds. One hundred and thirty-nine well-separated sites are set in the heart of a scenic hardwood hammock dominated by live oaks, red cedar, and sabal palms. Huge oak limbs decorated with dense patches of resurrection fern stretch out in all directions, effectively canopying the entire area, keeping it seemingly in perpetual shade. Only the sea breezes penetrate the forest cover, rustling the leaves and providing a hint of coolness even on hot midsummer days.

The campground is divided into seven loops, most of which

have between 15 and 20 sites. Restrooms and showers are within easy distance of each site, and two of the loops have several sites that are specially designed for the physically disabled.

This is also one of the few Florida parks that actually enforces the "registered campers only" rule. If you want to take your vehicle into the campground, you must request a visitor's pass from the park office.

Nature Trail

The Ancient Dunes Trail is the park's only nature walk. It is a circular route that may be reached from either of the campground loops. Reaching it requires walking into the campground or requesting a campground visitor's pass so you can drive in.

The trail's northern terminus begins across from the Sea Bean loop. After passing under a canopy of low-growing red bay with twisted, lichen-covered trunks you are immersed in a densely vegetated coastal forest that was once a seaside dune field. In a higher stand of the sea the region probably appeared much as the park's beachside does today. As the sea fell, maritime forest plants began to take hold in the mounds of shifting sand, resulting in today's forest of oaks, American holly, yaupon, southern magnolia, saw palmetto, and red cedar. A list of the park's trees can be obtained from the entrance station and will help you identify the more common species.

Birding

Anastasia boasts a bird list of more than 170 species. A number of these are transient visitors that pass through the park only during fall or spring migration. The most interesting of these seasonally present migrants include the roseate spoonbill, sandhill crane, Tennessee warbler, red knot, stilt sandpiper, glaucous gull, roseate tern, burrowing owl, and rose-breasted grosbeak.

As might be expected, Anastasia is also good for gulls, terns, and shorebirds; the best place to see them requires a drive or walk north along the beach to the inlet. Marbled godwit, whimbrel, greater yellowlegs, spotted sandpiper, and common snipe are some of the more sought-after winter shorebirds. Wintering gulls and terns include the great black-backed and herring gulls, and the sandwich and Caspian terns.

Other interesting wintering species include the seaside and sharp-tailed sparrows, northern junco, American goldfinch, Virginia rail, sora, and whip-poor-will. Summer birders can find the brightly colored painted bunting nesting in the edges, and the least tern and Wilson plover nesting on the beach or in the dunes.

Best Time of Year

Any time of year has something to offer for birders. Camping, canoeing, and sea kayaking are also good year-round. Swimming is best in summer.

Pets

Allowed on a 6-foot leash; not allowed on the beach or in the campground.

BULOW CREEK STATE PARK

If you're looking for interpretive trails, colorful dioramas, well-stocked visitors center, or organized events, Bulow Creek State Park is not for you. But if you prize mature woodlands, trickling brooks, towering trees, lush ground cover, and tranquil hiking trails, you will not want to miss this outstanding sanctuary. What this park lacks in interpretation, it more than makes up for in sheer beauty.

Bulow Creek was acquired by the state in 1981 to preserve one of the best remaining examples of northeast Florida's coastal hardwood hammock community. It is situated in an old-growth area that supports a large number of ancient live oaks, many of which are more than 200 years old. Walking into the park's holdings from either the north or the south immerses you almost

Bulow Creek

immediately into an enchanted forest that is reminiscent of the types of woodlands William Bartram probably experienced in his pioneering treks through Florida's wildlands over 200 years ago.

One good way to see part of this park is by paddling the Bulow Creek Canoe Trail. See Chapter 7 for directions to the put-in points and for a brief description of the route.

Location, Mailing Address and Phone

The main entrance is located off Old Dixie Highway in northern Volusia County, just before the highway turns west and intersects with I-95; the second entrance is off Walter Boardman Ln. just before it crosses the bridge; Walter Boardman is part of the Volusia County Ormond Scenic Loop and turns east off Old Dixie Highway just north of the park's lower entrance.

Bulow Creek State Park, 3351 Old Dixie Highway, Ormond Beach, FL 32174; (904) 677-4645.

Facilities and Activities

Hiking, birdwatching, nature trail, botanizing, Fairchild Oak, scenic drives.

Fairchild Oak

Many people stop at this park just to see the ancient Fairchild Oak, named in honor of botanist David Fairchild. Entering the park from Old Dixie Highway, then turning left at the sign brings you to a small parking lot adjacent to the tree. This giant is estimated to be over 800 years old and is in outstanding condition. Huge branches stretch for nearly 100 feet from the trunk; some are so old and heavy that they now rest on the ground and appear to have taken root. The opportunity to see this magnificent tree is reason enough to stop here, but those who leave without exploring the rest of the park miss a wondrous place.

Hiking and Nature Trails

Two trails originate within the park; the termini of both are visible from the Fairchild parking lot. The Wahlin Nature Trail is the shorter of the two but provides a nice entry into a mature hardwood hammock. The entire route is probably less than 0.5 miles long and passes through a mature woodland of American elm, ironwood, southern red cedar, red mulberry, and hickory. Lizard tail and fern grow along the creek bottom below the boardwalk, and you can find a few specimens of the primitive coontie if you keep your head down.

The Fairchild Oak Trail is a much longer jaunt that connects Bulow Creek State Park with Bulow Plantation State Historic Site. It was constructed with the assistance of the Florida Trail Association (FTA) and is included in the FTA's official guidebook. This trail is about 6 miles long and passes through hardwood hammock, pine plantation, and along the edges of the saltmarsh. It offers level hiking on a well-marked trail and is a must for those who want to fully explore the area. You can leave a car at both ends of this trail if you want to make a one-way trip. However, the trail is open only for day use and the Historic Site closes early, so be sure to complete your hike in time to retrieve your vehicle.

Driving Trails

The Pumphouse Road turns right at the sign, just a few yards after entering the park from the Dixie Highway access. It borders the park's boundary for several miles and offers a scenic, though jostling, ride. There are a number of places to pull off and wander into the park, but there are no designated trails here. The road eventually leads to the northern edge of the Tomoka Basin, which is not part of the park.

Walter Boardman Lane is part of Volusia County's Scenic Ormond Loop. Although not part of the park, it runs through the park, around the eastern edge of the Tomoka Marsh, and back to Ormond Beach. Immediately after turning off Dixie Highway, Walter Boardman passes through a lush canopied area that offers outstanding scenery as well as easy access to the hammock. Again, there are no trails here, so those who venture off the road will need to be prepared.

The two-lane dirt road that turns south off Walter Boardman

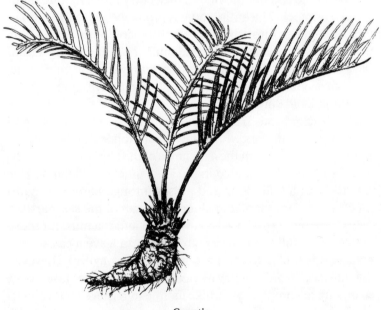

Coontie

Lane just west of the bridge that crosses Bulow Creek is part of the park's hiking trail but is also driveable. Following the road to its dead end (about 0.8 mile) leads to a good place to launch a canoe, kayak, or small boat. It also offers a good place to take in the scenery of the Tomoka Marsh.

Botanizing

This is a great place for studying the native vegetation of north Florida's coastal hardwood hammock. Much of the area is still in a nearly natural state; few exotic plants have gotten a toehold here. You will want to bring a good tree and shrub book with you, as well as your favorite wildflower guide.

Best Time of Year

Winter, spring, and fall are probably best for hiking, though the shady parts of the trail make summer walks enjoyable, especially in the early part of the day. However, there is usually a good supply of ticks during the summer months. Spring, summer, and fall are best for flowering plants and deciduous trees. Spring is best for birding.

Pets

Allowed but must be leashed.

CARY STATE FOREST

The Cary State Forest encompasses approximately 3,400 acres of typical north Florida terrain on the western outskirts of Jacksonville. Like many of Florida's state forests, Cary is a multiple use area. It is managed primarily for timber production but also supports a variety of other recreational uses including hiking, camping, hunting, environmental education, and nature study.

Cary was one of Florida's first state forests. In 1935 President Theodore Roosevelt encouraged then-Florida governor David Sholtz to appoint a Conservation Committee to develop guidelines for the protection of the state's natural areas. This committee drafted legislation that was passed in 1935 and established Florida's system of parks and forests. Most of the lands that currently define the Cary State Forest were purchased between 1935 and 1942 as a direct result of the funding provided by this new law. Nearly 1,900 acres of this land were purchased from the George F. and Charlotte C. Cary family, hence the forest's name. The remaining land was purchased from several other families at an average price of $4 per acre.

Location, Mailing Address and Phone

On the east side of US 301, 7.3 mi. north of US 90.

Division of Forestry, 8719 W. Beaver St., Jacksonville, FL 32220; (904) 693-5055.

Facilities and Activities

Hiking, nature trails, wildlife observation tower, open-air interpretive pavilion, primitive camping, picnicking, bath house with showers.

The southeastern corner of the Cary State Forest is dedicated to environmental education. Hunting is not permitted in this part of the forest and four nature trails, some with boardwalks, allow access to the area. An open-air environmental education interpretive pavilion is located at the end of a short trail near the intersection of Pavilion Drive (the entrance road) and Fire Tower Road. Exhibits at the interpretive center include a display of North American pine cones and a number of murals detailing the dynamic relationships that exist between plants, animals, soil, water, oxygen, and light. The pavilion is visited regularly by classroom groups from the Duval County School District, and the entire environmental education portion of the forest serves an important role in the natural science education of many area children.

The primary habitats here are pine flatwoods, cypress sloughs, and bay swamps. About two-thirds of the forest is dominated by flatwoods, the other third by swamps and wetlands.

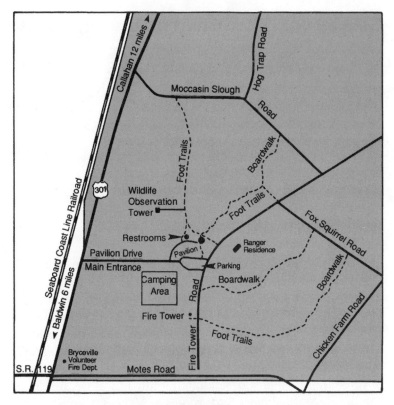

Cary State Forest

Two of the nature trails are essentially flatwoods routes that pass through typical pinelands; the other two trails include long stretches of bay swamp and cypress pond communities.

The flatwoods trails are lined with a variety of woody and herbaceous plants that are typical of north Florida pinelands. The most conspicuous plant in early summer is tar-flower, a woody heath that is closely related to the rhododendrons and blueberries. Its spreading, showy flowers are easy to spot among the dense, shrubby vegetation. Other plants along the trail include highbush blueberry, St. John's-wort, staggerbush, fetter-bush, redroot, hooded pitcher plant, gallberry, red maple, and at least two species of meadow beauty. The wetlands along the bay

Brown-headed Nuthatch

swamp trails are dominated by loblolly bay, swamp bay, and myrtle-leaved holly.

The environmental education area is only a small part of the entire Cary State Forest. In addition to the trails described above, there are also about 18 miles of woods roads that can be used as hiking trails. Most of these roads are improved for driving and are accessible to most types of vehicles. However, at least some of these thoroughfares deteriorate rapidly in wet weather and can become quite boggy. Such routes as Moccasin Slough, Hog Trap, Big Oaks, Deer Track, and Fox Squirrel Roads all make good walking trails for inquisitive naturalists.

This forest supports a variety of the state's native wildlife. White-tailed deer, American alligator, raccoon, and bobcat are fairly common, and a number of bird species frequent the area. Brown-headed nuthatch, Bachman sparrow, yellow-throated vireo, and summer tanager are the more sought-after avian species. The federally endangered red-cockaded woodpecker has historically been reported for Cary, but none have been seen here for several years. A number of other threatened species are likely to be present in the forest, including the indigo snake, canebrake rattlesnake, and spotted turtle. However, no official survey has been conducted to establish the presence of these animals.

Camping is possible in this forest but must be prearranged. It

Hooded Pitcher Plant

is probably wise to request information and permission from the Division of Forestry office in Jacksonville before depending on the availability of campsites.

Best Time of Year

Summer is best for Bachman sparrow and summer tanager; spring, summer, and fall are best for wildflowers. Hunting is permitted during the winter hunting seasons; other recreational users should be careful and wear bright colors during this part of the year.

Pets

Allowed.

DEVIL'S MILLHOPPER
STATE GEOLOGICAL SITE

The 120-foot descent into Devil's Millhopper is like a descent into another world. The sandy pine woods at the giant sinkhole's rim give way to several levels of vegetative communities and an increasing diversity of plants as one moves closer to the huge chasm's deepest extent.

The 63 acres that make up this small park constitute Florida's only designated geological site. Purchased by the state in 1974 to protect the area from increasing degradation brought on by a plethora of unauthorized explorations, the site is now carefully managed to insure its conservation. It has been designated a National Natural Landmark and is well known among scientists as a repository of important archaeological findings. Shortly after its acquisition, a 232-step boardwalk was constructed that leads to the floor of the massive depression. Though this zigzag stairwell is an unnatural addition to an otherwise magnificent natural feature, it is an essential ingredient in protecting the sinkhole from further erosion, while continuing to allow visitors to witness its beauty.

The age of the sinkhole itself is somewhat conjectural. Experts have estimated that its upper walls were formed as much as 15,000 years ago, while its lower walls may be less than 1,000 years old. The basis for this assessment lies in the interpretation of the sinkhole's vegetative communities as well as its topographic relief. The upper part of the sink harbors a number of remnant plant species that tie its age to a bygone era, and the upper slopes display the more gentle topographic features that are indicative of older landforms. The lower walls, on the other hand, are more steep, indicating that they are younger and have been subjected to fewer years of erosion.

As a unit, the sink's walls also provide a cut-away cross-section of perhaps 20 million years of Florida's historical record. Studying the layers of sediments from rim to base has allowed geologists and archaeologists to unravel and reconstruct much about central Florida's ancient past. The lower levels of the sink

Devil's Millhopper

have revealed fossilized remains that date from the time when the Florida peninsula was completely covered by the sea, while the uppermost walls have revealed fragments from more recent eras.

The Devil's Millhopper takes its name from its distinctive shape, which is reminiscent of the funnel-like hopper used to feed corn to a grist mill. It is 500 feet wide at its rim, but narrows to about 100 feet at its base. Folklore holds that the many fossilized bone fragments that have been found in the sink are actually the remains of souls that were fed to the devil.

Location, Mailing Address and Phone

From exit 78 on I-75 take 441 south toward Gainesville to its intersection with SR 121 (about 12.5 mi.); turn south on 121, then west on NW 53rd Ave. (less than 1 mi.); then continue for approximately 2 mi. to the entrance to the park.

Devil's Millhopper State Geological Site, 4732 Millhopper Rd., Gainesville, FL 32653; (904) 955-2008.

Facilities and Activities

Picnicking, nature trail, interpretive center, boardwalk, botanizing, birding.

Boardwalk and Nature Trail

The main attraction for most visitors is the huge sink and steep stairwell. For botanists, birdwatchers, and amateur naturalists alike, the descent can be an exciting adventure. Huge live oaks, chestnut oaks, and hickories tower over the upper rim, undergirded by an understory of eastern hophornbeam, red mulberry, ironwood, pawpaw, and Carolina ash. Further downslope, the calcareous walls support a lush herbaceous and woody vegetation that includes a number of colorful wildflowers, as well as elderberry, cork elm, needle palm, and a dense of covering of native fern. The clatter of woodpeckers reverberates in the natural echo chamber, and the normally subdued chatterings of native songbirds seem amplified and easier to hear. The air becomes cooler as you near the sink's lowest levels, and the air waves are dominated by a cacophony of gurglings and tricklings as if literally hundreds of seepages were dribbling their waters in unison on the fungus-covered limerock. At its lowest level the boardwalk flattens and terminates at a widened observation platform that overlooks the sink's floor and offers an ant's-eye view of the slopes above.

For those who choose not to make the walk to the bottom, or, perhaps more to the point, who choose not to make the walk back to the top, there is a flat, easy-to-follow nature trail that encircles the Millhopper's upper edge. One side of this trail passes through a typical hammock forest of hardwoods and spruce pine. The other side passes through a pine upland with an understory of American holly, devil's walking stick, saw palmetto, muscadine, persimmon, spurge nettle, black cherry, and gum bumelia.

Interpretive Center

Near the entrance to the trail there is a visitor and interpretive center that is worth visiting. The rangers here are very helpful and there is usually someone available to answer questions. The interpretive center is a covered, open-air collection of exhibits that explain the origin and formation of the Devil's Millhopper as well as the subsurface geology of the region. Other displays highlight the archaeological finds that have been discovered here and also include life-size photographs of the park's typical habitats. The park also offers regularly scheduled guided walks into the sink. These are typically slated for weekends and offer an easy way to learn about the Millhopper's cultural and geologic history.

Best Time of Year

There is something of interest year-round.

Pets

Allowed on a hand-held leash.

FAVER-DYKES STATE PARK

Faver-Dykes is an out-of-the-way and lightly used park that supports a variety of typical, near-coastal northeast Florida habitats. Pine flatwoods, hardwood hammock, and marshes are all available for exploration. The park was donated to the state in 1950 by Hiram Faver. Faver's wife's maiden name was Dykes, hence the park's somewhat interesting name.

Part of the reason this park is lightly used stems from its location on the mainland rather than the seaward side of the Intracoastal Waterway. Most people traveling along A1A simply miss it. Another reason may stem from its primitive setting. Unlike many state parks, there are no paved roads at Faver-Dykes, and not as much in the way of developed facilities. The sandy, canopied entrance road leaves first-time visitors with the feeling that they are heading into the no-frills world of a backwoods wilderness. Those who stay find a delightful park in a natural setting with plenty of opportunities for unhurried exploration.

Faver-Dykes currently contains 752 acres but is in the throes of expansion. A cooperative purchase by the Florida Department of Environmental Protection and the St. Johns River Water Management District will soon double the park's size and extend its boundaries all the way to the Intracoastal Waterway.

Location, Mailing Address and Phone

At the intersection of US 1 and I-95, about 15 miles south of St. Augustine.

Faver-Dykes State Park, 1000 Faver Dykes Rd., St. Augustine, FL 32086; (904) 794-0997.

Facilities and Activities

Camping, birding, canoeing, fishing, nature trails.

The park's main campground has 30 sites, each with water and electricity. The campground is located in the heart of a hardwood hammock; wooded buffers between sites offer privacy and a sense of solitude. There is also a less-developed youth camping area that can accommodate about 100 people.

Two short trails are available for nature study. Both require about 30 minutes of leisurely walking but can take longer. One begins in the campground and passes through a mesic hammock of oaks and cabbage palm; the other originates near the picnic area and follows along Rooton Branch. The latter trail features examples of salt- and freshwater vegetation, as well as an example of coastal hammock and longleaf pine flatwoods. Both paths are delightful walks that offer the opportunity to study the park's major habitats.

There are also park roads that are available for walking. The entrance road, which passes through a mature pineland, makes a particularly nice walking trail.

Canoeing is available along Pellicer Creek, a slow-moving canoe trail that passes through tidal marsh. Long-legged wading

Bald Eagle

birds are abundant along the creek, as are alligators and bald
eagles. The latter are known to nest near the park. The marsh is
typical of those along the east coast's inland lagoons. The canoe
trail is a 4-mile paddle from the park to US 1, the terminus of the
trail, but the current is so mild that it is possible to make the
excursion a round-trip to avoid shuttling vehicles. In addition,
the park operates a canoe-rental service. If you plan to use this
service, call the park and leave your arrival time on the recorder;
a ranger will meet you at the canoe launch.

Wildlife watching is good at this park. In spring and fall the live oak hammock woodlands can be filled with a variety of migrating songbirds, including an assortment of warblers and vireos. Hawks are common over the marsh and in the edges of the woodlands, and eagles and osprey are common along the creek. Rooton Branch is a good place to look for river otter. White-tailed deer, bobcat, gray fox, and wild turkey are also fairly common but are seen most often only by quiet, patient observers.

Best Time of Year

Spring and fall are best for seeing migrating birds. Winter is the best time to paddle the creek. Camping is good year-round but high summer temperatures make winter preferable.

Pets

Allowed on a 6-foot leash. Not allowed in the campground.

FT. CLINCH STATE PARK

Ft. Clinch State Park is the northernmost of Florida's state parks and is one of several that protect the fragile seaside habitats of the state's northeastern coast. It is located on a north-facing peninsula that is separated from Cumberland Island, Georgia, by Cumberland Sound, and is bordered on the west and east by the Amelia River and Atlantic Ocean, respectively. More than 12,000 feet of shoreline border the park's northern and eastern edges, and an expansive system of tidal marsh borders it on the west.

Ft. Clinch was one of the earliest installments in the state's park system and was purchased in 1935 to preserve the old Union fort from which the park takes its name. As with a number of Florida's early parks, workers from the Civilian Conservation Corps initially developed the site. The park was first opened to the public in 1938.

Location, Mailing Address and Phone

On Atlantic Ave. in Fernandina Beach, just off A1A.

Ft. Clinch State Park, 2601 Atlantic Ave., Fernandina Beach, FL 32034; (904) 277-7274.

Facilities and Activities

Camping, hiking, birding, botanizing, swimming, shelling, bicycling, picnicking, nature trail, bath house, fishing pier, boardwalk.

Camping

Ft. Clinch has two campgrounds. The 21-site beachside campground is the smaller of the two and is located in a completely open, sparsely vegetated area near the beach. A boardwalk connects the campground to the shoreline.

The river-area camp is about twice as large as the beach-area camp and is situated in an attractive hammock on the edge of the Amelia River. Many sites are shaded by large live oaks, but some are more open.

Hiking, Biking, Nature Trails

There are plenty of places to walk and peddle at Ft. Clinch. The park's 3-mile-long entrance road leads from the ranger station to the old fort and is a canopied thoroughfare that winds through a scenic coastal hammock. Many visitors bicycle this route, stopping periodically to check the treetops for birds. More intense birders walk along the road's edges.

The Willow Pond Nature Trail, which is located on the east side of the main road about 0.5 mile before reaching the fort, is the park's only developed trail. It is composed of two circular routes that pass through hardwood hammock and around a small, marshy pond. Alligators are commonly seen in the pond, but you may have to look closely to spot them. The surface of the water is generally covered with a dense layer of duck weed which provides the 'gators an effective camouflage.

For plant enthusiasts, the Willow Pond Trail offers the opportunity to study the vegetation of the hammock community.

Coral bean, American holly, southern magnolia, small fruited pawpaw, red bay, yaupon, American beautyberry, poison ivy, hackberry, coastal plain willow, red maple, red cedar, rattan vine, white-topped sedge, sabal palm, buttonbush, red mulberry, and thistle are just a few of the plants encountered along the trail edges. A plant list is available at the entrance station; be sure to ask for it.

There are at least three other nature walks you can take in this park, none of which are designated trails. To follow the most obvious of the three, start at the parking lot adjacent to the pier, then walk back down the parking lot's entrance road to the beach-area campground road. The road to the campground is bordered by back dune habitat with a plethora of low-growing plants. At the campground a boardwalk leads to the beach. Following the boardwalk, then turning right at the beach, leads back to the pier. There can be a variety of shorebirds and gulls along this beach. The more conspicuous plants include sea oats and railroad vine.

The picnic area across from the entrance to the old fort is a good place to access the hammock. Entering the picnic area from the parking lot, then turning left immediately, leads to an unmarked trail that drops down behind an old live oak with a particularly gnarly base. The path quickly leads to what appears to be an old abandoned service road. A handful of unmarked but walkable paths turn off this old road and allow explorers to wander the hammock. The service road eventually intersects the River Area Campground road.

At the end of the parking lot adjacent to the fort, a hardpacked clay road leads for a short distance to a sandy parking lot. A boardwalk from the parking lot provides access to the beach below the fort. Most people who use this area are fishing enthusiasts. Swimming is not permitted here due to the strong currents, and most sunbathers prefer the beaches that front the Atlantic. However, for nature enthusiasts this is one of the best places in the park to explore the scrub–hammock ecotone and the fascinating landscape that lies behind the dunes.

Turning left for a short distance after reaching the beach leads to several openings into the sparsely vegetated back dune habitat. Making your way inland through the initial thicket leads to large areas of open sand bordered on one side by sandy scrub and on the other by huge, ancient, densely vegetated dunes that rise sharply in steep vertical ascents. Though currently clothed with a dense covering of trees and shrubs, these old dunes are actually shoreline remnants that once bordered directly on the water. Climbing to the apex of one of these mountainous mounds will perch you atop a narrow crest that, on one side, drops off precipitously into the hammock woodlands, and on the other provides a bird's-eye view of Cumberland Sound.

Birding

Like much of the northeast Florida coast, Ft. Clinch can be an outstanding birding location. The edges of the entrance road and the Willow Pond Nature Trail are good places to look for songbirds during the spring and fall migration; the latter is also a good place to find nesting painted buntings during the summer.

Sea- and shorebirds are one of the park's main attractions. The huge fishing pier that extends far out into the Atlantic provides an outstanding place to look for offshore species such as northern gannet, black scoter, goldeneye, greater scaup, and bufflehead. A number of gull and tern species can also be seen along the pier, including the great black-backed, bonaparte's, herring, laughing, and ring-billed gulls, and the royal, least, gull-billed, black, caspian, sandwich, and common terns.

The jetty that follows along the pier sometimes harbors small flocks of purple sandpiper in the winter. Though somewhat drab and inconspicuous in its winter attire, the purple sandpiper's dumpy form, yellow legs, and slightly downcurved bill which is yellowish near the base help in identifying the species.

Ft. Clinch's unique location also results in some unlikely species showing up at the park from time to time. Horned lark and lapland longspur have been reported from the sandy dunes near the fishing pier, and smooth-billed ani, whip-poor-will, and old squaw have been reported from other locations within the park. At least 19 species of warblers have also been reported, including the worm-eating and black-throated blue warblers, and blackpoll. Be sure to ask for the bird list as you enter.

Ft. Clinch

History buffs will want to visit old Fort Clinch. Situated near the confluence of the Amelia River and Cumberland Sound, it was originally constructed by the federal government in 1847 and later played a small part in the Civil War. It is well preserved and open for inspection for a small fee. Rangers at the fort dress in period garb and are available to answer questions for visitors.

Best Time of Year

Any time of year is a good time to visit this park. However, birders usually visit in fall, winter, or spring. The campground is likely to be busiest during summer but camping is good year-round. Water-related activities are generally confined to late spring, summer, and early fall, though some mild winter days can also be pleasant.

Pets

Allowed on a 6-foot leash; not allowed in campground, the fort, in any structures, or on the bathing beaches.

GAINESVILLE'S NATURE PARKS

Some cities seem to be more successful than others at establishing passive nature parks; the city of Gainesville must certainly be ranked in the first of these categories. At this writing, there are six such parks in the city and the designation of still others is in process. Though none of these parks could be classified as wilderness, and none are out of earshot of typical urban noises, all are important. Each one preserves a remnant of north-central Florida, and each makes a statement about the importance of conserving our natural heritage. Three of these parks—Morningside Nature Center, Bivens Arm Nature Park, and Gum Root Park—are particularly good places to study the Gainesville area's native communities. The other three—Boulware Springs, Alfred A. Ring Park, and Palm Point—are smaller and less important installations that are mentioned below only for completeness.

Location, Mailing Address and Phone

Information about any of Gainesville's nature parks may be obtained by writing Department of Cultural and Nature Operations, Box 490-30, Gainesville, FL 32602.

Facilities and Activities

Hiking, nature trails, picnicking, wildlife observation, birding, botanizing, bicycling.

Birding

The city of Gainesville is situated in a region of the state that is well known to birdwatchers. At least 200 avian species are known to occur in the region, many of which can be found in one or more of the city's nature parks. At least 25 warblers have been recorded in the area, as well as a large number of hawks, woodpeckers, and thrushes. The Louisiana waterthrush, wood thrush, broad-winged hawk, and hooded, chestnut-sided, magnolia, black-throated blue, black-throated green, bay-breasted, and blackburnian warblers are among the more interesting but difficult-to-find species. Morningside and Bivens Arm are probably the better parks for birding, though Gum Root also has some prime birding habitat.

Botanizing

Botanizing is also good in the Gainesville area. The city is located at the southernmost range for many northern species, and at the northernmost range of others. The more common woody plants include the Florida maple, red maple, devil's walking stick, pignut hickory, black tupelo, black cherry, American basswood, red bay, sweetgum, hackberry, gallberry, buttonbush, gopher apple, and hearts-a-bustin'-with-love. The more interesting herbaceous plants include green dragon, lobelia, rosebud orchid, rain lily, ladies tresses, sundew, hooded pitcher plant, butterwort, bladderwort, grass-pink, meadow beauty, a large variety of asters, and several hundred additional species.

Morningside Nature Center

3540 E. University Ave.

Morningside Nature Center is a 278-acre nature park that is by far the best known, most used, and best interpreted of Gainesville's passive parks. It offers approximately 7 miles of nature trails through a variety of north-central Florida habitats. Many of these trails are circular in design but intersect with other trails to allow for extended walking opportunities. Some paths cross over boardwalks that pass through or adjacent to cypress domes, wet prairies, and tupelo gum swamps; other trails traverse sandy upland woods dominated by pine–oak forests. All of the trails are well maintained, easy to follow, and provide a variety of wildlife watching opportunities. An observation blind on one of the trails allows easy viewing of native species, and an observation deck allows visitors to sit quietly and observe the goings-on in a shallow, wetland marsh. One loop is specifically managed for fall wildflowers and another for butterflies. An easy-to-follow map helps visitors find their way along the trails. For those who choose to spend the day here, there is also a large picnic area with restroom facility.

Morningside also serves as a regional environmental education center for area children. The small office complex includes an activity room with aquaria, environmental education books and materials, and interesting hands-on exhibits. School groups take field trips here during the school year, and environmental education day camps are offered during summer. There is also a working farm complete with farm animals that helps children understand life in early Florida.

Morningside is the only one of Gainesville's parks that publishes extensive bird and wildflower lists. Both of these are available at the park's office and are very useful. The bird list contains more than 130 species that include the wood stork, bald eagle,

1. Nothing signifies the onset of a north Florida winter better than the arrival of numerous species of wintering waterfowl.

2. Peacock Springs State Recreation Area offers some of north Florida's most picturesque springs.

3. The picnic area and reflecting pool at Ravine State Gardens is a good starting point for an extended walk along the floor of this giant natural ravine.

4. Boardwalks along parts of the Osceola section of the Florida National Scenic Trail help hikers keep their feet dry.

5. This ancient live oak is one of many mature trees at Andrews Wildlife Management Area.

6. The willet is one of Florida's loudest and easiest to identify shorebirds.

7. The brown pelican is one of the east Florida coast's most conspicuous birds.

8. Bulow State Park's Fairchild Oak, named for Dr. David Fairchild, is over 800 years old.

9. The dangling fruit of eastern hophornbeam is common and conspicuous in early summer in upland mixed forests.

10. The tarflower takes its common name from its sticky flowers.

11. Capturing dragonflies and butterflies on film can be an amateur photographer's delight.

12. Northeastern Florida offers some of the east coast's best preserved beaches; the sea oats seen in the foreground can grow to great depth and help bind beach sands to stabilize dunes and reduce erosion.

13. The mountainous sand dunes at Ft. Clinch State Park offer a bird's-

13. The mountainous sand dunes at Ft. Clinch State Park offer a bird's-eye view of Cumberland Sound.

14. This view from the observation deck at Lower Suwannee River National Wildlife Refuge is a typical scene along the lower reaches of Florida's most famous river.

15. Paynes Prairie, near Gainesville, bursts into a sea of color during spring and fall.

16. Several species of diminutive violets are some of spring's earliest

16. Several species of diminutive violets are some of spring's earliest bloomers.

17. The showy rose pogonia is fairly frequent in bogs, marshes and pine flatwoods from Canada to central Florida.

18. It's not difficult to see how the meadow beauty gets its name.

19. The tangled woodlands in the Morman Branch scenic area of the Ocala National Forest are evidence of its pristine aspect.

American woodcock, red-cockaded woodpecker, and 24 species of warblers. The wildflower list is neatly organized by flower color, family, and blooming season, and doubles as a species guide for much of the Gainesville area.

Bivens Arm Nature Park

3650 S. Main St.

The entrance to Bivens Arm contains an informative collection of open-air exhibits that tell the story of sinkholes as well as the natural history of the Bivens Arm area. A wooden deck overlooks a small marsh that is a good location for seeing alligators. Pig frogs are often heard calling from the grasses, and a variety of wildlife visit the marsh for food and cover. Several species of wading birds as well as a number of songbirds are easily observed here during spring and fall migration.

Bivens Arm contains a scenic boardwalk and two easy-to-follow nature trails that pass through several habitats. The upland part of the trail traverses a typical north-central Florida hammock with a variety of trees and shrubs including hackberry, yaupon, beautyberry, pawpaw, Florida maple, black

Biven's Arm Nature Park

117

tupelo, black cherry, and bald cypress. Barred and great-horned owls are common along the trails and not particularly difficult to find. The boardwalk passes over the edges of a swampy wetland that is also good for birdwatching, as well as for seeking out a variety of frogs and toads.

Gum Root Park

There are two entrances to Gum Root; one is at the intersection of SR 26 and NE 27th Ave., the other on the east side of 26, just north of the same intersection.

Gum Root Park is one of Gainesville's newest, largest, and potentially most important nature parks. Its 741 acres makes it larger than many state parks, and its strategic location makes it a critical ecological preserve. Gum Root is a jointly owned and managed project of the St. Johns Water Management District (SJWMD) and the city of Gainesville. The city owns the 369 acres that lie to the west of Florida 26, and SJWMD owns the 372 acres to the east. Several old roads that lead through the area are now closed to vehicles but make nice walking paths. The entrance on the east side of 26 leads to the northern end of the lake.

The park is situated in the watershed of an important surface water system which includes both Newnans and Orange Lakes, as well as tributaries of the Oklawaha and St. Johns Rivers. This location alone places it in an ideal position for insuring the quality of the water that feeds these lacustrine and riverine systems.

Newnans, Orange, and Lochloosa Lakes are three large lakes that comprise the main surface-water reservoirs for the Orange Creek drainage basin. All three have long been recognized for their beauty, wildlife value, and outstanding bass fishing opportunities. As a unit, the Orange Creek watershed supports virtually all of inland north Florida's mammal, bird, reptile, and amphibian species, including bald eagles, wood storks, river otters, alligators, sandhill cranes, limpkins, large populations of herons and egrets, several species of bullfrogs and tree frogs, a large number of snakes, and an assortment of warblers and other songbirds.

As with many of Florida's developing areas, the Orange Creek basin is in danger of losing its pristine quality. Increased nutrient supply threatens to hasten the natural eutrophication process and the introduction of aquatic weeds threatens to clog the constituent lakes' open waterways. Staff at the St. Johns Water Management District are grappling with these and related problems in an effort to insure the area's integrity. Preservation of the Gum Root Swamp Park and Conservation Area is one of their solutions.

Boulware Springs Park

SE 15th St.

Boulware Springs is a small installation with a nature trail and covered picnic area. It is best known as the trailhead for the Gainesville–Hawthorne State Trail, a 17-mile horseback, biking, and walking trail that passes through Paynes Prairie State Preserve (see p. 146) as well as the Lochloosa Wildlife Management Area (see p. 181). The day-use-only trail was established as part of a program that converts old railroad beds to recreational walking and riding trails. Paynes Prairie lies less than 3 miles south of the Boulware Springs parking lot. The trail is open from 8:00 A.M. to sunset.

Palm Point

Lakeshore Dr.

Palm Point is a small 20-acre park located on the southwestern shores of Newnans Lake, a 7,427-acre lake that is known as an important birding site. Prothonotary warblers nest along the lake's edge in summer, and both the golden-winged and blue-winged warblers can be regular visitors in the fall. It is not unusual to record a dozen or more warbler species during fall or spring migration, including blackburnian and worm-eating warblers, redstarts, and northern parula. Lakeshore Drive, on which the park is located, is a scenic byway that skirts the edge of the lake; its curving roadway makes for a relaxing drive.

Palm Point takes its name from the small stand of sabal palm that is found there. The sabal palm is Florida's state tree and is one of the state's most widespread and picturesque palms.

Alfred Ring Park

2002 NW 16th Ave.

Alfred Ring is billed as a neighborhood park. One visit tells you why. The park is sandwiched between two large subdivisions and there is no designated parking lot at the park's entrance gate. "You'll just have to find a place to park on one of the side streets, then walk back to the park," one of the 16th-Avenue residents told me, "or you can enter off Northwest Twenty-second Street near Northwest Twenty-third Avenue." Two creeks trickle through this park, which also offers a wildflower garden, nature trail, and covered picnic area.

Best Time of Year

Birding is best in spring and fall; walking is good year-round.

Pets

Allowed on a leash.

GAMBLE ROGERS MEMORIAL STATE RECREATION AREA AT FLAGLER BEACH

Florida's smaller parks often harbor well-hidden treasures that are easily overlooked by the average patron. This is certainly true for the 145-acre Gamble Rogers State Recreation Area. Probably best known for its beachside campground and popular day-use swimming area, the areas to which most visitors confine their visits, it also supports an attractive and readily accessible expanse of coastal scrub that gives a firsthand look at this important but diminishing habitat.

Gamble Rogers was previously known as Flagler Beach State Recreation Area because of its close proximity to Flagler Beach, a stretch of northeast Florida shoreline that was named for railroad magnate Henry Flagler. However, its name was changed in the early 1990s in honor of Gamble Rogers, a well-known Florida folk singer who drowned at the park while attempting to rescue an imperiled park visitor. The area was first acquired by the state in 1954 and was opened to the public in 1961. Since then, it has been a favored spot for beachgoers.

There are actually two parts to Gamble Rogers. The beach side, which contains the campground and swimming area, lies east of A1A. The other part of the park, which contains the nature trail, picnic area, and boat launch, lies on the west side of the highway.

Location, Mailing Address and Phone

Located along SR A1A in Flagler Beach.

Gamble Rogers Memorial State Recreation Area at Flagler Beach, 3100 S. A1A, Flagler Beach, FL 32136; (904) 439-2474.

Facilities and Activities

Swimming, camping, picnicking, boating, fishing, nature trail.

The camping area, which sits atop the dunes that line the eastern side of A1A, is very popular because it directly overlooks the Atlantic Ocean. All sites are open, sunny, and can be very hot in summer or late spring. Nevertheless, the campground is always filled and can be difficult to get into without reservations.

The swimming area is located opposite the campground and is also often extremely crowded. A restroom facility and small parking lot (both of which are reached by the same entrance road as the campground) are connected to the beach by a boardwalk. It is important for the preservation of the fragile dune vegetation that beachgoers use the boardwalk to cross the dunes.

A picnic area is located on the west side of A1A and is reached by entering the park's main access road. There are covered tables along the Intracoastal Waterway as well as restrooms.

In winter the beach is a good place to scan the horizon for northern gannets or to study wintering shorebirds. During

Blanketflower

winter storms, or when there are strong onshore winds, it is sometimes possible to see pelagic birds that have moved closer to land.

The west side of the park also has a boat landing and boat basin that opens onto the Intracoasal Waterway. Fishing is possible in or along the edges of the Waterway, and manatees sometimes visit the boat basin during summer.

Nature Trail

Amateur naturalists, in particular, will enjoy the nature trail that winds through the dune scrub on the west side of A1A. One entrance to the trail leads off the main park road just before the entrance station. The trail is also accessible by driving through the picnic area to the point at which the road is closed to further vehicle traffic. Parking and walking from here leads to several sandy roads that intersect the trail.

The trail passes through an attractive salt-pruned woodland that is typical of northeast Florida's coastal scrub. Myrtle oak, sabal palm, and prickly ash are common and there are some particularly impressive treelike saw palmetto, a shrubby palm that is more often seen growing prostrate than upright. It is also possible to see Florida scrub jays here, though they are not common. Spring and fall migrants also frequent the trail area.

The sandy meadows that stretch away from the woodlands are beautiful when in bloom. In late spring the multicolored flowers of the firewheel or blanketflower and bright yellow blossoms of the prickly pear cactus add an attractive show of color to the park.

Best Time of Year

Late spring, summer, and early fall are best for swimming. Winter and spring are best for exploring the trail. Cold-weather walks on the beach, especially immediately following the passage of a strong cold front, can be both invigorating and captivating.

Pets

Allowed on a 6-foot leash; not allowed in the campground, on the beach, or in any buildings.

GOLD HEAD BRANCH STATE PARK

The 2,099-acre Gold Head Branch State Park is a plant lover's paradise. Its prime location in the deep sand uplands of Florida's central ridge, coupled with the sandy sinkhole lakes and distinctive natural ravine that dominate its landscape, sets the stage for a diversity of natural communities that support an interesting array of both woody and herbaceous plants. A walk into the ravine that runs nearly the length of the park is a descent through a series of vegetative levels. The typical upland terrain that borders the ravine's rim gives way first to rich mesic woodlands along the steeply slanting slopes, then to spring-fed wetlands at the ravine's lowest levels. All of these combine to produce a richly diverse collection of native flora.

The origin of the ravine that dominates this park is as interesting as the plant communities it supports. The ravines of the central ridge all occur on sandy slopes that angle downward toward rivers or drainage-filled lakes. At Gold Head Branch, the underground water flows toward Little Lake Johnson but intersects the land surface and forms a small, clear, spring-fed creek long before reaching its destination. The first of these springs is at the head of the ravine and is eroding the ravine slope from below, causing it to grow headward toward the source of the subsurface water. As with most geologic processes, the speed with which this growth is taking place is much slower than we humans can appreciate. Its result, however, is a natural feature that no north Florida explorer should miss.

In addition to its natural endowments, Gold Head Branch State Park is also rich in cultural history and is one of only a handful of Florida parks that got their start through the labor of the Civilian Conservation Corps (CCC). Twenty-five craftsmen as well as a large number of CCC youth came to the park in the 1930s for the purpose of clearing and establishing the park. Many of the park's cabins, roads, and buildings were built by this work force. Each spring, the remaining veterans of this project get together at the park for an annual reunion.

Location, Mailing Address and Phone

Take SR 100 east from Starke to Keystone Heights (13 miles), then left (northeast) on SR 21 for 6 miles to the park entrance.

Gold Head Branch State Park, 6239 State Road 21, Keystone Heights, FL 32356; (904) 473-4701.

Facilities and Activities

R.V. and tent camping, primitive camping, cabins, nature trails, swimming, birding, botanizing, bicycling, and canoeing.

Camping and Cabins

Gold Head Branch supports three campgrounds, two in the center of the park and another overlooking the southern corner of Big Lake Johnson. Together these campgrounds offer 74 campsites, most with water, electricity, grills, and tables. There is also a youth camp and a primitive camp (see below).

By virtue of being constructed by the CCC, Gold Head Branch is one of the few Florida parks that offers furnished cabins. A total of 14 cottages in two sizes are available by reservation (up to one year in advance). Spring, summer, and early fall are the park's busiest seasons and the cabins are usually in great demand during these times, particularly on weekends. The cabins are clean, cooled with a window air conditioner, equipped with linens, and include a kitchen with utensils.

For those who wish to get away from developed camp-grounds, Gold Head Branch offers a primitive camping area that is devoid of modern conveniences. Situated at the terminus of a 0.5-mile trail, the primitive area overlooks Big Lake Johnson and is accessible only by foot. Primitive campers must register at the office and pay a nominal fee for using the area.

Nature Trails

A single system of three trails traverses the steepsided ravine that stretches from near the park's entrance to the northern border of Little Lake Johnson. The first access to these footpaths is at a parking lot adjacent to a wooden platform that overlooks the head of the ravine. The overlook offers an important perspective on the depth and breadth of a chasm that appears without warning in the upland woods. A short walk (or drive) down the main park road from the overlook leads to the stairway parking area.

An old cement stairway zig-zags to the bottom of the ravine and allows easy access to the trail. Though a nonnatural addition to the park, the stairway helps protect the fragile walls of the ravine from erosion. It is important to remain on the trail at all times to preserve the ravine's integrity. Leaving the established route to make one's own path injects a dangerous dynamic into the ravine's natural system. Such unnecessary tramping alters the normal drainage pattern and encourages erosion which can radically change the ravine's aspect.

At the bottom of the stairway, Fern Loop leads off to the left on a jaunt that passes over several boardwalks and encircles the headwaters of a tiny stream. Needle palm, southern magnolia, swamp bay, loblolly bay, devil's walking stick, sweetgum, Virginia willow, American beautyberry, and an assortment of ferns are the most obvious plants on this short circuit.

The Ridge Trail leads off to the right at the base of the stairway, then crosses the stream where a small population of possumhaw grows adjacent to the bridge. Agarista, highbush blueberry, hickories, and several species of oaks become dominant as the trail angles upslope. The rim supports a typical upland sand plant assemblage including staggerbush, flag pawpaw, and Florida rosemary, as well as myrtle, bluejack, and turkey oaks.

Farther on, the Ridge Trail intersects with the Loblolly Trail for the final stretch to the picnic area. An attractive area at the intersection is the site of an old mill and provides a nice respite on a hot day. An access trail at this location also leads back to the main park road.

A short section of the Florida Trail also cuts through the park. It begins near the park entrance and is confined mostly to the uplands. It is another outstanding way to experience the park's varied plant communities.

Birding

Gold Head Branch's bird list contains about 130 species, a respectable number for a park located along the state's interior. At least 16 warblers are known to occur here as well as three vireos and all of north Florida's woodpeckers. While many species are considered uncommon, or frequent the park only during certain times of year, at least one hard-to-find species is considered common: The Florida scrub jay, a blue-and-brown, highly vocal, endangered species, is most regularly spotted in the upland scrub.

Best Time of Year

Spring and fall are best for flowering plants and birds. However, the park is enjoyable at almost any time of year.

Pets

Allowed on leash in some areas; not allowed on trail, in campground, in swimming area, or in any structure.

GUANA RIVER STATE PARK AND WILDLIFE MANAGEMENT AREA

Be sure to bring your walking shoes and binoculars when you visit Guana River. There are over 12,000 acres to explore here and more than 20 miles of trails to explore them with. Walking or biking are about the only ways to cover this area during most of the year, and the scenery is as good as you'll find anywhere on the central east coast.

Guana River State Park and Guana River Wildlife Management Area actually constitute two distinct governmental subdivisions that share opposite ends of the same intriguing natural area. Located along the Atlantic shoreline, the preserved region consists of a narrow peninsula of coastal landscape squeezed between the ocean on one side and the Tolomato River on the other. At least seven distinctive habitats are represented within the combined installations, including beaches, dunes, coastal scrub, flatwoods, both salt- and freshwater marshes, and luxuriant maritime hardwood hammocks.

Guana River itself is a tidally influenced brackish water tributary of the Tolomato and is well known for the birds and wildlife it supports. The northern part of the river, which is usually referred to as Guana Lake, has been separated from the lower river by an earthen dam and is primarily a freshwater habitat.

Fishermen come to both places to test their skills, and birders come to witness the huge numbers of long-legged wading birds, shorebirds, and waterfowl that flock to the lake in winter.

Location, Mailing Address and Phone

On A1A about 15 mi. north of St. Augustine. The South Beach and North Beach Use Areas provide parking and access to the Atlantic; Guana Dam Use Area provides access to the trails of both the park and the wildlife management area.

For park information: *Guana River State Park, 2690 S. Ponte Vedra Blvd., Ponte Vedra Beach, FL 32082; (904) 825-5071.*

For wildlife management area information: *Florida Game and Fresh Water Fish Commission, 620 S. Meridian St., Tallahassee, FL 32399-1600; (904) 488-3831.*

Facilities and Activities

Birding, hiking, fishing, botanizing, wildlife observation.

Hiking and Biking

Guana River's hiking trails are accessed from the Guana River Dam Use Area. A locked gate blocks the roadway near the end of the parking lot but allows entrance for pedestrians and bicyclists. The short stretch of dikeway that extends beyond the gate disappears quickly into a mature coastal woodland. The system of old service roads that crisscross this hammock are easy to follow and are perfect for walking or peddling.

Just inside the woodland there is an information box that contains maps of the trails on the state park side; maps of the wildlife management area can be obtained by writing the Florida Game and Fresh Water Fish Commission or by following the state park trail to the entrance of the management area.

It should be noted that the wildlife management area allows hunting and vehicular access during some parts of October, November, and December. Other recreational uses should probably be avoided during these times. However, hunting is never allowed along the nearly 9 miles of trail on the state park side, and winter is a perfect time to explore this area.

There are seven trails in the state park that traverse nearly all of the peninsula's habitats. The Timucuan Trail passes through mature hammock, the Guanaloop leads along the edges of pine flatwoods, a boardwalk crosses a freshwater marsh, and the South Point Loop leads near the edge of the Tolomato River.

A Game and Fresh Water Fish Commission observation deck and interpretive exhibit lie just outside the park's boundaries and offer a nice vantage to observe the goings-on in Big Savannah Pond. The latter site is a good place to hear moorhens cackling in the dense vegetation, marvel at the bright pink plumage of summering roseate spoonbills, listen for the deep, staccato grunts of the southern pig frog, or watch for the American bald eagles that nest in the woods just beyond the marsh. Not far beyond Big Savannah Pond, the Capo Road Tower offers another opportunity for observing marsh birds, raptors, and long-legged waders. The latter observation tower, in particular, offers an outstanding vista of a typical east coast tidal marsh.

During nonhunting season, Hammock Road makes a nice walk through the management area. The two-lane path passes through a beautiful hammock woodland, but also follows close along the edge of Guana Lake just inside several nice sabal palm islands. An observation tower is located along the lake about 4.5 miles from the management area–state park boundary and offers an ideal location for surveying the lake for birds and other wildlife.

Plant enthusiasts will find a variety of vegetation to keep them busy. Live oak, hickory, southern magnolia, prickly ash, devil's walking stick, persimmon, red bay, sabal palm, wax myrtle, sparkleberry, loblolly pine, coral bean, gaura, red cedar, winged sumac, American holly, fetterbush, gallberry, a variety of sedges and grasses, and huge prickly pear are but a few of the more dominant plants. Spending an entire day in these woods with a backpack full of field guides can be a rewarding botanical experience.

Birding and Wildlife Observation

There are two access points to the ocean side of the park: the North Beach Use Area and South Beach Use Area. Each supports a single parking lot and provides access to the ocean and beaches. As might be expected, the beach areas can be crowded with sunbathers and water enthusiasts during holiday weekends in summer. In winter, however, the raised portion of the deserted boardwalk that crosses over the dunes at the North Beach Use Area is an excellent place to set up a spotting scope and scan the horizon for loons, sea ducks, northern gannets, peregrine falcons, and northern right whales. (It is important to note that the dunes here are extremely fragile; walking on or across them should be strictly avoided.)

The parking lot at the North Beach Use Area is also a good location for birding the northern end of Guana Lake. The shallow waters here can be outstanding for shorebirds. Black-necked stilt, marbled godwit, solitary sandpiper, and lesser and greater yellowlegs are the more outstanding species, but a variety of others, including dunlin, western sandpiper, least sandpiper, and both long- and short-billed dowitchers are usually present.

The southern end of the lake is accessed by the road to Guana River Dam Use Area. This is the southern terminus of Guana Lake and provides a vantage point to scan both the lake and the river. Several thousand ducks winter in this area and are sometimes easily seen from the dam. Long-legged waders, marsh birds, and raptors are also common here during parts of the year; sightings typically include wood stork, white pelicans, grebes, and peregrine falcons. Even the fulvous whistling-duck has occasionally been reported.

In addition to birds, the Guana River area supports a variety of other wildlife. White-tailed deer are common and easy to see, as are raccoons, alligators, and a variety of poisonous and nonpoisonous snakes. Even the gopher tortoise is resident here. Look for the large, sandy, oval openings that mark the entrance to their underground burrows.

Prickly Pear Cactus

Best Time of Year

There are birds here year-round, but fall, winter, and spring are the seasons with the widest variety and largest numbers. Fall is especially productive for migratory songbirds. Hiking and biking are also good in late fall and winter, when the weather is cooler. However, summer can also be good for hiking, if you drink plenty of water and don't mind the heat.

Pets

Allowed on a 6-foot leash; not allowed on the beaches.

ICHETUCKNEE SPRINGS STATE PARK

The tiny Ichetucknee just may be Florida's most beautiful river. The phosphorescent hue of its emerald green headwater springs and the crystalline clarity of its shallow run seem like surrealistic additions to the surrounding woodlands, almost as if someone had installed artificial lights immediately below the water's surface, then pumped the rippling currents through a filtering system to ensure the river's translucence. Large and impressive populations of wild rice line much of the upper river, and the long, ribbonlike leaves of tape grass, a submerged aquatic angiosperm whose tiny white flowers float at the surface when in bloom, pulsate in the invisible currents. Cypress, blackgum, red maple, and swamp chestnut oaks lean over the water's edge, shading the river from the sun and providing a scenic backdrop to its banks.

Ichetucknee Springs State Park preserves virtually all of the Ichetucknee River's watershed. The park's 2,241 acres encompass the river's nine major springs, as well as the first 3.5 miles of its 6-mile length. Approximately 233 million gallons of water per day issue from the subterranean cracks and crevices that underlie its headwaters, then flow freely through an outstanding collection of swamps and hardwood hammocks before eventually emptying into the Santa Fe River, south of US 27.

As might be expected, this state park is one of north Florida's major outdoor recreation attractions, particularly during the summer months. Thousands of people visit here in an average year, most of whom come for swimming or tubing in the river's sparkling clear water. Its popularity as a tubing run (floating lazily down the river atop the inflated inner tube of an automobile or truck tire) has placed significant demand on the river's natural resources. As a result, the Florida Park Service currently restricts access to a seemingly liberal 750-person daily limit at the north entrance, a maximum that is typically reached before 10 A.M. on summer weekends. The south end has a limit of 2,250 people per day at mid-point landing and no limit at Dampiers Landing. (The limits apply only to tubers and snorkelers; other

132

visitors may still enter the park to swim in the springs or walk the nature trails.)

In addition to controls on the number of tubers, the Park Service has also constructed special launch platforms at several places along the river's course which help keep tubing enthusiasts from trampling the fragile vegetation and further encouraging streamside erosion.

The limestone exposed at this park was laid down in the Eocene Epoch, or about 40 million years before present. This makes it older than many similar outcrops in the region and poses questions about its origin. Either younger sediments were never deposited here, or they have been eroded away over time.

Location, Mailing Address and Phone

The north entrance is located on CR 238 off either SR 137 or 47, a few miles north of US 27; the south entrance is located off US 27, about 5 mi. west of Fort White.

Ichetucknee Springs State Park, Rt. 2, Box 108, Ft. White, FL 32038; (904) 497-2511.

Facilities and Activities

Tubing, swimming, snorkeling, canoeing, cave and cavern scuba diving (must be certified), picnicking, birding, botanizing, nature trails.

Tubing, Canoeing, Swimming, and Snorkeling

Most people who visit this park do so for the water, and tubing is, by far, the park's most popular water-related activity. During times of peak use, the river can be a boisterous place, overrun with people and inner tubes. However, on uncrowded days, which occur most often during mid-week, or on weekends if you can be one of the first parties down the river, a tubing and snorkeling excursion can also be a great way to study the river's plants and animals and to appreciate the park's scenic beauty. Alligator snapping turtles and a variety of freshwater fish including both bream and bass are common in the water, while otters are some-times seen along the bank. Limpkin are also present along the river's course and are easily seen, and the day's earliest tubers commonly flush wood duck from the river's marshy edges.

There are three access points for tubers, one via the park's north entrance and two via the south. For those fortunate enough to be one of the first 750 people admitted to the north entrance, the 3-mile trip to the lower take-out point offers about three hours of unhurried floating. The park service requires all tubing parties that launch at the north entrance to first deposit their gear near the put-in point, then select one driver to ferry the vehicle to the south entrance and take the park-provided shuttle back to the launch site. The north entrance is open for tubing only from June 1 to Labor Day.

Tubing is permitted from the south entrance year-round. There is a large parking lot, a bathhouse and concession, and a park-operated tram during the summer season (when funds are available) that carries tubers to and from the launch and termi-nation points. The two launch sites may also be reached by foot-path; one requires a five-minute walk, the other about a 20-minute walk.

Tubing is an enjoyable but potentially environmentally destructive activity. Tubers are specifically prohibited from leaving the water between the launch sites and termination points because climbing or jumping from the river's banks serves to hasten erosion and destroy the river's pristine beauty. In addition, food, beverage, and tobacco products are not allowed on the river. Preventing the presence of such products serves to reduce the risk of both intentional and inadvertent litter, as well as to prevent the introduction of nonnatural food sources into the river's ecosystem.

Some visitors choose to paddle rather than tube the river. Though the distance from the north entrance to the lower take-out point is short, the trip can be very rewarding. Due to the intense use by tubers during warm weather, most canoeists choose a mid-week or winter day. During these times there are few people on the water, which ensures a more pleasurable pad-dling excursion.

Ichetucknee Spring, the river's main headwater, is located adjacent to the picnic area in the park's northern unit. It is about 75 feet wide, 105 long, and 14 feet deep. It is easily accessible from the parking lot and is one of the park's most used swimming and snorkeling areas. It discharges about 30 million gallons of water a day into the small pool, and its water temperature averages about 73 degrees Fahrenheit.

Nature Trails

There are four nature trails at Ichetucknee Springs, three in the north unit and one in the south. The three in the north are the longer and less crowded of the four; the southern trail also doubles as an access route for tubers.

The boardwalk and footpath from the north unit's picnic area leads to Blue Hole, one of the park's favorite snorkeling spots. The trail follows through a scenic hardwood hammock that is lined with ironwood, hackberry, hickory, southern sugar maple, Virginia willow, poison ivy, and several species of grape vines before terminating at a wooden platform overlooking the spring. Blue Hole is about 85 feet wide, 125 feet long, and 37 feet deep at its deepest point. The clearly visible boil at the center of the pool issues about 60 million gallons per day directly into the Ichetucknee River and is an outstanding place for beginning snorkelers to enjoy their hobby. Cave-certified scuba divers also use Blue Hole as a dive site.

The Trestle Point and Pine Ridge Nature Trails, the north unit's longer walking paths, pass through about 2 miles of hardwood hammock and upland sandy woods. The Trestle Point Trail follows along the river for part of its course and is essentially a hammock path that is dominated by an overstory of laurel oaks, live oaks, hickory, sweetgum, and southern magnolias, with an understory and ground cover of pawpaw, red bay, American beauty berry, strawberry bush, American basswood, green dragon, and red buckeye.

As its name suggests, the Pine Ridge Trail passes through a stretch of restored sandy, pine-studded uplands that support wiregrass, longleaf pine, chinquapin, and several species of scrubby oaks. The ground cover along the trail can be filled with wildflowers, including climbing butterfly pea, lupine, twin flower, goldenrod, blazing star, and several species of asters. Gopher tortoise burrows are also common, as well as several species of woodpeckers, sparrows, and hawks.

The only trail of interest at the south entrance is the relatively short walkway that leads to what is called the midway launch point. The trail can be overrun with tubers early in the day but is an otherwise interesting place to visit. Eastern hophornbeam, red bay, black oak, southern magnolia, and southern sugar maple are common along the walk, and red maple, blackgum, and cypress are found near the river. The opposite, triangular-shaped leaves of wood-vamp or climbing hydrangea hug the trunks of some of the trees at the launch site; its spreading cymes of creamy flowers and resulting greenish brown fruit are distinctive field marks.

Birding

Ichetucknee's bird list is similar to most of north-central Florida's natural areas. Over 25 warblers have been recorded here, most during spring and fall migration, as well as a number of other songbirds. Limpkin, ground dove, Mississippi kite, red-tailed hawk, wild turkey, orchard oriole, and scarlet tanager are some of the more interesting species. The trails at the north entrance are generally quieter and more varied than the ones at the south entrance, and provide the better opportunities for finding land birds. The river can also be good in early morning or on uncrowded days.

Best Time of Year

For land-loving naturalists, the best time to visit the north unit is between Labor Day and June 1, preferably on a weekday. Tubing is not allowed during these months and the park has a more unhurried aspect. Early or mid-afternoon is the best time for a summer visit to the north entrance. Most of the day's tubers are already on their journeys by this time and the park seems less crowded.

Late afternoon, after the trail to the midway launch point is closed, is the best time to visit the south unit. Most tubers have left the park by 4:00 P.M. and it is permissible for nontubers to walk the trail to the midway landing.

Pets

Allowed on a 6-foot leash; not allowed in the river, springs, or inside any structures.

MANATEE SPRINGS STATE PARK

The name of this 2,075-acre park denotes two of its major attractions: West Indian manatees and the clear, refreshing waters of a typical Florida spring. While the first of these attractions is probably the more interesting of the two, it is the latter that attracts the most visitors.

Manatee Springs is one of Florida's 27 first-magnitude springs and has long figured prominently in the cultural history of the Levy County area. It produces nearly 120 million gallons of water daily, all of which flow into a short run that intersects with the Suwannee River about 0.25 mile from the headwaters. The main spring serves as one of the park's major recreation areas and is heavily used during summer by swimmers, snorkelers, and scuba divers. One side of the spring is bordered by a developed stone and concrete walkway and diving platform, the other side by a clay and sand beach.

These springs have long been a center of cultural activity. Their clean, fresh water and abundance of wildlife must certainly have been an important natural resource for the state's aboriginal Indian population, and the area's interesting plant community attracted the attention of naturalist William Bartram who visited the area in the late 1700s. The park takes its current name from the West Indian manatee, a large freshwater mammal that sometimes enters the run in winter to bask in the spring's constant 72-degree water.

Location, Mailing Address and Phone

At the end of SR 320, west of Chiefland.

Manatee Springs State Park, Rt. 2, Box 617, Chiefland, FL 32626; (904) 493-6072.

Facilities and Activities

Canoeing, camping, swimming, birding, botanizing, hiking, nature trail, boardwalk, scuba diving, snorkeling, bathhouse, canoe rentals, food concession.

The park's two campgrounds are located in the middle of a hardwood hammock, on opposite sides of the main park road. Both are near several of the park's major activity areas including the picnic area, swimming area, canoe rental concession, and the Sink Nature Trail. Together, the two campgrounds contain 86 campsites; 45 have both water and electrical hookups; the remainder have only water. All are accessible to bathrooms and showers.

Hiking, Nature Trail, and Boardwalk

Manatee Springs has an assortment of hiking and nature trails that traverse all of the park's major habitats.

The most often walked path is probably the short boardwalk that follows along the spring run from the canoe landing to the Suwannee River. Most of the wooden walkway passes above a riverine hammock of cypress, red maple, stiffcornel dogwood, blackgum, buttonbush, planer tree, and Carolina ash. Bromeliads adorn the trunks of many of the trees and the usually wet ground cover is dominated by lizard tail. Several overlooks along the way allow outstanding views of the crystal clear water of the spring run, and the boardwalk terminates at a partially covered manatee-viewing platform. As many as 80 West Indian manatee sightings have been reported in a single month, though the number of animals spotted is usually smaller than this. Winter and spring, from about November to April, are the best months for seeing these huge creatures. Park staff have been keeping sighting records since 1988 and each month post the latest records on the bulletin board at the viewing platform.

The Sink Trail is the other of the two short trails. It leaves the main park road at a designated trailhead near the entrance to the Magnolia Campground. The trail leads through a stretch of upland hammock woods and adjacent to a number of sinkholes. In addition to typical dry hammock plant species, this trail also includes a particularly impressive specimen of the uncommon bluff oak, as well as a small population of the typically shrubby Carolina or sand holly. The flaking whitish bark of the former and bright red berries of the latter are distinctive field marks.

For extended hiking or bicycling opportunities the north trail system provides the best opportunities. More than 8 miles of hard-packed woods roads lead through sandhill and hammock uplands. Shrubby specimens of sweetleaf and Carolina silverbell line many of these old roadways. The yellowish, ball-like flower clusters of the former and the white, bell-shaped flowers of the latter make a beautiful show during their early spring flowering periods. There is an excellent and easy-to-follow map of these trails available at the trailhead which includes the road's names and the distances between intersections.

Birding and Wildlife Observation

The park's trail system offers the best opportunities for observing wildlife. White-tailed deer are commonly seen year-round, as are wild turkey and bobwhite quail. The park also supports a large population of gopher tortoise. The oval openings to their sandy burrows are easy to spot, but the tortoises themselves are somewhat shy, generally remain close to home, and are not particularly tolerant of people. Nevertheless, quiet, persistent observers are sometimes rewarded for their diligence by a tortoise that emerges from its cavity to search for food or to tamp down the sand surrounding the burrow's entranceway. Other common reptiles include the six-lined racerunner and the fence swift, both of which scamper across the top of the sand with amazing speed and dexterity.

Manatee Springs' bird list is not particularly large but includes enough interesting species to make a visit here worthwhile. The hooded, prothonotary, and parula warblers nest during summer and the black-and-white, orange-crowned, yellow-rumped, and palm warblers, as well as the ovenbird, are common in winter. Another dozen warblers are either permanent residents or pass through during migration, along with a variety of other song-birds that include both the Swainsons and gray-cheeked thrushes, as well as the veery. Other notable species include the swallow-tailed and Mississippi kites, both of which are most likely to be seen swooping and soaring in open areas over the river.

Canoeing

This park is outstanding for canoeing and sea kayaking. There is a landing on the spring run just outside of the swimming area, and the run is strictly reserved for nonmotorized traffic. A canoe rental concession is available at the landing, or paddlers can bring their own craft. The water in the run is very clear and the fishes and underwater vegetation are easy to see. It is only a short paddle from the landing to the Suwannee River which allows greater access to more open waters.

For longer trips it is possible to launch from the wayside park located near the US 19 bridge at the little village of Fanning Springs. The park is only about 7 miles below this put-in, a moderate distance for a river with the velocity of the Suwannee. It is easy to find the park from the river; just look for the observation deck, floating dock, and spring run on the river's eastern side. Paddlers must make their own transportation arrangements; no shuttle service is available at the park.

Best Time of Year

Summer is best for swimming and snorkeling; any time is good for canoeing or walking the trails.

Pets

Allowed on a 6-foot leash; not allowed in the swimming area, campground, or near concessions.

O'LENO STATE PARK

The name O'Leno is a contraction of Old Leno, the historical appellation of a now-defunct mid-1800s village. The original town bore the name Keno, after the popular game of chance that is still a favorite in many modern-day gambling casinos. Though the town's name was eventually changed to Leno in deference to its more God-fearing successors, its first name must certainly indicate something about the spirit and personalities of the settlement's earliest pioneers.

Today, O'Leno is one of Florida's largest state parks. More than 6,000 acres of prime north-central Florida terrain is encompassed within its boundaries, including outstanding examples of nearly every one of the region's native communities and vegetative assemblages.

A short stretch of the Santa Fe River, one of north-central Florida's finest canoeing streams, enters the park from the northeast but disappears almost immediately into a giant swallow hole before passing through most of the remainder of the park under the cover of a densely vegetated natural bridge. Both the sink and the subsequent rise are within the park's boundaries. The river, which originates at Santa Fe Lake a few miles northeast of Gainesville, is a major tributary of the Suwannee River and a stream of significant geological interest. It flows westwardly across two of the state's major topographic provinces, making the transition from the Northern Highlands to the Gulf Coastal Lowlands at about the location of the park. At least 35 springs, including the group that comprises the headwaters of the Ichetucknee River (see Ichetucknee Springs State Park, p. 132), feed into the tannin-stained waterway. Though its cultural history is long and varied, its use today is confined primarily to fishing, swimming, paddling, and other recreational uses.

O'Leno is also one of the state's Civilian Conservation Corps parks and was built by the CCC in the 1930s to serve as a summer forestry camp. A suspension bridge which spans the river near the swimming and picnic area was originally constructed when the park was established and now serves as an access point for the park's expansive trail system.

Location, Mailing Address and Phone

Off US 441, about 5 mi. south of I-75 and 6 mi. north of High Springs.

O'Leno State Park, Rt. 2, Box 1010, High Springs, FL 32643; (904) 454-1853.

Facilities and Activities

Camping, cabins, hiking, backpacking, birding, botanizing, picnicking, swimming, canoeing, nature trails, horseback trails, fishing.

Campground and Cabins

Like most CCC parks, O'Leno offers cabins as well as campsites. The cabins are rustic affairs that offer few amenities—bring your own towels, washcloths, linens, and pillows—but are close to the river and help patrons gain an appreciation of the park's history. There are also two developed campgrounds, one near the entrance and one closer to the river. Together, they offer 61 campsites, each with water and electricity. Youth and primitive campsites are also available.

Hiking, Backpacking, Horseback Riding, and Nature Trails

Several trails of varying lengths traverse O'Leno State Park, including one that is suitable for backpacking and primitive camping. All of these trails offer interesting walking opportunities and are excellent for exploring the region.

The Limestone Trail is the shortest of these footpaths and takes less than an hour to explore. It exits the main park road just past the entrance station, then winds through hammock woodlands to the site of an old limestone quarry. The stones mined from this site were used to build fireplace chimneys for early residents. The limestone boulders that are evident along the trail are approximately 40 million years old and were probably deposited before the beginning of the Oligocene Epoch.

The River Sink Trail begins at the old suspension bridge near the swimming area. Crossing the bridge then turning left leads through a calcareous woodland along the river's edge for about 0.25 mile before turning toward the sink. About 1,500 feet from the suspension bridge the trail passes Ogden Pond, a small, narrow lake that is in some ways an extension of the river. There are sometimes moving currents evident on the pond's surface, and its level fluctuates with the groundwater.

Beyond Ogden Pond, the trail circles around the large swallow hole into which the river disappears for its 3-mile subsurface excursion. Huge, 140-foot-deep vertical conduits channel the water down through the limestone and into a labyrinth of underground cavities and passageways. Though these subterranean features are not visible from the surface, the boardwalk platform that hangs out over the river at this point allows you to see the slowly swirling surface currents and to imagine all of that water being fanned out into the natural limestone network below you. Beyond the overlook the trail follows along the river's edge and back to the trailhead.

Pareners Branch Loop is a longer path that turns off the River Sink Trail at Ogden Pond. Its circular, 3.5-mile route leads through pine flatwoods and sand hills as well as hammock woodlands. Part of its course leads along the edges of several ponds and sinkhole depressions before intersecting with Wire Road, an 1800s wagon route that passes through the park.

The intersection of Pareners Loop and the Wire Road is the beginning point for the Sweetwater Lake and River Rise Trails, primitive backpacking and hiking trails that lead to Santa Fe River Rise. A primitive camping area has been established at Sweetwater Lake and includes a campfire ring and privy; however, backpackers are required to bring their own water supply. The primitive camp is limited to 12 people per night and requires a small usage fee. Day hikes to River Rise are also possible but may require several hours, depending on how thoroughly you explore the area.

In addition to walking, the 6,000 acres of O'Leno River Rise State Preserve also contain many miles of horse trails. Riders must bring their own horses.

Swimming and Paddling

The park's swimming area is located adjacent to the suspension bridge at the end of the main park road. The Santa Fe River's tannin-stained waters are a refreshing summertime retreat and a favored haunt of nearby residents.

A canoe rental concession is also available that allows paddling excursions on the river. It is possible to put in near the swimming area, paddle upstream against the gentle currents, then float leisurely back. However, no boats or canoes are allowed below the swimming area toward the sink.

It is also possible to put a canoe in at the US 441 bridge and make the easy 2-mile paddle up to River Rise. This entire route is within the park's boundaries and is quite scenic.

There are several other routes available for longer adventures, only one of which passes through the park. It is only a 5-mile float to the park from the Florida 241 bridge and the scenery is worth the trip. High banks line much of the route and the tea-colored water is delightful. The river narrows a little as it enters the park. The few telltale signs of civilization that are scattered along some portions of the upper river disappear completely and are replaced, instead, by scenic wooded bluffs.

Below the park, the Santa Fe twists and turns for another 30 miles before finally emptying into the Suwannee just west of US 129. There are a number of access points along this route including bridges at US 441, US 27, Florida 47, and US 129.

Botanizing

All of O'Leno's walking trails and canoe routes allow plenty of opportunity to study the park's plant life. A large number of north-central Florida's native species are present here. American holly, black tupelo, pignut hickory, Carolina silverbell, live oak, sweetgum, Carolina ash, blackgum, titi, and cypress are the more common trees; small-fruited pawpaw, wild azalea, winged sumac, buttonbush, sebastian bush, sweetleaf, dangleberry, sparkleberry, and highbush blueberry are the more common shrubs. There are also a number of herbaceous flowering plants including blazing star, deer tongue, wild buckwheat, and sneezeweed, as well as a selection of native ferns. All plants and animals in the park are protected.

Birding

O'Leno's bird list includes approximately 135 entries that represent an assortment of both wetland and woodland species. The hammock woodlands that line much of the park's trail system can be good for songbirds during fall and spring migration; 27 different warblers have been reported from the park. Hooded and prothonotary warblers nest here, as does the Bachman sparrow. Chuck-will's-widows and common nighthawks are frequently heard on summer evenings, and the whip-poor-will passes through and is sometimes heard in spring. Four owls have been reported from the park, including the barn, screech, great horned, and barred. The raucous hooting of the latter is a common nighttime sound. At least ten raptors also visit the park, including the bald eagle, osprey, Mississippi kite, and American swallow-tailed kite.

Best Time of Year

Summer is best for swimming; canoeing and hiking are good year-round. Backpacking is probably best during cooler winter weather. Spring, summer, and fall are best for birding and botanizing.

Pets

Allowed on a 6-foot leash; not allowed in the river, camping area, cabins, or inside structures.

PAYNES PRAIRIE STATE PRESERVE

William Bartram may have been one of the first American naturalists to see the lands now encompassed by Paynes Prairie State Preserve. The chronicles of his 1774 travels in Florida and the Carolinas describe a serenity unsurpassed by even the most outstanding modern-day remnants of our natural lands.

"The extensive Alachua Savanna is a level green plain," he wrote, "above fifteen miles over, fifty miles in circumference, and scarcely a tree or bush of any kind to be seen on it. It is encircled with high, sloping hills covered with waving forests and fragrant orange groves, rising from an exuberantly fertile soil. The towering Magnolia grandiflora and transcendent palm stand conspicuous amongst them.

"At the same time are seen innumerable droves of cattle; the lordly bull, lowing cow, and sleek capricious heifer. The hills and groves re-echo their cheerful, social voices. Herds of sprightly deer, squadrons of the beautiful fleet Seminole horse, flocks of turkeys, civilized communities of the sonorous watchful crane, mix together, appearing happy and contented in the enjoyment of peace."

Its easy to understand Bartram's exuberance at first seeing Paynes Prairie. The huge wet basin, hemmed in on all sides by conspicuous patches of upland forest, is a sight unlike any other in the state. On an early spring day, when the ground is carpeted with wildflowers and the sky is clear and blue, it is one of north Florida's most delightful locations.

The Alachua Savannah, as Bartram termed it, is essentially a large wetland depression that lies as much as 20 meters below the elevation of the surrounding uplands. It is a seasonally wet area that is characterized by a mosaic of plant communities including freshwater marshes, pastures, wet meadows, and shrubby wetlands. Much of the basin's central region is dominated by picturesque open flatlands that support a variety of sedges, grasses, rushes, and other monocotyledonous plants. The subsoil below these communities is composed primarily of impermeable clays that retard the downward percolation of rain

The observation tower at Paynes Prairie State Preserve

and runoff, and assure the presence of standing water during much of the year.

Healthy wet prairies are noted for rapidly changing conditions and equally rapidly changing natural communities. Paynes Prairie is no exception. Extreme annual fluctuations in both temperature and ground water are common occurrences in such places and lead to noticeable changes in the composition of a prairie's plant communities. During dry years, aquatic and wetland plants suffer and their dominance in the ground cover is diminished; in wet years, however, they recover quickly, making visible advances in only a single growing season, usually to the detriment of other species.

The Department of Environmental Protection manages Paynes Prairie Preserve to reflect these historical fluctuations and to insure biological diversity in its natural communities. Rainfall and water level are monitored as much as possible, and prescribed burning is used to simulate natural conditions and to discourage the expansion of shrubs and other shading species. Both of these management strategies are designed to insure the advantage of the myriad low-growing herbaceous species that naturally inhabit the area.

Paynes Prairie is a birder's and wildlife observer's hotspot. About 350 vertebrates are known to inhabit the area, including more than 40 reptiles, over 20 amphibians, and nearly 30 mammals. The preserve's bird list is extensive and includes large numbers of ducks, long-legged waders, and shorebirds, as well as 27 species of warblers; the latter are more likely to be seen during spring or fall migration. A variety of hawks hunt over the open grasslands during various times of the year, and both wood storks and sandhill cranes can be seen year-round.

The preserve also supports over 750 plant species, including a large number of trees, woody shrubs, vines, and herbaceous plants. In spring the meadows burst into bloom with an array of wildflowers too numerous to list. Even the most accomplished amateur botanists can fill many hours poring over their field guides, trying to identify the plants contained within only a small part of the prairie.

Location, Mailing Address and Phone

The main entrance is located on US 441, about 10 miles south of Gainesville. Other access points are described below.

Paynes Prairie State Preserve, Rt. 2, Box 41, Micanopy, FL 32667-9702; (904) 466-3397.

Facilities and Activities

Hiking, camping, canoeing, birding, wildlife observation, botanizing, horseback riding, bicycling, visitor center, nature trails.

Lake Wauberg Recreation Area

Off US 441, about 10 miles south of Gainesville.

The Lake Wauberg Recreation Area is much like a typical Florida state park and is the preserve's most developed recreation area. Camping, hiking, horseback riding, and fishing are all available here. Just beyond the ranger station, the main park drive provides a scenic thoroughfare that leads northward to a visitor center and observation tower. Turning left at the only intersection leads to a boat landing on Lake Wauberg. No gasoline motors are allowed on the lake; electric trolling motors, sails, and oars provide the preferred methods of locomotion. There is also a very nice picnic area near the landing, complete with pavilions, a covered outdoor cooking area, and plenty of parking.

Visitor Center

The Visitor Center is located at the end of the main park drive and is a good place to learn about the preserve's natural history and special endowments. A collection of exhibits highlights both the natural and cultural history of the area and a covered porch off the rear of the center offers a picturesque view of the prairie through a grove of old live oaks. Park staff are usually on hand to answer questions and are very cooperative in helping visitors locate the preserve's more scenic locations.

A short walk beyond the visitor center leads to a three-story, covered observation tower that overlooks the prairie's southern rim; each level of the tower offers a more enchanting vista than the one below. The gentle breezes that blow through the topmost deck of this rustic vantage point, even on hot summer days, make the tower a respite that is difficult to relinquish. It is also a great place to spend a summer rain shower. Bring binoculars and telescopes when visiting the tower; its an outstanding place to scan for birds and other wildlife.

Camping

The Puc Puggy campground, which is located near the eastern edge of Lake Wauberg, is the preserve's only developed camping area. The camp's unusual name is in honor of William Bartram. After giving Bartram the privilege of searching for native plants in the area, the Seminole Cowkeeper gave him the name Puc Puggy, which translates to English as Flower Hunter.

There are 50 sites (35 for RVs; 15 for tents) at the campground, each with a table, grill, electric hookup, and running water. All sites are located in a scenic hammock and most are well separated for privacy. Puc Puggy provides a perfect base camp for a several-day exploration of the preserve.

Trails

The Lake Wauberg area provides extensive walking and horseback riding opportunities. The Chacala Trail, which leads east off the main park drive, is an interconnecting system that encompasses over 8 miles of pathways. A parking area at the trailhead is suitable for horse trailers, and a kiosk offers maps and other user information. The trail passes through a variety of habitats including pine flatwoods, mixed forests, and bay gall. This is an excellent route for all-terrain bicyclists.

The northern end of Chacala intersects the access to Cone's Dike, a 6-mile route that leads across the southeastern end of the prairie. The official trailhead for Cone's Dike is located at the Visitor Center parking lot near the end of the main park road. The trail leads first through hammock woodlands before turning northward, then dropping down onto the prairie. A walk along the dike is an excellent way to experience the prairie's animal and plant life. Both sides of the trail are lined with a variety of rushes, sedges, and other herbaceous plants, and the bird life here can be extraordinary.

The Wacahoota Trail is the shortest of the Lake Wauberg Recreation Area's trails but is very interesting. It is a 0.5 mile walk that passes below the observation tower described above, then circles through a mature hammock woodland with some particularly old live oaks. Bicycles and horses are not permitted on this trail.

Bolen Bluff Trail

On US 441, a few miles north of the Lake Wauberg Recreation Area.

The Bolen Bluff Trail is a 2.88-mile loop that begins at US 441 and circles through an attractive hammock of mixed upland woods. A spur route near the trail's halfway point leads into the prairie and terminates at a low observation deck that provides a

360-degree view of the prairie. This is a good place to look for birds, especially fall migrant warblers. The shrubby edges attract sparrows and other secretive species, and the observation deck provides a good vantage to survey for cranes, hawks, and other larger species. Because of its ease of access, this trail is an often-used pathway. Birders and bicyclists come here regularly.

Boardwalk and Observation Platform

On US 441, 1 mile north of Bolen Bluff Trail.

This is a short boardwalk with a paved parking lot adjacent to the highway. An observation platform at the end of the walk allows a vista of the prairie. Though this is a nice place to stop, it does not even begin to introduce visitors to all this preserve has to offer.

La Chua Trail and Alachua Sink

Accessed via the Gainesville-Hawthorne Trail from the city of Gainesville's Boulware Springs Park (see p. 119 for directions).

The La Chua Trail turns off to the south about 1 mile from the Boulware Springs trailhead of the Gainesville-Hawthorne Trail. It is 3 miles long (roundtrip) and traverses mostly prairie habitat. The trail passes the Alachua Sink area, a densely vegetated ever-green–deciduous hardwood hammock that supports a southern mixed hardwood forest. The area is rich in sinkholes, some of which have visible limestone along their slopes. Live oak, pignut hickory, sweetgum, red bay, Carolina ash, winged elm, soap-berry, wafer ash, and cornel are the dominant overstory and understory species. Shrubs and vines include tough bumelia, poison ivy, Virginia creeper, smilax, cross vine, trumpet creeper, and trifoliate orange. Bicycles and horses are not permitted on this trail. Access to this area is provided by ranger-led programs including the Rim Ramble and overnight backpacking trip. Call the Visitor Center at (904) 466-4100 for details.

Best Time of Year

Birding is best in fall, winter, and spring. Wildflowers are most abundant in spring but there always seems to be something in bloom. Cool winter days are best for hiking the more open trails.

Pets

Where allowed, dogs must be kept on a 6-foot leash. Pets are not allowed in the campground, visitor center, pavilions, recreation area, or on any trail; they are permitted along the 3.5-mile-long main park drive.

PEACOCK SPRINGS STATE RECREATION AREA

The expansive karst plain that stretches across much of northwestern Florida supports an enchanting terrestrial landscape as well as one of the world's most intriguing underground ecosystems. Below ground, intricate water-filled passageways weave through ancient formations of subsurface limestone, while aboveground the calcium-rich soil supports a lush hammock community where diminutive and little-known plants intermingle with those more typical of the Florida landscape.

Peacock Springs State Recreation Area, acquired by the state in 1987 with the help of The Nature Conservancy, is touted as one of the world's most pristine karst plain preserves. Used primarily by water enthusiasts, its tiny picnic areas and two freshwater springs can be filled to capacity on warm weekends by an unlikely combination of cave-certified scuba divers out to explore the area's expansive subsurface cavern system, and nearby residents out only for an afternoon of fun, frolic, and relaxation.

Location, Mailing Address and Phone

Drive south from Live Oak on SR 51 for about 16.8 miles. Turn east onto 180th Street at the settlement of Luraville (the Luraville Store is directly across the highway and provides a good landmark). Follow 180th for about 2.5 miles to the park entrance. Note: This is not an easy park to find. No signs point the way until you reach the park's entrance.

Peacock Springs State Recreation Area, Rt. 4, Box 370, Live Oak, FL 32060; (904) 776-2194.

Facilities and Activities

Diving, snorkeling, picnicking, swimming, botanizing.

There are not many facilities at this park. Two small picnic areas complete with portable restrooms, a few signs warning of the dangers inherent in cave diving, and two unpaved parking lots are all the amenities you will find. There is no organized nature trail, no campground, no running water, and no pavilion. However, for those who enjoy wandering freely in mature, old-growth woodlands, or exploring the ground cover for interesting herbaceous plants, or learning the identity of north Florida's native trees and shrubs, or sinking below the surface to marvel at sights most people never experience, this park's lack of creature comforts can be one of its most appreciated characteristics.

Diving and Snorkeling

Cave and cavern divers are, by far, the most consistent users of this park. Two major springs and one major sinkhole provide the main enticements. Peacock and Bonnet Springs, both of which are third-magnitude springs that feed Peacock Slough, are clear-water areas that provide beautiful open-water diving and snorkeling conditions. The rock crevices and many freshwater fishes make these two spots particularly attractive.

More serious divers use the above two springs as well as Orange Grove Sink to access the deepwater tunnels and caves that make up part of more than 28,000 feet of mapped passageways. Many of these passageways alternate between huge rooms with cathedral ceilings and narrow corridors just large enough to provide passage. Many of the more popular trails are marked by permanent guide lines put in place by experts from the National Speciological Society; all have no natural light and require significant skill to explore safely. Open-water divers are not permitted to carry lights or to enter this extensive cave system, and solo dives are not allowed. The floors of many of the areas are covered with fine silt that can engulf the unwary in a murky fog if disturbed. Signs bordering the walkways to these areas warn that 45 divers have lost their lives in the underground system since 1960, a somber editorial on the dangers of this fast-growing sport.

Orange Grove Sink is one of the more popular jumping-off points for certified divers. At first glance, this sink doesn't look particularly inviting. Most of its surface is covered with duck weed, a small-leaved, free-floating aquatic plant that is common on many of north Florida's quieter waters. Such ponds often look as though they have completely succumbed to a kind of slimy scum. In reality, the tiny plants are restricted only to the water's surface and are not the least bit offensive to the touch.

One of Orange Grove Sink's most popular destinations is a large cavern whose floor lies about 100 feet below the surface. The 7-by-15-foot entrance to the room is located at a depth of about 50 feet; the room itself measures about 60 by 85 feet. A number of divers come here just for this attraction. The cavern's popularity has led to it being used extensively as an outdoor classroom for organized courses designed to teach aspiring cave divers the intricacies of their sport.

For the more experienced and adventurous, the numerous passageways that constitute the Peacock Springs system can provide a veritable lifetime of exploration opportunities. There are many unmapped and completely unexplored corridors in this expansive labyrinth, and the system's maximum extent is still not well understood.

Botanizing

Underground attractions are not all that this park offers. At least four natural plant communities are found here including both xeric and upland hammocks and floodplain and bottomland forests. The plants found here include such interesting and relatively uncommon species as green dragon and cedar elm as well as the more common water and pignut hickories, red buckeye, Florida dogwood, sweetgum, little silverbell, red maple, Florida maple, southern magnolia, American holly, bald cypress, buttonbush, swamp privet, and Carolina ash. Those who can't resist fingering the leaves, fruits, and flowers of low-growing herbaceous plants should be warned: the ground cover here has an extremely healthy population of poison ivy.

The best way to explore the plants contained within the park's 252 acres is by leaving your vehicle at the Orange Grove Sink parking lot, then walking the woodlands along the roadside. Crisscrossing the area all the way to the parking lot at Peacock Springs will reveal many interesting plants as well as five additional sinkholes and numerous small depressions. Beyond Peacock Spring you can walk through a parklike woodland along the edges of Peacock Slough. Though there are no trails, the woodlands here are easy to traverse and there is little chance of getting lost.

Best Time of Year

Diving is good year-round; snorkeling is best in warmer weather; botanizing is best in spring, summer, and fall, but is likely to be more enjoyable on weekdays rather than weekends.

Pets

Generally allowed; not allowed in the springs, sinks, or swimming areas.

RAVINE STATE GARDENS

It doesn't take an astute observer to recognize the significant impact that human hands have had on Ravine State Gardens. Footpaths, brick-lined roadways, suspension bridges, landscaped courtyards, stone stairways, nonnative ornamentals: the evidence is abundant. Yet, even with all this modification, the unique geological and cultural resource that this park preserves is an important component of Florida's state park system, and one that may one day again reflect more natural vegetative patterns. Even today it is a great place to study the northern peninsula's native plants.

Ravine State Gardens was first established in 1933 as an activity of the Works Project Administration, a post-Depression government jobs program designed to put people to work on projects that benefitted the country. Once completed, the gardens were turned over to the city of Palatka and managed as a city park until 1970 when they became part of the state park system. The WPA planted a large number of azaleas, camellias, palms, ferns, and banana trees within the park, most of which are still very much in evidence. Large numbers of tropical plants were also planted but have long since disappeared.

Ravine State Gardens takes its name from the huge canyon that dominates its landscape. Similar in structure to most central peninsula ravines, the dominant landform of Ravine Gardens was created by water flowing down gradient toward the St. Johns River basin. Much like the process described for the development of Gold Head Branch (see p. 124), the subsurface water flowing toward the river intersects the surface of the land prior to reaching its destination, eroding the sandy soils from below and creating a mammoth chasm that supports a variety of native flora. A number of trails now criss-cross the ravine, allowing easy access to its slopes and interior.

Location, Mailing Address and Phone

Turn south onto Moseley Ave. from US 17/SR 100 in Palatka. Continue on Moseley for 0.9 mile to Twigg St. Turn left at the park directional sign; the entrance to the park is on the right about 0.2 mile from the intersection.

Ravine State Gardens, P.O. Box 1096, Palatka, FL 32178-1096; (904) 329-3721.

Facilities and Activities

Walking trail, driving trail, plant study.

Driving Trail

The ravine is encircled by a 1.8-mile-long one-way drive that hugs the rim for nearly its entire route. There are several places to park along the roadway that allow access into the ravine. Some of these locations have rock stairways leading down the steeper slopes; others have moderately descending footpaths.

There are also several picnic areas along the way. Near the end of the trail the road crosses the low end of the ravine adjacent to a landscaped garden and reflecting pool. Stopping here allows easy access to the trail system.

Walking Trails

The ravine contains an extensive trail system that allows access to all parts of the park. The longest of these trails essentially parallels the roadway but at a much lower level. Two suspension bridges cross the stream that cuts through the ravine floor and allow access from one side of the ravine to the other. Although much of the trail is lined with nonnative azaleas, there are still a number of native species that are common to the ravine ecosystem.

The Bamboo Springs Trail is an interpretive walk that begins adjacent to the building that houses the park office and civic center. Be sure to pick up a trail guide from the small rack attached to the front of the building. The Bamboo Springs Trail is one section of the more extensive trail but differs by containing 17 numbered markers along its route. The markers are keyed to the trail guide and identify 14 of the more common native plants found in the park, including the endangered coontie, a plant that the original Florida Indians used to make flour. The trail is not long, but the dense vegetation along the way encourages you to move slowly.

Best Time of Year

February through April, when the azaleas and camellias are in bloom, are the months of maximum color. However, almost any time in spring, summer, or fall will find at least some blooming plants. Winter is also a great time for walking the trails.

Pets

Allowed on a 6-foot leash.

SAN FELASCO HAMMOCK STATE PRESERVE

San Felasco Hammock ranks among the most important of north Florida's preserved natural lands. Located just beyond the outskirts of metropolitan Gainesville, it seems only marginally removed from the bustling activity of urbanization. Yet, in its deepest reaches, in those places reached only with significant commitment of time and energy, the hammock precipitates a sense of being far removed from the nearest vestiges of civilization.

This state preserve's 6,500 acres encompass at least 18 biological communities that include nearly all of north Florida's major forest cover types, as well as a wide array of plants and wildlife. Unlike nearby Paynes Prairie State Preserve, there are no facilities except for three sparsely interpreted but easy-to-follow trails that circle through the park and provide access to the more remote areas. Though the walking paths get plenty of use, the management objective here is focused less on recreation and interpretation than on preservation, protection, and restoration. Controlled burning is used to maintain the delicate balance of the preserve's upland pine forests, and restoration projects are underway to insure the integrity of the wetlands. Intensive steps have also been taken to reduce erosion along the park's fragile slopes. Trailside markers admonish walkers to remain on the path, a difficult challenge given the near irresistible temptation to strike out through the relatively open understory of mature hardwood forests, or to sneak a peek at what might lie at the bottom of a nearby ravine.

San Felasco Hammock State Preserve was purchased by the state in 1974 under Florida's Environmentally Endangered Lands Program. It was acquired along with several other, widely separated sites that included Paynes Prairie, Rock Springs Run, and Cape St. George. In addition to its ecological importance, the area is also known for its cultural significance. Archaeological evidence suggests that Florida's original Indians used this area at least as early as 10,000 years ago, and at least some of Florida's more recent Spanish history was also played out here.

Location, Mailing Address and Phone

Alachua CR 232, about four miles west of Devil's Millhopper State Geological Site.

San Felasco Hammock State Preserve, c/o Devil's Millhopper State Geological Site, 4732 Millhopper Rd., Gainesville, FL 32653; (904) 462-7905.

Facilities and Activities

Hiking, birding, botanizing, wildlife observation, nature trail.

Hiking Trails

Three trails provide access. All are accessible from the preserve's only parking area located on the north side of CR 232.

The nature trail, which begins at the eastern end of the parking lot, is like a chef's sampler of what this preserve contains. After passing initially through a short stretch of pine–turkey oak uplands, the trail begins a gentle but steady descent which grades into a hardwood hammock of sweetgum, hickory, black cherry, red bay, eastern hophornbeam, at least two species of haw, American basswood, eastern redbud, sweetleaf, ironwood, American holly, chestnut oak, live oak, red mulberry, green dragon, and partridge berry. The path winds downward across a small stream adjacent to a swallow- or sinkhole before circling back toward the starting point. The trail is only about a mile in length but can take several hours for those who come armed with their field guides. The ground cover alone is enough to keep most plant lovers busy for a good while, and birders will find many woodland species, particularly during spring and fall migration. A variety of warblers, thrushes, vireos, and woodpeckers can be common during the right time of year.

The other two trails, both of which begin directly across CR 232 from the parking lot, are for the adventurous walker who has a penchant for seeing much more of what this preserve has to offer. The Old Spanish Trail, which is marked in blue, circles for 4.83 miles in the eastern part of the preserve; the Spring Grove Loop is a yellow marked circular path that traverses 5.66 miles near the western edge of the preserve. The two trails share the same canopied footpath for a mile or so, then diverge for the remainder of their routes. Even on a hot day the air feels cooler as you move deeper into the hammock, and quiet walkers have plenty of opportunity to see wildlife. White-tailed deer are often encountered along the trail's edge; many seem unconcerned about human visitors, as if they are aware of their protected status in these special woodlands. Bobcats, wild turkey, and gray fox are also common. Bicycles are specifically prohibited along these trails, and dogs must be restrained on a 6-foot leash.

Botanizing

Plant lovers should bring all of their north Florida field guides when walking these trails. Approximately 150 tree species are found within the preserve's boundaries, over half the number native to Florida and nearly 75 percent of those native to north Florida. Scores of shrubs and herbs and an assortment of both woody and herbaceous vines fill the understory. No matter the time of year, there is nearly always something in flower or fruit.

The most widespread vegetative community at San Felasco, and the one that attracts the most visitors, is the mixed hardwood hammock. The trees, shrubs, and vines found in the hammock include those listed above for the nature trail, with the addition of prickly ash, devil's walking stick, hearts-a-bustin'-with-love, may haw (including the national champion), several species of elm and ash, southern magnolia, diamond leaf oak, southern red oak, cross vine, wild olive, spruce pine, red maple, and mockernut hickory.

Sanchez Prairie, located in the preserve's northwestern quadrant, is one of the more botanically interesting areas. The large basin is forested with a population of Carolina ash and planer tree. The latter plant, which is named for German botanist Johann Jacob Planer, is the only living member of its genus and is more typically thought of as bordering rivers, backwaters, and oxbow lakes than inhabiting wetland marshes.

Best Time of Year

Any time of year is good here. Summer can be hot and buggy, but early morning hikes are delightful. Spring and fall are good for birding; winter for extended hiking.

Pets

Allowed on a 6-foot leash.

TALBOT ISLANDS STATE PARKS

Few of Florida's coastlines are better preserved than the stretch of pristine woodlands that lines the state's northeasternmost corner. Driving northward along A1A from the Mayport ferry is like driving through the Sunshine State in its earliest days. Large expanses of undisturbed coastal landscape line the old roadway, and few gaudy billboards or garish signs inhibit the view.

Much of this area's outstanding scenery can be directly attributed to the state's aggressive land acquisition program. Few methods are better for conserving our natural resources than adding to the reservoir of publicly protected lands, and those parcels that lie along the northeast Florida coast constitute some of the state's finest holdings. Unlike many similar landforms along the United States' eastern seaboard, northeast Florida's barriers are relatively undeveloped and free of the blight that unbridled human encroachment can cause. Much of what has been developed in this part of the state has been done so tastefully, and much of what isn't developed is protected as part of the Talbot Islands State Parks.

The Talbot Islands State Parks constitute a collection of four important natural areas that are currently managed under a single administrative unit. Consisting of large portions of Ft. George Island, much of Big Talbot Island, all of Little Talbot Island, and the southernmost tip of Amelia Island, these four parks preserve the southernmost members of the chain of sea islands that line the east coast from New York to Florida.

Florida's members of this Atlantic coast barrier chain constitute a unique and fragile resource and are certainly deserving of protection. They are young landforms that are only a few thousand years old and are constantly subject to powerful natural forces. Strong Atlantic waves beat regularly against their beaches, and the powerful winds of occasional hurricanes or violent winter storms erode their faces, altering the appearance of their shorelines as well as of the vegetative communities that inhabit their interiors. Even the slightest change in sea level can change an island's shape and extent, or even its physical location. Coastal geologists tell us that we can expect continued changes in these places over the next centuries. The parks in the Talbot Islands group help insure that these changes will come only through natural processes rather than at the hands of us humans.

Location, Mailing Address and Phone

All four of these parks are located on or off A1A north of Jacksonville; Ft. George Island State Cultural Site is the southernmost of the four and can be reached by turning left off A1A at the roadside marker; Little Talbot Island is just north of Ft. George Island and the entrance to the park is well-marked; Big Talbot Island State Park is just north of Little Talbot; Amelia Island State Recreation Area is just north of Nassau Sound.

Little Talbot Island State Park, 12157 Heckscher Dr., Jacksonville, FL 32226; (904) 251-2320.

Facilities and Activities

Birding, hiking, botanizing, swimming, shelling, camping, canoeing, bicycling, nature trails, historic sites.

The Talbot Islands State Parks offer a variety of outdoor exploration opportunities in an array of natural settings. Taken as a unit, these four parks can be lumped together as representatives of a single ecosystem, each with a variety of overlapping qualities. Taken individually, each has its own unique attributes that readily distinguish it from the others.

The one thing that all of these sites have in common is their attraction to birders. Nearly 200 bird species frequent this area annually, and there is something to attract the attention of avid birders nearly any time of year. Spring and fall are best for migrating shorebirds and songbirds, and winter is best for grebes, loons, and waterfowl. Herons, egrets, and ibises are common year-round and are most easily observed along grassy shorelines or in freshwater marshes. Specialties in the area include the great black-backed gull, painted bunting, and bobolink; rarities include the short-eared owl, horned lark, greater shearwater, red-throated loon, purple sandpiper, and water pipit.

In addition to the expansive variety of birds, these islands also support an astonishing number of reptiles and amphibians. More than 30 species of salamanders, tree frogs, turtles, tortoises, lizards, skinks, and snakes abound in the islands' varied habitats. Many of these secretive creatures are difficult to find by the average observer, particularly in the daylight hours. Others, such as the 6-lined racerunner or anole, are much more commonly encountered.

FT. GEORGE ISLAND STATE CULTURAL SITE

Facilities and Activities

Bicycling, hiking, scenic and historic driving trail, birding, historic site.

Ft. George has been the site of human habitation for over 7,000 years. The Timucuan Indians were probably the first to live here, finding sustenance in the plethora of shellfish that thrived in the shallow coastal waters. The huge shell mounds that are found on the island today are evidence of this prehistoric preoccupation with Florida's bounteous seafood supply.

In more recent centuries the island has undergone various changes in ownership and development. During the 1600s and

1700s Europeans colonized the island in an attempt to convert the Indians to Christianity. The mission of San Juan del Puerto, which is listed on the National Register of Historic Places, was established in 1587 and served the region for over 100 years.

In 1814, Zephaniah Kingsley brought his family to Ft. George and established a plantation home on the island's northern edge, overlooking Ft. George River. The plantation house and its related buildings are still intact and now constitute the Kingsley Plantation area of the Timucuan Ecological and Historic Preserve. The state turned the site over to the federal government in the early 1990s, which now manages it under the auspices of the National Park Service. In addition to its historical significance, the plantation area is a good place to look for migrating songbirds as well as to scan the river for least terns.

Following the demise of the plantation the island became the playground of the affluent. The Ribault Club, a golf and yacht club, opened in 1928. Golf became a mainstay of the island's identity for the next six decades but ended in 1991 when the golf course was permanently closed.

Today, about 700 acres of the island are under state control as the Ft. George State Cultural Site. In addition to preserving the island's historic value, the Florida Department of Environmental Protection is allowing the island's once-developed areas to regain their natural character, an attribute that is beginning to draw as many naturalists as historians. The old fairways that have now partially grown up are a major enticement to bird and wildlife watchers who use them to gain access to the island's central hammock. Gopher tortoise burrows are common among the fairways and the tortoises themselves are not particularly difficult to find, if you are blessed with a little luck.

There is also a 4.4-mile interpretive driving trail that loops around the island and includes 28 stops. The trail begins at the ruins of the Ribault Clubhouse, which is located on the east side of the island and can be reached by continuing northward (or straight ahead) at the island's only intersection. A well-done map and interpretive booklet describing each stop is available for pick-up at the clubhouse. Be sure to take the time to walk the paths that lead down to the saltmarsh, shoreline, or into the island's interior.

Visiting the island during spring or summer migration will certainly yield many interesting bird sightings. Walk the old fairways or along the loop road and scan the trees for songbirds, or walk down to the marsh behind the Ribault Club to look for waders, shorebirds, and sparrows. There is also a large expanse of marsh in the latter location that includes sea oxeye, saltwort, glasswort, sea purslane, marsh elder, and saltgrass. Fiddler crabs are also abundant here.

Painted buntings nest on the island and can be seen in full color during summer, especially on the east side of the island near Haulover Creek and the Rollins Bird and Plant Sanctuary. These brightly colored avians are often seen darting across the road or dropping down to the edges of the asphalt to forage.

LITTLE TALBOT ISLAND STATE PARK

The 2,500-acre Little Talbot Island offers the most developed recreational facilities of the Talbot Islands Parks and serves as the de facto headquarters for the entire group. It is the only one of the four that has a developed campground, paved beachside parking, elevated boardwalks, bathhouses, and complete restroom facilities. There is also an observation deck and picnic areas complete with grills. The observation deck on the south end of the park is a good place to look for northern gannets, gulls, terns, and shorebirds, as well as offshore ducks such as bufflehead, goldeneye, and scoters.

Little Talbot's campground is located on the west side of A1A, directly across from the park's main entrance gate. The facilities include 40 campsites situated in a shady coastal hammock, a dump station, two restrooms with showers, a small boat landing on Myrtle Creek, an observation platform, a 1.5 mile nature trail, and canoe rentals.

The nature trail exits the campground between sites 38 and 40 and offers a delightful walk through the island's hammock and saltmarsh habitats. It is a loop trail that doesn't require visitors to retrace their steps. However, walking the trail in both directions offers a different perspective on familiar territory and helps insure that explorers do not miss anything the trail has to offer. The marsh portion of the trail treats visitors to a variety of long-legged wading birds as well as to a large population of fiddler and hermit crabs. Raccoons and opossums are also common along the trail, and bobcat tracks are sometimes observed in the sandy soil.

The east side of the park offers an even longer, 4-mile hiking trail that begins between A1A and the entrance station. There is a sign marking the trailhead. The first 2 miles of the trail pass through a changing topography that includes hammock, scrub, and wet coastal swales. The path is wide and easy to follow. Trail-edge vegetation includes sparkleberry, chickasaw plum, tough bumelia, wild olive, red bay, yaupon, red cedar, myrtle oak, American holly, American beautyberry, ironweed, spurge nettle, sabal palm, and southern magnolia; wildlife includes rattlesnakes, gopher tortoise, painted bunting, and a variety of songbirds at different times of year.

The final 2 miles of trail follows southward along the beach to the boardwalk. This beach route offers an outstanding sampling of the more than 5.5 miles of Atlantic shore along the island's eastern rim. Shorebirds and gulls are common along this strip, and northern gannet are often seen diving into offshore waters. Loggerhead turtles are known to nest here during summer; the V-shaped trails that lead to their nests are most easily recognized early in the day when they are still fresh.

The female loggerhead approaches the beach at high tide, generally during cover of darkness, then digs a nest cavity with her rear flippers. She will likely deposit more than 100 eggs before returning to the safety of the sea. It takes about 60 days for the eggs to hatch and for the tiny hatchlings to begin their treacherous journey toward the water. Raccoons, in particular, are ferocious predators of hatchlings and unhatched eggs; on some beaches they have been known to destroy virtually every egg laid. Needless to say, suspected nest sites should not be disturbed.

BIG TALBOT ISLAND STATE PARK

Big Talbot is the least developed holding in the Talbot Islands Parks group. It is separated from Little Talbot Island by Long Island, a narrow, completely undeveloped strip of land bordered on the east by Myrtle Creek and the west by Simpson Creek. The only facilities on Big Talbot are two picnic areas, a boat landing, and several hiking trails. A1A bisects the island from south to north and offers scenic views of saltmarshes, dune scrub, and coastal flatwoods forests.

The lack of facilities here should certainly not be a deterrent to visitors, particularly to those who are looking for undisturbed natural habitat. There are hundreds of acres of open land here with relatively easy access from several points along the highway. The eastern side of the island is bounded by an impressive strip of Atlantic coastal beach; the western side supports expanses of typical east coast tidal marsh.

A primary access to the island's eastern edge is along the Blackrock Trail, a cleared footpath that leads through coastal woods to the Atlantic shore. A small parking area and state park sign marks the trailhead.

Plant lovers will particularly enjoy this relatively short walkway. There is an assortment of native shrubbery along the way which includes the attractively flowered tarflower, a member of the same botanical family that includes the rhododendrons, laurels, and blueberries. Tarflower blossoms are distinctive accoutrements that appear in profusion in early summer across much of northeast Florida's wet pinelands. The seven narrow petals are white, sometimes tinged with pink, and radiate from a central collection of long, showy stamens. The plant's leaves are whitish to bluish green and stand stiffly erect along the branches, making it a somewhat easy plant to identify even when not in bloom.

The Blackrock Trail terminates at the beach after passing through a particularly scenic grove of leaning live oak trees. The final few feet of the trail drop down the bluff to a shoreline littered with the whitened remains of old stumps, roots, and stems of dead trees that have succumbed to the naturally eroding shoreline, or to the ravages of past storms and hurricanes. Walking northward along the beach from the trail's end leads along a scenic Atlantic shoreline that overlooks the mouth of Nassau Sound and is backed by a continuous line of majestic wave-cut bluffs.

Big Talbot's other hiking trails traverse various portions of the island and pass through dune scrub, flatwoods, and along the edges of the saltmarsh. All are accessible from A1A and are easy to follow.

AMELIA ISLAND STATE RECREATION AREA

Amelia Island State Recreation Area is the smaller and northern-most of the four parks in the Talbot group. Its 229 acres are situated on the southern tip of Amelia Island, across Nassau Sound from Big Talbot. It was acquired by the state in July 1983 and is of particular interest to beachcombers, marsh lovers, fishing enthusiasts, and birders. The beach is easy to access just north of the bridge and the southernmost point of land can be outstanding for shorebirds. In addition to the tip of the island, the recreation area also encompasses several acres of saltmarsh along Amelia's western edge.

The only concession on the island is Sea Horse Stables, a private concern that leads guided horseback rides along the Atlantic beaches. Sea Horse is touted as one of the only places in the eastern U.S. that offers horseback riding on the beach.

Best Time of Year

There is something to do in these parks year-round. Birding is especially good during spring and fall migrations but a variety of wintering and nesting species make other times of the year productive as well. Camping is coolest during winter, but the campground is also well used in summer. For those who like beach-combing in relative solitude, cold winter days are probably best.

Pets

Allowed on a 6-foot leash; not allowed in the campground, in concessions, or on the bathing beaches.

TOMOKA STATE PARK

The influence of Florida's early Indians runs much deeper than just a name at this park. Indeed, in some ways, Tomoka State Park is the center of Indian history for northeast Florida and contains some of the most important archaeological sites in Volusia County.

Evidence suggests that the Tomoka Peninsula, the current site of the park, was home to aboriginal Floridians as long as 14,000 years ago. Known today as the Timucua Indians, an appellation given them by early European explorers, this relatively small band of primitive people was one of at least six loosely organized tribes scattered across the Florida landscape. Though their original territory was expansive and is generally considered to have extended from the Aucilla River eastward across southern Georgia and southward to about Cape Canaveral, their last stronghold was likely in the vicinity of Tomoka. Spanish explorer Alvaro Mexia documented the Timucuan village of Nocoroco in his 1605 survey of the Tomoka Peninsula, and current archaeological evidence points to the area as a centerpiece of Timucuan culture.

Though history seems to be one of the most important contributions of this park, the rapidly disappearing ecosystem it preserves is equally portentous. Most of the park is covered with rich, coastal hammock woodlands, much like those that William Bartram must have found when he traveled through Florida in the 1700s. The natural area set aside at Tomoka is one of the few remaining examples of this special habitat and is as important to an appreciation of our natural history as the understanding of our earliest peoples is to that of our cultural history.

Location, Mailing Address and Phone

Three miles north of Ormond Beach; turn east onto SR 40 off US 1, then left onto North Beach St. just before the bridge. Continue north for about 3.2 miles to the park.

Tomoka State Park, 2099 N. Beach St., Ormond Beach, FL 32174; (904) 676-4050.

Facilities and Activities

Visitor center and museum, camping, picnicking, birding, boating and canoeing, nature trails, fishing, botanizing.

Visitor Center and Museum

The Fred Dana Marsh Museum is a small but well-done collection of exhibits that depicts both the natural and cultural history of the Tomoka area. Fred Dana Marsh, for whom the museum is named, was a turn-of-the-century sculptor and painter who settled in Ormond Beach in the late 1920s. The central part of the museum houses a collection of his work. A huge piece of statuary which is located near the picnic area at what is believed to be the site of the village of Nocoroco was completed by Marsh when he was in his late 70s and stands as his last achievement.

In addition to Marsh's art, the museum includes dioramas that trace and explain the geologic history of the area as well as depict its native wildlife. One exhibit includes lifelike examples of the bobcat, wild turkey, wood stork, pygmy rattlesnake, cottonmouth, black-crowned night heron, and several of the more common rodents. Other exhibits trace the cultural history of the area from the time of the Timucuans through the occupations by Spain, England, and the United States.

Camping

The campground is located in an attractive, shaded hammock of oaks, hickories, palms, and magnolias. Nearly 100 large camping spots line the one-way road that encircles the area, and one of three large restroom facilities complete with showers is convenient to each site. Mosquitoes can be fierce here during the summer, or during wet years. Otherwise, the campground has few detractions.

Boating and Canoeing

Tomoka State Park is located at the confluence of the Halifax and Tomoka Rivers; the spit of land adjacent to the picnic area marks the point at which the two streams meet. The park operates a canoe rental concession at the boat landing on the Tomoka River side. Paddling up the Tomoka (which is actually southward in direction) leads under the Old Dixie Highway, then past the park's pristine hammock on one side, and large expanses of salt-marsh on the other. Manatees are known to frequent this river, and the stretch that extends from the Tomoka Basin to I-95 is one of the state's designated manatee protection zones.

The Halifax River is much larger than the Tomoka and more difficult to negotiate in a canoe. It is part of the Intracoastal Waterway and sometimes carries significant powerboat traffic. Nevertheless, for seasoned and energetic canoeists, or sea kayakers, it offers another interesting paddling option.

Note: swimming is not permitted in these rivers and the taking of shellfish is prohibited due to contamination of surrounding waters.

Nature Trails and Hiking

The park has only one designated nature trail that begins adjacent to the museum and terminates at the picnic area. The trail corridor passes through typical northeast Florida coastal woodlands that include live oak, loblolly pine, sabal palm, pignut hickory, red bay, coral bean, pawpaw, American beauty berry, southern magnolia, American holly, sparkleberry, deerberry, yaupon, laurel oak, wild coffee, red cedar, black cherry, and saw palmetto. Walking the short trail in one direction, then returning along the park's main road (which is hard-packed sand) makes an interesting jaunt and offers an overview of the park's natural features.

In addition to the designated trail, Tomoka offers an extensive hammock that invites exploration. There are several places to pull off the main park road, or even the Old Dixie Highway, and just wander into the woods. The hammock here is mature and supports a fairly open understory which makes it easy to move about and almost impossible to get lost. Spring and fall can bring waves of migrating land birds that flit through the treetops, and the progression of native blooms throughout spring, summer, and fall make the park a place to be visited periodically throughout the year.

Best Time of Year

Camping is best in late fall, winter, and early spring. Birding is best during migration. Canoeing and botanizing are good year-round.

Pets

Allowed on a 6-foot leash; not allowed in the campground or concession area, or inside the museum.

WASHINGTON OAKS STATE GARDENS

Washington Oaks State Gardens offers a unique blend of natural habitats and horticultural specialties. Stretching from the coquina rock-strewn beaches of the Atlantic Ocean to the shores of the Matanzas River, the park was once part of the Bella Vista Plantation owned by Gen. Joseph Hernandez, a northeast Florida militia commander who served during the Second Seminole War. George Lawrence Washington, Hernandez's son-in-law, established extensive orange groves which were expanded significantly by General Electric Chairman of the Board Owen Young after he and his wife acquired the property in 1936. While Mr. Young gave his interest and attention to the citrus groves, Louise Young established the garden plantings. Flowering plants from around the world were imported to the area and became part of an attractive landscape design that currently includes winding foot trails, reflecting pools, and a large number of showy azaleas, camellias, and roses. Following Mr. Young's death, the land was donated to the state by Mrs. Young in honor of her husband.

Though many visitors are first attracted here by the manicured gardens, the landscaped portion of the park is in some ways overshadowed by the equally outstanding examples of two of northeast Florida's most important habitats.

On the east side of A1A approximately 85 acres of undisturbed coastal scrub separate the beach from the highway. The short road that leads through this part of the park terminates at a parking lot that provides access to the beach via a boardwalk. On either side of the road lies an interesting expanse of low-growing, shrubby plants that supports one of northern Florida's few remaining scrub jay populations. In contrast, the west side of the road is dominated by a lush coastal hammock that supports a forest of live oak, red cedar, hickory, red mulberry, red bay, American holly, magnolia, cabbage palm, and yaupon.

Location, Mailing Address and Phone

On SR A1A, just south of Marineland.

Washington Oaks State Gardens, 6400 N. Oceanshore Blvd., Palm Coast, FL 32137; (904) 445-3161.

Facilities and Activities

Visitor center, garden, hiking, birding, botanizing, swimming.

Visitor Center

The former home of the property's last owners has been converted into a visitor and interpretive center. Located adjacent to the gardens and overlooking the Matanzas River, the small center contains mostly oversized photos of the park as well as northeast Florida habitats and wildlife.

The lawn behind the visitor center slopes gently to the river where fishermen can angle off the sea wall. Redfish, spotted sea trout, whiting, flounder, and mangrove snapper are a few of the species caught seasonally. A small picnic area with cooking grills is also located at the sea wall.

Garden

The garden is located adjacent to the visitor center and is a delightful place to wander among both native and exotic plants. In addition to the azaleas and camellias, there are large patches of ferns as well as hackberry, lantana, coral bean, wax myrtle, eastern red bud, and a number of large and impressive live oaks. A small courtyard is filled with roses that are beautiful when in bloom, and a flowing artesian well fills an attractive reflecting pool along one portion of the walkway. A wide array of colorful flowering annuals line the meandering paths.

Hiking

In addition to the casual walkways that wind through the gardens, there are two other trails, each of which passes through more natural terrain.

The Mala Campra Trail starts opposite the gardens trail and leads through a thin coastal woodland before turning toward the edge of the river. A wooden footbridge crosses a small creek along the back side of the trail and leads to a small island that fronts on the river. A large colony of sand fiddler crabs that live near the end of the bridge scurry toward their tiny burrows as you step onto the sand, and a healthy patch of sea oxeye lines the trail as it approaches the water. The tiny canal below the bridge provides good habitat for long-legged wading birds, and a picnic table under the oaks provides a good place to stop for a snack. Other parts of the Mala Campra Trail contain populations of the common seaside elder as well a shrubby collection of black mangrove, one of the northernmost populations of this latter species. The Mala Campra Trail links the gardens to the spacious picnic area, which is shaded by a scenic hardwood hammock.

The other trail, which is nearly 2 miles long, is much longer than the Mala Campra and offers access to the relatively unused northern part of the park. This latter trail begins just before reaching the gardens and was developed in cooperation with the

Florida Trail Association. An unpaved portion of the park road also extends northward into the same region and even intersects the designated hiking trail in at least two places. This unpaved road is not open to driving and makes pleasant walking. It is possible to spend the better part of a day exploring the coastal hammock that lines the trail and either side of the old road.

Best Time of Year

Spring is best for the gardens due to the profusion of blossoms. Fall, winter, and spring are best for hiking; spring, summer, and fall for studying the native flora.

Pets

Allowed on a leash; not allowed on the beach or in the gardens.

VII
ADDITIONAL SITES
AND INFORMATION

ANNOTATED LIST OF
ADDITIONAL NATURAL AREAS

There are a number of other natural places within northern Florida that are excellent for exploration. While a few of these sites have well-developed facilities or offer interpretive trails or exhibits, many do not. However, for those who wish to get away from developed parks and embark on personally defined explorations, these latter sites often provide outstanding opportunities. In an attempt to make this guide as complete as possible, the better of these sites are described below. Please note that state forests, wildlife management areas, and state reserves allow hunting as well as nonconsumptive use; care should be taken when visiting such areas during hunting season.

For information and maps of those listed as wildlife management areas (WMA), contact the Florida Game and Fresh Water Fish Commission, 620 S. Meridian St., Tallahassee, FL 32399-1600; (904) 488-3831.

For information about state forests, contact the Florida Department of Agriculture and Consumer Services, Division of Forestry, Forest Management Bureau, 3125 Conner Blvd., Tallahassee, FL 32399-1650.

Camp Blanding Wildlife Management Area

Size: 62,340 acres
Location: Clay County
Ownership: Public
Camp Blanding is a training site for the National Guard and requires a permit. It is an expansive area with a variety of natural

areas including turkey oak woods, pine flatwoods, hardwood hammocks, sinkholes, cypress swamps, and steep-sided ravines. The area is near Goldhead Branch State Park (see p. 123).

Caravelle Wildlife Management Area

Size: 11,607 acres
Location: Marion and Putnam Counties
Ownership: Public
Carravelle includes marshes, flatwoods, live oak hammocks, and river-bottom woodlands. It is bordered on the east by the St. Johns River, and the south and west by the Oklawaha River. SR 19 divides the area east and west and provides the major access. The two main drive-in entrances are located on either side of SR 19 about 2 miles south of Rodman Road. Both lead to a system of improved roadways. A designated walk-in entrance is located on the east side of 19 about 1 mile south of the drive-in entrances.

Cedar Key Scrub Wildlife Management Area and State Reserve

Size: 4,720 acres
Location: Levy County
Ownership: Public
Cedar Key Scrub is located adjacent to the Lower Suwannee River National Wildlife Refuge, just north of the intersection of CR 347 and SR 24. Access is by foot only. A system of old road-ways provides a network of walking paths. The eastern half of the reserve offers an outstanding example of easily accessible dune scrub; the western half is wetland and borders coastal marsh.

Fort Matanzas National Monument

Size: 298 acres
Location: St. Johns County
Ownership: Public
Fort Matanzas can be great for birding. The Florida scrub jay is easily seen here, and both wood stork and roseate spoonbill are

occasional visitors. The wooded hammock is a good songbird hotspot during spring and fall migration, and the beaches and sandbars of Matanzas Inlet, just south of the park entrance, can be outstanding for gulls, terns, skimmers, and shorebirds. The entrance to the park is on A1A, about 14 miles south of St. Augustine. The fort is located across the Matanzas inlet and is reached by ferry.

Goethe State Forest and Wildlife Management Area

Size: 43,614 acres
Location: Levy County
Ownership: Public
The Goethe State Forest consists of a wide variety of habitats that include upland pine woods, hardwood hammocks, and cypress-studded wetlands. A well-developed system of woods roads provide access to the area but are open for driving only sporadically outside of hunting season. Wildlife found here includes, but is certainly not limited to, the red-cockaded woodpecker, Bachman's sparrow, wood stork, bald eagle, gopher tortoise, eastern indigo snake, eastern coral snake, bobcat, and white-tailed deer. Prior to the 1940s, the time at which the area was purchased by the Goethe family, the acreage within this forest was typical cut over pinelands. Timber harvesting was nearly eliminated after the Goethes acquired the property, and the area has been relatively free from any disturbance for the past 50 years.

Gulf Hammock Wildlife Management Area

Size: 24,685 acres
Location: Levy County
Ownership: Private and Public
Gulf Hammock Wildlife Management Area is owned by Georgia-Pacific Corp. and is located in southern Levy County. It is open to the public and is accessible from several points off CR 40A and US 19, just north of the tiny town of Inglis. Butler Road, which turns northward off 40A about 1.1 mile west of US 19 bisects the

management area and provides an interesting several-mile drive through what remains of this once magnificent and nearly inaccessible hammock. Large boulders line the roadway along much of the route, indicating how thin the soil mantle is above the subsurface limestone. Numerous side roads lead east and west from the main route; most of these are open to vehicular travel but are also suitable for walking or biking. Clearcut areas are intermingled with mature, second-growth hammock woodlands which provide thousands of acres of wilderness exploration opportunities. A large variety of trees, shrubs, vines, and herbaceous plants exist here and wildlife, including white-tailed deer, bobcat, opossum, raccoon, and wild turkey, is abundant. Though the area is open for hunting during parts of the fall and winter months, white-tailed deer are commonly seen along the roadways during the summer. Though there is no developed bird list, a drive through this management area in spring and fall can yield a surprising number of migrating songbirds as well as a variety of hawks.

The cabbage palm–hardwood hammocks that are found in this WMA constitute some of its more scenic forest cover types. At least a few of these vegetative assemblages are visible from Butler Road; others require slogging through wilderness woodlands. The captivating charm of these more secluded forests is well worth the energy expended to find them.

It is important to procure the map of this area when exploring it. The roads are generally driveable but not well marked and some of the highway entrances are not open during certain parts of the year. The Butler Road entrance is about the only access point that can be counted upon year-round.

Jennings State Forest and Wildlife Management Area

Size: 19,990
Location: Clay County
Ownership: Public
Jennings State Forest is located east of Clay CR 217, just south of the Duval/Clay County line. The area is criss-crossed by a

number of creeks, all of which are in good condition. An extensive system of unimproved roads provide walking access to the area and many miles of scenic hiking opportunities. A number of wildlife species are found within the forest, including the Florida gopher frog, gopher tortoise, Florida green water snake, eastern coral snake, Sherman fox squirrel, bobcat, and white-tailed deer.

Lochloosa Wildlife Management Area

Size: 31,751 acres
Location: Alachua County
Ownership: Private
This area is similar in many ways to close-by Paynes Prairie State Preserve. There are good examples of hardwood hammock, lake edge, and wet prairie habitats here. Access is via Alachua CR 325, 346, and 234. US 301 borders the WMA's eastern edge. The last few miles of the Gainesville to Hawthorne State Trail passes along the area's northern edge and provides good walking, bicycling, and horseback access to at least some of the area. An expansive system of improved and unimproved roads provide access to other locations within the WMA.

Nassau Wildlife Management Area

Size: 40,160 acres
Location: Nassau County
Ownership: Private
Nassau WMA is a large, mostly pinewoods area located just south of the Florida state line. It is bordered on the east by I-95, and is divided north and south by A1A. South of A1A the WMA encompasses several creeks that eventually empty into the Nassau River. Edwards Road, which turns south off A1A about 2 miles west of I-95, leads to a campsite and boat landing that provides access to these waterways.

Rice Creek Sanctuary and Georgia-Pacific Wildlife Management Area

Size: 11,149
Location: Putnam County
Ownership: Private

Rice Creek Sanctuary is a private preserve managed and maintained by Georgia-Pacific Corporation. Several miles of loop trails pass through the sanctuary as well as the adjacent portions of the WMA. Part of the trail follows along Rick Creek for a good distance. The trail is open for hiking year-round, but hikers must stay on the path. Hunting is allowed in those parts of the WMA outside of Rice Creek Sanctuary. The best access to the trail is from Florida 100, about 1 mile west of its intersection with CR 309, a few miles west of Palatka.

Santa Fe Swamp Wildlife and Environmental Area

Size: 5,492 acres
Location: Alachua County
Ownership: Public

This WMA preserves the expansive wetland that feeds Santa Fe Lake and eventually the Santa Fe River. The swamp is of major importance to the continued health of this outstanding Florida waterway. There is little developed access here, other than a few unimproved roads off SE 35th Street, which turns off SR 100 near the WMA's eastern boundary. A parking area is provided near the road and walking is allowed along the old roadways.

Silver River State Park

Size: 4,432 acres
Location: Marion County
Ownership: Public

This will be the site of an outstanding state park in a few years. There are about 5 miles of frontage on the Silver River which begins at famed Silver Springs. Facilities and trails are in the planning stages.

Theodore Roosevelt Area—Timucuan National Ecological and Historic Preserve

Size: 640 acres
Location: Duval
Ownership: Public

This site includes outstanding examples of fresh- and saltwater marsh, hardwood hammock, and dune scrub. Several miles of hiking trail, and an observation tower provide a variety of observation opportunities. Common wildlife include painted bunting, wild turkey, cottontail rabbit, six-lined racerunner, brown pelican, wood stork, osprey, and a variety of long-legged wading birds. Great blue heron, great egret, and black-crowned night heron rookeries are also located within the preserve. The preserve's uplands support a maritime hammock that is composed of oaks, hickories, southern magnolia, red bay, and wild olive, while lower elevations are dominated by buttonbush, wax myrtle, and fetterbush. The preserve is located 12 miles east of Jacksonville. Take Atlantic Boulevard, then turn north onto Girvin Road, then onto Mt. Pleasant Road.

Tiger Bay State Forest and Wildlife Management Area

Size: 6,981 acres
Location: Volusia County
Ownership: Public

Tiger Bay State Forest is composed chiefly of swamps and pinelands. Flatwoods make up about 1,800 acres of the forest while over 4,300 acres are contained within hardwood/cypress swamps. Tiger Bay Swamp makes up about 60 percent of the forest. The Florida Division of Forestry is working to reforest and restore this area. Access is from US 92 between Daytona Beach and DeLand.

Twin Rivers Wildlife Management Area

Size: 9,340 acres
Location: Hamilton, Madison, and Suwannee Counties

Ownership: Public

This WMA takes its name from the confluence of the Withlacoochee and Suwannee Rivers. The five management units
border various portions of each of these fascinating waterways
and preserve important remnants of north Florida's hardwood
hammock and river swamp communities. The area is owned by
the Suwannee River Water Management District and managed
in conjunction with the Florida Game and Freshwater Fish Commission. Much of the area is open to hunting as well as to nature
study. There are few facilities, but lots of beautiful scenery. All
five units provide either walking or driving access to one of the
rivers. Both the Ellaville and Mill Creek North Units have designated picnic areas on the Withlacoochee and Suwannee Rivers,
respectively. The Ellaville picnic area can be reached from the
extension of CR 141 by turning south onto the first graded road
west of the Withlacoochee River bridge, then continuing south
for about 0.8 mile before turning east toward the river. The Mill
Creek picnic area is located at the terminus of the unit's main
entrance road. Both of these sites provide good places to leave a
vehicle while exploring the adjacent woodlands.

Waccasassa Bay State Preserve

Size: 30,784 acres
Location: Levy County
Ownership: Public

Waccasassa Bay State Preserve is a large area of saltmarsh dotted
with pine islands that lies along the Gulf coast just south of the
Cedar Keys. It is most easily accessible by boat from Cedar Key,
or from the boat ramp on the Waccasassa River at the end of
Levy County 326, off U.S. 19 (be aware that this river also carries
powerboat traffic which can be challenging to canoeists). The
area includes a number of shallow tidal creeks which offer good
sea kayaking opportunities for strong, experienced paddlers
with significant commitment. Paddlers should pay close attention to local tides; outgoing tides can leave boaters high and dry,
especially on days with a strong north wind.

DESIGNATED NORTH FLORIDA CANOE TRAILS

Florida has 36 officially designated canoe trails; seven are within the area covered by this book. The Florida Recreational Canoe Trails System is managed by the Florida Department of Environmental Protection in conjunction with several other agencies. A brochure is available for each trail, as well as a map that shows the location of each stream. These items are available by writing: Division of Recreation and Parks, Florida Department of Environmental Protection, 3900 Commonwealth Blvd., Tallahassee, FL 32399-3000; (904) 488-2850.

St. Marys River

Mileage: 51
Location: Baker and Nassau Counties
Difficulty: Easy
Access Points: State Rd. 121; Stokes Bridge; State Rd. 2; Thompkin's Landing, State Rd. 121; Trader Hill, GA; US 301.
The official canoe trail portion of this river is relatively wide and slow moving. There are numerous sandbars along the route that make good camping as well as scenic woodlands along the bank. Some portions have little access and seem quite remote. Part of the river receives its waters from the Okefenokee Swamp in southern Georgia. For information on paddling the narrow, upper portion of this river, see the section on the Osceola National Forest, p. 78.

Suwannee River (Upper)

Mileage: 64
Location: Columbia, Hamilton, Suwannee Counties
Difficulty: Easy to strenuous
Access Points: State Rd. 6; Cone Bridge Rd.; US 41; State Rd. 136; US 129; State Rd. 249; Suwannee River State Park.

The upper Suwannee River canoe trail begins in Georgia and ends at the Suwannee River State Park on the west side of the river. This is a beautiful run with numerous springs, outstanding woodlands, scenic limestone banks, and even a set of rapids locally known as Big Shoals. There are white sand beaches at many of the river's major bends which make good camping spots. For a short trip it is also possible to put into the Suwannee near its confluence with the Alapaha River for an 8-mile run downriver to the park. There are intermittent houses along the banks on this stretch, which somewhat mitigates the wilderness scenery, but the trip is still an enjoyable paddle.

Suwannee River (Lower)

Mileage: 62
Location: Hamilton, Lafayette, and Madison Counties
Difficulty: Easy
Access Points: Suwannee River State Park; US 90; State Rd. 250; State Rd. 51; US 27.
The lower Suwannee River Canoe Trail begins at the Suwannee River State Park on the west side of the river and ends near the Gulf of Mexico. The trip is along a large, fully mature river. Springs and creeks are common, especially in the section within a few miles of the park. Even though the distance from the park to the Gulf exceeds 100 miles, there are numerous state, federal, and county roads that provide termination points along the way. Planning shorter trips that begin at the park poses little difficulty.

Santa Fe River

Mileage: 26
Location: Alachua, Columbia, Gilchrist, and Suwannee Counties
Difficulty: Easy
Access Points: US 41/441; US 27; State Rd. 47; US 129
The Santa Fe is a tannin-stained waterway that traverses the central part of north Florida before emptying into the Suwannee River. The official trail lies along that portion of the river below O'Leno State Park, but the section above the park from about

Worthington Springs is canoeable, but often strenuous, when there is enough water. More information about this river, both above and below the state park, is found in the description of O'Leno State Park, p. 141.

Pellicer Creek

Mileage: 4
Location: Flagler and St. Johns
Difficulty: Easy
Access Points: U.S. 1; Faver-Dykes State Park.
This is a round-trip paddle on a slow-moving, essentially tidal marsh creek. It is possible to begin at either Faver-Dykes State Park (see p. 107) or at the bridge on US 1. There is an abundance of wading birds and waterfowl in season.

Bulow Creek

Mileage: 13
Location: Flagler and Volusia Counties
Difficulty: Easy to moderate
Access Points: Bulow Ruins State Historic Site; Walter Boardman Lane; High Bridge Park on High Bridge Rd.
This is another coastal marsh river that is excellent for birding and allows close observation of Florida's large wading birds. Osprey are regularly seen along some of the trail and alligators are also common. Most of Bulow Creek is open-water paddling, so be sure and bring sunscreen.

Tomoka River

Mileage: 13
Location: Volusia County
Difficulty: easy to moderate
Access Points: SR 40; US 1; Tomoka State Park Bridge; Tomoka State Park Boat Landing.
See the description of Tomoka State Park (p. 169) for information about canoeing this stream.

WILDLIFE CHECKLISTS

The following checklists were compiled from *Checklist of Florida's Birds, A Checklist of Florida's Mammals*, and *A Checklist of Florida's Amphibians and Reptiles* distributed by the Nongame Wildlife Program of the Florida Game and Fresh Water Fish Commission. They are intended to include the known native and some of the more common naturalized species found in north Florida.

Population status is given in relative terms as follows:

abundant–likely to be seen in the right habitat
common–often seen in the right habitat
occasional–sometimes seen
uncommon–infrequently seen
rare–not likely to be seen
resident (bird checklist only)–present year-round
migrant (bird checklist only)–passes through on way to wintering/ summering grounds
visitor (bird checklist only)–north Florida is the final migration destination
E–endangered species

BIRD CHECKLIST

Loons
☐ **Red-throated loon** (*Gavia stellata*)–uncommon winter visitor; offshore
☐ **Arctic loon** (*Gavia arctica*)–occasional in winter in coastal waters
☐ **Common loon** (*Gavia immer*)–fall to spring; common offshore and in saltwater bays along the coast, occasionally on inland lakes

Grebes
☐ **Pied-billed grebe** (*Podilymbus podiceps*)–resident; freshwater ponds and saltwater bays along both coasts

☐ **Horned grebe** (*Podiceps auritus*)–winter visitor; typically in salt-water

☐ **Red-necked grebe** (*Podiceps grisegena*)–winter; occasional offshore and in coastal waters

☐ **Eared grebe** (*Podiceps migricollis*)–rare winter visitor in Gulf coastal waters

☐ **Western grebe** (*Aechmophorus occidentalis*)–occasional along the Gulf coast in winter

Petrels and Shearwaters

☐ **Black-capped petrel** (*Pterodroma hasitata*)–spring to fall; occasional offshore

☐ **Cory's shearwater** (*Calonectris diomedea*)–occasional in spring through winter in offshore Atlantic waters

☐ **Greater shearwater** (*Puffinus gravis*)–occasional spring through winter in offshore Atlantic waters

☐ **Sooty shearwater** (*Puffinus griseus*)–occasional year-round in offshore Atlantic waters

☐ **Manx shearwater** (*Puffinus puffinus*)–occasional fall to spring in offshore Atlantic waters

☐ **Audubon's shearwater** (*Puffinus iherminieri*)–occasional in spring through winter in offshore Atlantic waters

Storm-Petrels

☐ **Wilson's storm-petrel** (*Oceanites oceanicus*)–occasional in spring through winter in offshore Gulf and Atlantic waters

☐ **Leach's storm-petrel** (*Oceanodroma leucorhoa*)–occasional spring through winter in offshore Atlantic waters

☐ **Band-rumped storm-petrel** (*Oceanodroma castro*)–rare off Gulf and Atlantic coasts in August and December

Tropicbirds

☐ **White-tailed tropicbird** (*Phaethon lepturus*)–occasional in spring and summer off both the Gulf and Atlantic coasts

☐ **Red-billed tropicbird** (*Phaethon aethereus*)–occasional in fall along the Atlantic coast

Boobies and Gannets

☐ **Masked booby** (*Sula dactylatra*)–fairly common in summer in off-shore Gulf waters

☐ **Brown booby** (*Sula leucogaster*)–occasional year-round in offshore Gulf waters

☐ **Northern gannet** (*Sula bassanus*)–commonly seen along the Gulf and Atlantic coasts from early fall to summer

Pelicans

☐ **American white pelican** (*Pelecanus erythrorhynchos*)–variably common year-round in near-coastal and inland waters

☐ **Brown pelican** (*Pelecanus occidentalis*)–common residents along both coasts

Cormorants

☐ **Great cormorant** (*Phalacrocorax carbo*)–uncommon in winter along the Atlantic coast

☐ **Double-crested cormorant** (*Phalacrocorax auritus*)–common to abundant resident, chiefly along the coasts

Darters

☐ **Anhinga** (*Anhinga anhinga*)–common resident in freshwater habitats

Frigatebirds

☐ **Magnificent frigatebird** (*Fregata magnificens*)–uncommon in offshore waters; spring through early winter

Bitterns and Herons

☐ **American bittern** (*Botaurus lentiginosus*)–fairly common in dense marshlands but seldom seen due to secretive habitats; fall to spring

☐ **Least bittern** (*Ixobrychus exilis*)–fairly common in marshlands; spring to fall

☐ **Great blue heron** (*Ardea herodias*)–common resident in many fresh- and saltwater habitats

- ☐ **Great egret** (*Casmerodius albus*)–common resident in many fresh- and saltwater habitats
- ☐ **Snowy egret** (*Egretta thula*)–common resident in many fresh- and saltwater habitats
- ☐ **Little blue heron** (*Egretta caerulea*)–common resident in many fresh- and saltwater habitats
- ☐ **Tricolored heron** (*Egretta tricolor*)–common resident in many fresh- and saltwater habitats
- ☐ **Reddish egret** (*Egretta rufescens*)–variously common resident in shallow saltwater
- ☐ **Cattle egret** (*Bubulcus ibis*)–common to abundant resident in a variety of habitats
- ☐ **Green-backed heron** (*Butorides striatus*)–fairly common in fresh- and saltwater; spring to fall
- ☐ **Black-crowned night-heron** (*Nycticorax nycticorax*)–fairly common resident in fresh- and saltwater habitats
- ☐ **Yellow-crowned night-heron** (*Nycticorax violaceus*)–occasional in fresh- and saltwater; spring to fall

Ibises and Spoonbills

- ☐ **White ibis** (*Eudocimus albus*)–common resident in fresh- and saltwater habitats
- ☐ **Glossy ibis** (*Plegadis falcinellus*)–variously occasional to abundant resident in fresh- and saltwater marshes
- ☐ **Roseate spoonbill** (*Ajaia ajaja*)–rare to occasional from spring to fall along the Gulf coast

Storks

- ☐ **Wood stork** (*Mycteria americana*)–locally common in fresh- and saltwater wetlands; spring to early winter

Flamingos

- ☐ **Greater flamingo** (*Phoenicopterus ruber*)–rare along Atlantic and Gulf coasts; spring to fall

Swans, Geese, and Ducks

☐ **Fulvous whistling-duck** (*Dendrocygna bicolor*)–occasional winter visitor in freshwater marshes

☐ **Tundra swan** (*Cygnus columbianus*)–estuaries and lakes; winter to early spring

☐ **Greater white-fronted goose** (*Anser albifrons*)–casual winter visitor

☐ **Snow goose** (*Chen caerulescens*)–occasional winter visitor to coastal marshes

☐ **Brant** (*Branta bernicla*)–rare winter visitor in bays and estuaries

☐ **Canada goose** (*Branta canadensis*)–common winter visitor in fields and coastal marshes

☐ **Wood duck** (*Aix sponsa*)–fairly common resident in woodlands bordering ponds, sloughs, and rivers

☐ **Green-winged teal** (*Anas crecca*)–common winter visitor in brackish and freshwater ponds

☐ **American black duck** (*Anas rubripes*)–occasional winter visitor along both coasts

☐ **Mottled duck** (*Anas fulvigula*)–fairly common local resident in coastal marshes

☐ **Mallard** (*Anas platyrhynchos*)–fairly common winter visitor in coastal and inland marshes

☐ **White-cheeked pintail** (*Anas bahamensis*)–rare winter visitor in coastal marshes

☐ **Northern pintail** (*Anas acuta*)–common winter visitor in open fresh- and saltwater ponds

☐ **Blue-winged teal** (*Anas discors*)–common winter visitor on ponds and bays

☐ **Northern shoveler** (*Anas clypeata*)–fairly common winter visitor in marshes, ponds, and bays

☐ **Gadwall** (*Anas strepera*)–fairly common winter visitor on ponds and bays

☐ **Eurasian wigeon** (*Anas penelope*)–very occasional winter visitor along the coast

☐ **American wigeon** (*Anas americana*)–common in winter on ponds and bays

☐ **Canvasback** (*Aythya valisineria*)–fairly common winter visitor in lakes and marshes

☐ **Redhead** (*Aythya americana*)–abundant winter visitor along the coast, particularly offshore in shallow bays

☐ **Ring-necked duck** (*Aythya collaris*)–common winter resident in marshes, ponds, and lakes

☐ **Greater scaup** (*Aythya marila*)–common winter resident, chiefly offshore along the coast

☐ **Lesser scaup** (*Aythya affinis*)–common to abundant winter visitor in ponds, marshes, and bays

☐ **Harlequin duck** (*Histrionicus histrionicus*)–rare winter visitor along the coast

☐ **Oldsquaw** (*Clangula hyemalis*)–occasional winter visitor along the coast

☐ **Black scoter** (*Melanitta nigra*)–uncommon (to common in some years) along the coast

☐ **Surf scoter** (*Melanitta perspicillata*)–rare to occasional along the coast, winter to about midsummer

☐ **White-winged scoter** (*Melanitta fusca*)–occasional in winter along the coast

☐ **Common goldeneye** (*Bucephala islandica*)–fairly common in winter in bays and offshore

☐ **Bufflehead** (*Bucephala albeola*)–abundant winter visitor in bays and coastal lakes

☐ **Hooded merganser** (*Lophodytes cucullatus*)–fairly common to common winter visitor in ponds, marshes, and rivers

☐ **Common merganser** (*Mergus merganser*)–occasional in winter near the coast, especially in brackish waters

☐ **Red-breasted merganser** (*Mergus serrator*)–fairly common to common year-round in coastal waters

☐ **Ruddy duck** (*Oxyura jamaicensis*)–occasional to common year-round in lakes and shallow, saltwater bays

☐ **Masked duck** (*Oxyura dominica*)–rare along the Gulf coast in December

Vultures

☐ **Black vulture** (*Coragyps atratus*)–common resident through-out the state

☐ **Turkey vulture** (*Cathartes aura*)–common resident throughout the state

Kites, Eagles and Hawks

☐ **Osprey** (*Pandion haliaetus*)–fairly common to common resident, primarily coastal areas

☐ **American swallow-tailed kite** (*Elanoides forficatus*)–uncommon to common summer visitor in a variety of habitats

☐ **White-tailed kite** (*Elanus leucurus*)–rare winter visitor along the Gulf coast

☐ **Snail kite** (*Rostrhamus sociabilis*)–rare winter visitor **E**

☐ **Mississippi kite** (*Ictinis mississippiensis*)–fairly common summer visitor in a variety of habitats

☐ **Bald eagle** (*Haliaeetus leucocephalus*)–fairly common, nearly year-round

☐ **Northern harrier** (*Circus cyaneus*)–fairly common winter visitor in fields and wetland marshes

☐ **Sharp-shinned hawk** (*Accipiter striatus*)–fairly common to common from about August to May

☐ **Cooper's hawk** (*Accipiter cooperii*)–uncommon resident in woodland edges

☐ **Northern goshawk** (*Accipiter gentilis*)–rare in winter

☐ **Red-shouldered hawk** (*Buteo lineatus*)–fairly common to common resident in a variety of habitats including fields, marshes, and woodlands

☐ **Broad-winged hawk** (*Buteo platypterus*)–fairly common summer visitor in woodlands

☐ **Short-tailed hawk** (*Buteo brachyurus*)–rare summer visitor

☐ **Swainson's hawk** (*Buteo swainsoni*)–rare winter visitor

☐ **Red-tailed hawk** (*Buteo jamaicensis*)–fairly common resident in woodlands

☐ **Ferruginous hawk** (*Buteo regalis*)–very rare winter visitor

☐ **Golden eagle** (*Aquila chrysaetos*)–rare winter visitor

Caracaras and Falcons

☐ **American kestrel** (*Falco sparverius*)–common resident in fields, along roadsides, and in woodland edges

☐ **Merlin** (*Falco columbarius*)–uncommon but regular in winter, most often along the coast

☐ **Peregrine falcon** (*Falco peregrinus*)–uncommon but regular winter visitor, mostly along the coast E

Pheasants, Turkeys, and Quail

☐ **Wild turkey** (*Meleagris gallopavo*)–common resident in upland woods and turkey oak-pineland ridges

☐ **Northern bobwhite** (*Colinus virginianus*)–fairly common resident in open woods

Rails, Gallinules, and Coots

☐ **Yellow rail** (*Coturnicops noveboracensis*)–rare winter visitor in fresh and brackish marshes

☐ **Black rail** (*Laterallus jamaicensis*)–rare and secretive resident in brackish marshes and saltmarshes

☐ **Clapper rail** (*Rallus longirostris*)–common resident in salt- and tidal marshes

☐ **King rail** (*Rallus elegans*)–uncommon resident, chiefly in freshwater marshes

☐ **Virginia rail** (*Rallus limicola*)–uncommon winter visitor in salt- and brackish marshes

☐ **Sora** (*Porzana carolina*)–uncommon winter resident in freshwater and brackish marshes

☐ **Purple gallinule** (*Porphyrula martinica*)–fairly common spring to fall visitor, chiefly in freshwater marshes

☐ **Common moorhen** (*Gallinula chloropus*)–common resident in marshes

☐ **American coot** (*Fulica americana*)–common to abundant resident in fresh and saltwater marshes

Limpkins

☐ **Limpkin** (*Aramus guarauna*)–fairly common resident in clear water rivers

Cranes

☐ **Sandhill crane** (*Grus canadensis*)–uncommon to common resident in fields

Plovers and Lapwings

☐ **Black-bellied plover** (*Pluvialis squatarola*)–common resident along coastal shores

☐ **Lesser golden-plover** (*Pluvialis dominica*)–rare winter visitor in fields

☐ **Snowy plover** (*Charadrius alexandrinus*)–uncommon resident of sand beaches

☐ **Wilson's plover** (*Charadrius wilsonia*)–fairly common summer visitor to beaches and shores

☐ **Semipalmated plover** (*Charadrius semipalmatus*)–common to abundant resident of beaches and shores

☐ **Piping plover** (*Charadrius melodus*)–uncommon nearly year-round on beaches

☐ **Killdeer** (*Charadrius vociferus*)–common resident in fields, near coasts, on golf courses, large grassy areas

☐ **Mountain plover** (*Charadrius montanus*)–rare winter visitor

Oystercatchers

☐ **American oystercatcher** (*Haematopus palliatus*)–fairly com-mon resident along coasts

Stilts and Avocets

☐ **Black-necked stilt** (*Himantopus mexicanus*)–uncommon to locally common in summer, chiefly along the coast

☐ **American avocet** (*Recurvirostra americana*)–fairly common in fall, winter, and spring in shallow ponds and marshes near the coast

Sandpipers

☐ **Greater yellowlegs** (*Tringa melanoleuca*)–fairly common nearly throughout the year in coastal marshes and mud flats

☐ **Lesser yellowlegs** (*Tringa flavipes*)–fairly common nearly year-round in coastal marshes and mud flats

☐ **Solitary sandpiper** (*Tringa solitaria*)–uncommon summer visitor in brackish waters along the coast

☐ **Willet** (*Catoptrophorus semipalmatus*)–common resident along the coast

☐ **Spotted sandpiper** (*Actitis macularia*)–fairly common nearly year-round on shores of freshwater ponds, marshes, and streams

☐ **Upland sandpiper** (*Bartramia longicauda*)–rare summer visitor

☐ **Whimbrel** (*Numenius phaeopus*)–fairly common winter visitor, chiefly along the coast

☐ **Long-billed curlew** (*Numenius americanus*)–rare summer visitor, inland

☐ **Hudsonian godwit** (*Limosa haemastica*)–rare in spring and fall along the east coast

☐ **Marbled godwit** (*Limosa fedoa*)–uncommon but regular winter visitor along the coast

☐ **Ruddy turnstone** (*Arenaria interpres*)–common resident on coastal shores

☐ **Red knot** (*Calidris canutus*)–fairly common nearly year-round on beaches

☐ **Sanderling** (*Calidris alba*)–common resident along sandy beaches

☐ **Semipalmated sandpiper** (*Calidris pusilla*)–common migrant along the coast

☐ **Western sandpiper** (*Calidris mauri*)–common to abundant winter visitor along the coast

☐ **Least sandpiper** (*Calidris minutilla*)–common winter visitor to mud flats and coastal wetlands

☐ **White-rumped sandpiper** (*Calidris fusciollis*)–rare to un-common visitor along the coast during migration

☐ **Baird's sandpiper** (*Calidris bairdii*)–rare visitor during migration

☐ **Pectoral sandpiper** (*Calidris melanotos*)–fairly common visitor during migration, fields and marshes

☐ **Purple sandpiper** (*Calidris maritima*)–uncommon to rare winter visitor, chiefly along the east coast

☐ **Dunlin** (*Calidris alpina*)–abundant winter visitor along the coast

☐ **Curlew sandpiper** (*Calidris ferruginea*)–very rare in migration

☐ **Stilt sandpiper** (*Calidris himantopus*)–rare during migration, chiefly along the east coast

☐ **Buff-breasted sandpiper** (*Tryngites subruficollis*)–rare during spring and fall migration, chiefly along the east coast

☐ **Ruff** (*Philomachus pugnax*)–rare during spring migration

☐ **Short-billed dowitcher** (*Limnodromus griseus*)–common to abundant resident along coastal mud flats

☐ **Long-billed dowitcher** (*Limnodromus scolopaceus*)–uncommon winter visitor along coastal mud flats

☐ **Common snipe** (*Gallinago gallinago*)–fairly common to common in marshes

☐ **American woodcock** (*Scolopax minor*)–uncommon but regular winter visitor in thickets and moist woodlands

☐ **Wilson's phalarope** (*Phalaropus tricolor*)–rare spring and fall migrant

☐ **Red-necked phalarope** (*Phalaropus lobatus*)–rare spring and fall migrant

☐ **Red phalarope** (*Phalaropus fulicaria*)–rare spring and fall migrant

Jaegers, Gulls, Terns, and Skimmers

☐ **Parasitic jaeger** (*Stercorarius parasiticus*)–possible year-round in pelagic waters

☐ **Long-tailed jaeger** (*Stercorarius longicaudus*)–rare during winter in pelagic waters

☐ **Laughing gull** (*Latrus atricilla*)–common to abundant resident in coastal areas

☐ **Franklin's gull** (*Larus pipixcan*)–rare winter visitor along coast

☐ **Little gull** (*Larus minutus*)–rare winter visitor along the east coast

☐ **Bonaparte's gull** (*Larus philadelphia*)–common to abundant winter visitor along the coast

☐ **Ring-billed gull** (*Larus delawarensis*)–abundant resident along coasts and inland

☐ **Herring gull** (*Larus argentatus*)–common resident along the coast

☐ **Iceland gull** (*Larus glaucoides*)–rare winter visitor along the east coast

☐ **Lesser black-backed gull** (*Larus fuscus*)–rare midwinter visitor along the east coast

☐ **Glaucous gull** (*Larus hyperboreus*)–rare in midwinter along the east coast

☐ **Great black-backed gull** (*Larus marinus*)–uncommon winter visitor along the east coast

☐ **Black-legged kittiwake** (*Risa tridactyla*)–rare in midwinter, chiefly offshore

- [ ] **Gull-billed tern** (*Sterna nilotica*)–uncommon to common in summer along beaches and coastal marshes
- [ ] **Caspian tern** (*Sterna caspia*)–uncommon resident along the coast
- [ ] **Royal tern** (*Sterna maxima*)–common to abundant resident along the coast
- [ ] **Sandwich tern** (*Sterna sandvicensis*)–uncommon winter visitor along the coast
- [ ] **Roseate tern** (*Sterna dougallii*)–rare in spring and fall, offshore
- [ ] **Common tern** (*Sterna hirundo*)–rare to uncommon in winter
- [ ] **Forster's tern** (*Sterna forsteri*)–common in fall, winter, and spring, chiefly coastal
- [ ] **Least tern** (*Sterna antillarum*)–common to abundant summer visitor along the coast and inland
- [ ] **Bridled tern** (*Sterna anaethetus*)–rare in summer off the east coast
- [ ] **Sooty tern** (*Sterna fuscata*)–rare in summer off east coast
- [ ] **Black tern** (*Chlidonias niger*)–common to abundant in summer along the coast
- [ ] **Brown noddy** (*Anous stolidus*)–rare in summer and fall off the coast
- [ ] **Black skimmer** (*Rynchops niger*)–uncommon to abundant resident along the coast

Pigeons and Doves
- [ ] **Rock dove** (*Columba livia*)–abundant resident, cosmopolitan
- [ ] **White-winged dove** (*Zenaida asiatica*)–rare in winter
- [ ] **Zenaida dove** (*Zenaida aurita*)–rare in winter
- [ ] **Mourning dove** (*Zenaida macroura*)–common resident in fields
- [ ] **Inca dove** (*Columbina inca*)–very rare in spring or early summer
- [ ] **Common ground-dove** (*Columbina talpacoti*)–common resident of open woods, often along the coast

Cuckoos, Anis, and Allies
- [ ] **Black-billed cuckoo** (*Coccyzus erythropthalmus*)–rare in woodlands during migration
- [ ] **Yellow-billed cuckoo** (*Coccyzus americanus*)–fairly common but secretive summer visitor in woodlands
- [ ] **Smooth-billed ani** (*Crotophaga ani*)–rare in winter in open scrub

☐ **Groove-billed ani** (*Crotophaga sulcirostris*)–rare in winter in marsh edges

Barn-Owls

☐ **Common barn-owl** (*Tyto alba*)–occasional resident, chiefly in old buildings and barns

Typical Owls

☐ **Eastern screech-owl** (*Otus asio*)–fairly common resident in woodlands

☐ **Great horned owl** (*Bubo virginianus*)–fairly common resident in rich upland woods

☐ **Burrowing owl** (*Athene cunicularia*)–uncommon resident, chiefly near Jacksonville

☐ **Barred owl** (*Strix varia*)–fairly common resident in floodplain and lowland woods

☐ **Short-eared owl** (*Asio flammeus*)–rare winter visitor over fields and open marshes

☐ **Northern saw-whet owl** (*Aegolius acadicus*)–very rare winter visitor

Nightjars

☐ **Common nighthawk** (*Chordeiles minor*)–common in spring, summer, and fall in a variety of habitats

☐ **Chuck-will's-widow** (*Caprimulgus carolinensis*)–fairly common summer visitor in open, pine–oak woods

☐ **Whip-poor-will** (*Caprimulgus vociferus*)–uncommon in winter, most often heard and seen during spring migration

Swifts

☐ **Chimney swift** (*Chaetura pelagica*)–common summer visitor near cities and dwellings

☐ **Vaux's swift** (*Chaetura vauxi*)–very rare winter visitor

Hummingbirds

☐ **Broad-billed hummingbird** (*Cynanthus latirostris*)–very rare in winter

☐ **Ruby-throated hummingbird** (*Archilochus colubris*)–common summer visitor inland and along coast

☐ **Rufous hummingbird** (*Selasphorus rufus*)–rare in winter

Kingfishers

☐ **Belted kingfisher** (*Ceryle alcyon*)–common resident near wetlands

Woodpeckers

☐ **Red-headed woodpecker** (*Melanerpes erythrocephalus*)– fairly common resident of upland woods

☐ **Red-bellied woodpecker** (*Melanerpes carolinus*)–common resident in a variety of woodland habitats

☐ **Yellow-bellied woodpecker** (*Sphyrapicus varius*)–uncommon winter visitor in woodlands

☐ **Downy woodpecker** (*Picoides pubescens*)–fairly common resident in woodlands

☐ **Hairy woodpecker** (*Picoides villosus*)–uncommon resident in woodlands

☐ **Red-cockaded woodpecker** (*Picoides borealis*)–uncommon to locally common resident of mature longleaf pine woodlands and adjacent habitats

☐ **Northern flicker** (*Colaptes auratus*)–common resident in woodlands

☐ **Pileated woodpecker** (*Dryocopus pileatus*)–common resident in wetlands, swamps, and floodplains

Tyrant Flycatchers

☐ **Olive-sided flycatcher** (*Contopus borealis*)–occasional spring and fall migrant in woodlands

☐ **Eastern wood-pewee** (*Contopus virens*)–fairly common summer visitor in woodlands

☐ **Acadian flycatcher** (*Empidonax virescens*)–fairly common summer visitor in woodlands

☐ **Alder flycatcher** (*Empidonax alnorum*)–rare fall migrant in woodlands

☐ **Willow flycatcher** (*Empidonax traillii*)–rare fall migrant in woodlands

☐ **Least flycatcher** (*Empidonax minimus*)–rare spring and fall migrant in woodlands

☐ **Eastern phoebe** (*Sayornis phoebe*)–fairly common winter visitor near wetlands

☐ **Say's phoebe** (*Sayornis saya*)–rare fall migrant on east coast

☐ **Vermillion flycatcher** (*Pyrocephalus rubinus*)–rare but regular winter visitor on west coast

☐ **Ash-throated flycatcher** (*Myiarchus cinerascens*)–rare winter visitor in woodlands

☐ **Great crested flycatcher** (*Myiarchus crinitus*)–common summer visitor in a variety of woodland habitats

☐ **Brown-crested flycatcher** (*Myiarchus tyrannulus*)–very rare in midwinter

☐ **Western kingbird** (*Tyrannus verticalis*)–occasional winter visitor in open areas and along the coast

☐ **Eastern kingbird** (*Tyrannus tyrannus*)–common summer visitor in woodlands and fields

☐ **Gray kingbird** (*Tyrannus dominicensis*)–fairly common along the coast

☐ **Scissor-tailed flycatcher** (*Tyrannus forficatus*)–rare winter visitor along the coast

Larks

☐ **Horned lark** (*Eremophila alpestris*)–rare winter visitor in open areas along the coast

Swallows

☐ **Purple martin** (*Progne subis*)–common to abundant spring and summer visitor

☐ **Tree swallow** (*Tachycineta bicolor*)–nearly year-round, chiefly near large bodies of water

☐ **Northern rough-winged swallow** (*Stelgidopteryx serripennis*)–uncommon to fairly common summer visitor

☐ **Bank swallow** (*Riparia riparia*)–fairly common spring and fall migrant

☐ **Cliff swallow** (*Hirundo pyrrhonota*)–rare during spring and fall migration

☐ **Cave swallow** (*Hirundo fulva*)–very rare during spring migration and other times of the year

☐ **Barn swallow** (*Hirundo rustica*)–common to abundant summer visitor, often near bridges but also in other places

Jays, Magpies, and Crows

☐ **Blue jay** (*Cyanocitta cristata*)–abundant resident in a variety of habitats

☐ **Scrub jay** (*Aphelocoma coerulescens*)–uncommon and local in north Florida

☐ **American crow** (*Corvus brachyrhynchos*)–abundant and often-seen resident

☐ **Fish crow** (*Corvus ossifragus*)–abundant and often-seen resident

Titmice

☐ **Carolina chickadee** (*Parus carolinensis*)–common woodland resident

☐ **Tufted titmouse** (*Parus bicolor*)–common woodland resident

Nuthatches

☐ **Red-breasted nuthatch** (*Sitta canadensis*)–occasional winter visitor in woodlands

☐ **White-breasted nuthatch** (*Sitta carolinensis*)–fairly common resident in woodlands

☐ **Brown-headed nuthatch** (*Sitta pusilla*)–fairly common resident in pinelands

Creepers

☐ **Brown creeper** (*Certhia americana*)–occasional winter visitor in woodlands

Wrens

☐ **Carolina wren** (*Thryothorus ludovicianus*)–abundant resident in many habitats

☐ **Bewick's wren** (*Thryomanes bewickii*)–rare winter visitor

☐ **House wren** (*Troglodytes aedon*)–fairly common winter visitor in shrubby and brushy areas

☐ **Winter wren** (*Troglodytes troglodytes*)–rare winter visitor, chiefly near streams and wet areas

☐ **Sedge wren** (*Cistothorus platensis*)–uncommon but regular winter visitor in marshes and grassy meadows

☐ **Marsh wren** (*Cistothorus palustris*)–fairly common resident in marshes

Old World Warblers, Kinglets, etc.

☐ **Golden-crowned kinglet** (*Regulus satrapa*)–uncommon winter visitor in woodlands

☐ **Ruby-crowned kinglet** (*Regulus calendula*)–common winter visitor in woodlands

☐ **Blue-gray gnatcatcher** (*Polioptila caerulea*)–fairly common resident in woodlands

☐ **Eastern bluebird** (*Sialia sialis*)–common resident in open woodlands

☐ **Veery** (*Catharus fuscescens*)–uncommon spring and fall migrant, woodlands

☐ **Gray-checked thrush** (*Catharus minimus*)–uncommon spring and fall migrant, woodlands

☐ **Swainson's thrush** (*Catharus ustulatus*)–uncommon spring and fall migrant, woodlands

☐ **Hermit thrush** (*Catharus guttatus*)–uncommon to common winter visitor in woodlands

☐ **Wood thrush** (*Hylocichla mustelina*)–fairly common summer visitor in woodlands

☐ **American robin** (*Turdus migratorius*)–abundant winter resident in woodlands, fields, yards

Mimic Thrushes

☐ **Gray catbird** (*Dumetella carolinensis*)–fairly common to common winter resident in woodlands

☐ **Northern mockingbird** (*Mimus polyglottos*)–common resident in a variety of habitats

☐ **Sage thrasher** (*Oreoscoptes montanus*)–rare in winter and early spring

☐ **Brown thrasher** (*Toxostoma rufum*)–common resident in woodlands

Wagtails and Pipits
☐ **Water pipit** (*Anthus spinoletta*)–fairly common to common winter visitor, fields
☐ **Sprague's pipit** (*Anthus spragueii*)–occasional winter visitor, fields

Waxwings
☐ **Cedar waxwing** (*Bombycilla cedrorum*)–fairly common winter visitor in neighborhoods and woodlands

Shrikes
☐ **Loggerhead shrike** (*Lanius ludovicianus*)–fairly common resident in open areas near woodlands

Starlings
☐ **European starling** (*Sturnus vulgaris*)–abundant resident in many habitats

Vireos
☐ **White-eyed vireo** (*Vireo griseus*)–fairly common resident in dense moist woodlands
☐ **Bell's vireo** (*Vireo bellii*)–rare in spring and fall migration
☐ **Solitary vireo** (*Vireo solitarius*)–uncommon but regular winter visitor, woodlands
☐ **Yellow-throated vireo** (*Vireo flavifrons*)–fairly common summer visitor in rich woodlands
☐ **Warbling vireo** (*Vireo gilvus*)–rare spring and fall migrant in woodlands
☐ **Philadelphia vireo** (*Vireo philadelphicus*)–rare spring and fall migrant in woodlands
☐ **Red-eyed vireo** (*Vireo olivaceus*)–common summer visitor in woodlands
☐ **Black-whiskered vireo** (*Vireo altiloquus*)–rare spring and early summer visitor, chiefly along the coast

Wood Warblers

☐ **Blue-winged warbler** (*Vermivora pinus*)–occasional spring and fall migrant

☐ **Golden-winged warbler** (*Vermivora chrysoptera*)–occasional spring and fall migrant

☐ **Tennessee warbler** (*Vermivora peregrina*)–uncommon spring and fall migrant

☐ **Orange-crowned warbler** (*Vermivora celata*)–uncommon to fairly common winter resident in woodlands

☐ **Nashville warbler** (*Vermivora ruficapilla*)–rare spring and fall migrant

☐ **Northern parula** (*Parula americana*)–common summer resident in rich woodlands and hammocks

☐ **Yellow warbler** (*Dendroica petechia*)–uncommon spring and fall migrant

☐ **Chestnut-sided warbler** (*Dendroica pensylvanica*)– uncommon spring and fall migrant

☐ **Magnolia warbler** (*Dendroica magnolia*)–uncommon spring and fall migrant

☐ **Cape May warbler** (*Dendroica tigrina*)–uncommon spring and fall migrant

☐ **Black-throated blue warbler** (*Dendroica caereulescens*)–uncommon spring and fall migrant

☐ **Yellow-rumped warbler** (*Dendroica coronata*)–abundant winter visitor in a variety of habitats

☐ **Black-throated gray warbler** (*Dendroica nigrescens*)–occasional spring and fall migrant

☐ **Townsend's warbler** (*Dendroica townsendi*)–rare winter visitor

☐ **Black-throated green warbler** (*Dendroica virens*)–uncommon spring and fall migrant

☐ **Blackburnian warbler** (*Dendroica fusca*)–uncommon spring and fall migrant

☐ **Yellow-throated warbler** (*Dendroica dominica*)–fairly common resident in open woodlands

☐ **Pine warbler** (*Dendroica pinus*)–common resident in pine-lands and woodlands

☐ **Kirtland's warbler** (*Dendroica kirtlandii*)–rare spring and fall migrant E

☐ **Prairie warbler** (*Dendroica discolor*)–common summer visitor in woodlands

☐ **Palm warbler** (*Dendroica palmarum*)–common winter visitor in a variety of habitats

☐ **Bay-breasted warbler** (*Dendroica castanea*)–uncommon during spring and fall migration

☐ **Blackpoll warbler** (*Dendroica striata*)–occasional but regular spring and fall migrant in woodlands

☐ **Cerulean warbler** (*Dendroica cerulea*)–occasional spring and fall migrant, chiefly in the tops of trees

☐ **Black-and-white warbler** (*Mniotilta varia*)–uncommon to fairly common in fall, winter, and spring, woodlands

☐ **American redstart** (*Setophaga ruticilla*)–fairly common spring and fall migrant, woodlands

☐ **Prothonotary warbler** (*Protonotaria citrea*)–common sum-mer visitor, wet areas, never far from water

☐ **Worm-eating warbler** (*Helmitheros vermivorus*)–uncommon to fairly common spring and fall migrant

☐ **Swainson's warbler** (*Limnothlypis swainsonii*)–uncommon summer visitor, low woods

☐ **Ovenbird** (*Seiurus aurocapillus*)–uncommon to fairly common in open woodlands

☐ **Northern waterthrush** (*Seiurus noveboracensis*)–uncommon spring and fall migrant

☐ **Louisiana waterthrush** (*Seiurus motacilla*)–uncommon to fairly common summer visitor

☐ **Kentucky warbler** (*Oporornis formosus*)–uncommon sum-mer visitor in thickets

☐ **Connecticut warbler** (*Oporornis agilis*)–rare spring and fall migrant

☐ **Mourning warbler** (*Oporornis philadelphia*)–rare spring and fall migrant

☐ **Common yellowthroat** (*Geothlypis trichas*)–common resident, low, wet to moist woodlands

☐ **Hooded warbler** (*Wilsonia citrina*)–fairly common summer resident, rich woodlands and several other habitats

☐ **Wilson's warbler** (*Wilsonia pusilla*)–rare spring and fall migrant

☐ **Canada warbler** (*Wilsonia canadensis*)–rare spring and fall migrant

☐ **Yellow-breasted chat** (*Icteria virens*)–fairly common summer visitor, a variety of woodland habitats

Tanagers
☐ **Summer tanager** (*Piranga rubra*)–common summer visitor in woodlands and neighborhoods
☐ **Scarlet tanager** (*Piranga olivacea*)–uncommon spring and fall migrant, woodlands
☐ **Western tanager** (*Piranga ludoviciana*)–occasional in winter

Cardinals and Allies
☐ **Northern cardinal** (*Cardinalis cardinalis*)–abundant resident in woodlands and neighborhoods
☐ **Rose-breasted grosbeak** (*Pheucticus lucovicianus*)–uncommon spring and fall migrant, rich woodlands
☐ **Black-headed grosbeak** (*Pheucticus melanocephalus*)–rare spring migrant
☐ **Blue grosbeak** (*Guiraca caerulea*)–common summer visitor in thin woods, as well as shrubby and bushy areas
☐ **Indigo bunting** (*Passerina cyanea*)–common summer visitor in shrubby and bushy woodland edges
☐ **Painted bunting** (*Passerina amoena*)–locally common summer visitor, primarily east coast
☐ **Dickcissel** (*Spiza americana*)–occasional spring and fall migrant

Towhees, Sparrows, and Allies
☐ **Rufous-sided towhee** (*Pipilo erythrophthalmus*)–abundant resident in woodlands and thickets
☐ **Bachman's sparrow** (*Aimophila aestivalis*)–fairly common but secretive, pine woodlands
☐ **Chipping sparrow** (*Spizella passerina*)–common winter visitor, often seen at feeders
☐ **Clay-colored sparrow** (*Spizella pallida*)–occasional spring and fall migrant
☐ **Field sparrow** (*Spizella pusilla*)–fairly common resident along the edges of thin woodland and in fields

☐ **Vesper sparrow** (*Pooecetes gramineus*)–fairly common winter visitor in grasslands

☐ **Lark sparrow** (*Chondestes grammacus*)–occasional spring and fall migrant

☐ **Savannah sparrow** (*Passerculus sandwichensis*)–common winter visitor in grasslands and edges

☐ **Grasshopper sparrow** (*Ammodramus savannarum*)–rare winter visitor, pastures and fields E

☐ **Henslow's sparrow** (*Ammodramus henslowii*)–rare winter visitor, shrubby fields and edges

☐ **Le Conte's sparrow** (*Ammodramus leconteii*)–occasional winter visitor in wet grassy areas

☐ **Sharp-tailed sparrow** (*Ammodramus caudacutus*)–fairly common winter visitor in tidal and saltwater marshes

☐ **Seaside sparrow** (*Ammodramus maritimus*)–fairly common resident, tidal marshes

☐ **Fox sparrow** (*Passerella iliaca*)–rare in midwinter

☐ **Song sparrow** (*Melospiza melodia*)–common winter visitor, brushy areas, low thickets, and grassy areas with shrubs

☐ **Lincoln's sparrow** (*Melospiza lincolnii*)–occasional in winter

☐ **Swamp sparrow** (*Melospiza georgiana*)–fairly common to common winter visitor, generally in wet, grassy or shrubby areas

☐ **White-throated sparrow** (*Zonotrichia albicollis*)–common to abundant winter visitor in a variety of habitats

☐ **White-crowned sparrow** (*Zonotrichia leucophrys*)–rare winter visitor

☐ **Dark-eyed junco** (*Junco hyemalis*)–uncommon to common winter resident in edges and woodlands

☐ **Lapland longspur** (*Calcarius lapponicus*)–rare in winter, chiefly along grassy coastal beaches

☐ **Snow bunting** (*Plectrophenax nivalis*)–very rare in winter, beaches and open areas

Blackbirds, Orioles, and Allies

☐ **Bobolink** (*Dolichonyx oryzivorus*)–fairly common to common spring and fall migrant in open, grassy areas

☐ **Red-winged blackbird** (*Agelaius phoeniceus*)–abundant resident in wet grasslands and marshes

☐ **Eastern meadowlark** (*Sturnella magna*)–fairly common to common resident, grasslands and fields

☐ **Western meadowlark** (*Sturnella neglecta*)–rare winter visitor

☐ **Yellow-headed blackbird** (*Xanthocephalus xanthocephalus*)– rare spring and fall migrant, often near freshwater marshes

☐ **Rusty blackbird** (*Euphagus carolinus*)–fairly common to common winter visitor, wet woodlands

☐ **Brewer's blackbird** (*Euphagus cyanocephalus*)–fairly com-mon to common winter visitor in a variety of habitats

☐ **Boat-tailed grackle** (*Quiscalus major*)–abundant resident, chiefly coastal

☐ **Common grackle** (*Quiscalus quiscula*)–abundant resident in a variety of habitats

☐ **Brown-headed cowbird** (*Molothrus ater*)–abundant resident in a variety of habitats

☐ **Orchard oriole** (*Icterus spurius*)–fairly common to common summer visitor in open woods

☐ **Northern oriole** (*Icterus galbula*)–occasional winter visitor, suburbs and open woods

Northern Finches

☐ **Purple finch** (*Carpodacus purpureus*)–irregular but sometimes common winter visitor in a variety of habitats

☐ **Pine siskin** (*Carduelis pinus*)–uncommon to fairly common winter visitor

☐ **American goldfinch** (*Carduelis tristis*)–common to abundant winter visitor in woodlands and at feeders

☐ **Evening grosbeak** (*Coccothraustes vespertinus*)–rare winter visitor

Old-World Sparrows

☐ **House sparrow** (*Passer domesticus*)–abundant resident near cities and in suburban neighborhoods

MAMMAL CHECKLIST

☐ **Virginia opossum** (*Didelphis virginiana*)–abundant in most habitats, statewide

☐ **Southeastern shrew** (*Sorex longirostris*)–rare in wet forests, northern two-thirds of the state

☐ **Southern short-tailed shrew** (*Blarina carolinensis*)–common in forests, statewide

☐ **Least shrew** (*Cryptotis parva*)–common in fields, statewide

☐ **Eastern mole** (*Scalopus aquaticus*)–abundant in most habitats, statewide

☐ **Little brown bat** (*Myotis lucifugus*)–rare in caves and buildings, northern border of the state

☐ **Eastern pipistrelle** (*Pipistrellus subflavus*)–common in caves and trees, statewide

☐ **Rafinesque's big-eared bat** (*Plecotus rafinesquii*)–uncommon in trees and cabins, northern two-thirds of the state

☐ **Big brown bat** (*Eptesicus fuscus*)–rare in caves and trees, statewide

☐ **Hoary bat** (*Lasiurus cinereus*)–common in trees, northern one-third of the state

☐ **Red bat** (*Lasiurus borealis*)–common in trees, northern two-thirds of the state

☐ **Seminole bat** (*Lasiurus seminolus*)–common in trees, statewide

☐ **Yellow bat** (*Lasiurus intermedius*)–abundant in trees, statewide

☐ **Evening bat** (*Nycticeius humeralis*)–common in trees and buildings, statewide

☐ **Brazilian free-tailed bat** (*Tadarida brasiliensis*)–common in trees and buildings, statewide

☐ **Nine-banded armadillo** (*Dasypus novemcinctus*)–abundant in most habitats, statewide

☐ **Eastern cottontail** (*Sylvilagus floridanus*)–abundant in fields, statewide

☐ **Marsh rabbit** (*Sylvilagus palustris*)–abundant in marshes, statewide

☐ **Gray squirrel** (*Sciurus carolinensis*)–abundant in most forests, statewide

☐ **Fox squirrel** (*Sciurus niger*)–locally common in open pine and cypress woodlands, statewide

☐ **Southern flying squirrel** (*Glaucomys volans*)–abundant in oak forests, statewide

☐ **Southeastern pocket gopher** (*Geomys pinetis*)–abundant in upland areas, northern two-thirds of the state

☐ **Beaver** (*Castor canadensis*)–common in streams and lakes, northern one-third of the state

☐ **Eastern woodrat** (*Neottoma floridana*)–common in northern two-thirds of the state

☐ **Hispid cotton rat** (*Sigmodon hispidus*) abundant in fields, statewide

☐ **Eastern harvest mouse** (*Reithrodontomys humulis*)–uncommon in fields, northern two-thirds of the state

☐ **Marsh rice rat** (*Oryzomys palustris*)–common in marshes, statewide

☐ **Oldfield or beach mouse** (*Peromyscus polionotus*)–common in fields and coastal dunes, northern two-thirds of the state

☐ **Cotton mouse** (*Peromyscus gossypinus*) abundant in forests statewide

☐ **Golden mouse** (*Ochrotomys nuttalli*)–common in forests, northern two-thirds of the state

☐ **Pine vole** (*Microtus pinetorum*)–common in upland forests, northern one-third of the state

☐ **Meadow vole** (*Microtus pennsylvanicus*)–rare in saltmarshes along the coast of Levy County E

☐ **Round-tailed muskrat** (*Neofiber alleni*)–common in marshes and along lakeshores, peninsula and eastern panhandle

☐ **House mouse** (*Mus musculus*)–common in buildings, on farms and coastal dunes, statewide

☐ **Black or roof rat** (*Rattus rattus*)–abundant in buildings and on farms, statewide

☐ **Norway rat** (*Rattus norvegicus*)–common in buildings and on wharves, statewide

☐ **Nutria** (*Myocastor coypus*)–common in marshes, lakes, and streams, statewide

☐ **Florida black bear** (*Ursus americanus floridanus*)–rare in most habitats, statewide

☐ **Raccoon** (*Procyon lotor*)–abundant in most habitats, statewide

☐ **Mink** (*Mustela vison*)–rare in marshes, northern coasts

☐ **Long-tailed weasel** (*Mustela frenata*)–rare in most habitats, statewide

☐ **Striped skunk** (*Mephitis mephitis*)–common in most habitats, statewide

☐ **Eastern spotted skunk** (*Spilogale putorius*)–common in fields and open forests, statewide

☐ **River otter** (*Lutra canadensis*)–common in streams and lakes, statewide

☐ **Gray fox** (*Urocyon cinereoargenteus*)–common in most habitats, statewide

☐ **Red fox** (*Vulpes vulpes*)–common in uplands, statewide

☐ **Coyote** (*Canis latrans*)–rare in fields, northern two-thirds of the state

☐ **Bobcat** (*Felis rufus*)–common in most habitats, statewide

☐ **Harbor seal** (*Phoca vitulina*)–rare off the Atlantic coast

☐ **Hooded seal** (*Cystophora cristata*)–rare off the Atlantic coast

☐ **Rough-toothed dolphin** (*Steno bredanensis*)–rare in the Gulf of Mexico and Atlantic Ocean

☐ **Long-snouted spinner dolphin** (*Steno longirostris*)–rare in the Gulf of Mexico and Atlantic Ocean

☐ **Short-snouted spinner dolphin** (*Stenella clymene*)–rare in the Gulf of Mexico and Atlantic Ocean

☐ **Striped dolphin** (*Stenella coeruleoalba*)–rare in the Gulf of Mexico and Atlantic Ocean

☐ **Atlantic spotted dolphin** (*Stenella frontalis*)–common in the Gulf of Mexico and Atlantic Ocean

☐ **Pantropical spotted dolphin** (*Stenella attenuata*)–rare in the Gulf of Mexico and Atlantic Ocean

☐ **Saddle-backed dolphin** (*Delphinus delphis*)–common in the Gulf of Mexico and Atlantic Ocean

☐ **Fraser's dolphin** (*Lagenodelphis hosei*)–rare in the Gulf of Mexico and Atlantic Ocean

☐ **Bottle-nosed dolphin** (*Tursiops truncatus*)–abundant in the Gulf of Mexico and Atlantic Ocean

☐ **False killer whale** (*Pseudorca crassidens*)–rare in the Gulf of Mexico and Atlantic Ocean

☐ **Killer whale** (*Orcinus orca*)–rare in the Gulf of Mexico and Atlantic Ocean

☐ **Pygmy killer whale** (*Feressa attenuata*)–rare in the Gulf of Mexico and Atlantic Ocean

- [ ] **Risso's dolphin or grampus** (*Grampus griseus*)–rare in the Gulf of Mexico and Atlantic Ocean
- [ ] **Short-finned pilot whale** (*Globicephala macrorhynchus*)– abundant in the Gulf of Mexico and Atlantic Ocean
- [ ] **Harbor porpoise** (*Phocoena phocoena*)–rare in the Gulf of Mexico and Atlantic Ocean
- [ ] **Pygmy sperm whale** (*Kogia breviceps*)–rare in the Gulf of Mexico and Atlantic Ocean
- [ ] **Dwarf sperm whale** (*Kogia simus*)–rare in the Gulf of Mexico and Atlantic Ocean
- [ ] **Sperm whale** (*Physeter macrocephalus*)–rare in the Gulf of Mexico and Atlantic Ocean E
- [ ] **Goose-beaked whale** (*Ziphius cavirostris*)–rare in the Gulf of Mexico and Atlantic Ocean
- [ ] **Dense-beaked whale** (*Mesoplodon densirostris*)–rare in the Gulf of Mexico and Atlantic Ocean
- [ ] **Antillean beaked whale** (*Mesoplodon europaeus*)–rare in the Gulf of Mexico and Atlantic Ocean
- [ ] **True's beaked whale** (*Mesoplodon mirus*)–rare in the Gulf of Mexico and Atlantic Ocean
- [ ] **Fin whale** (*Balaenoptera physalus*)–rare in the Gulf of Mexico and Atlantic Ocean
- [ ] **Minke whale** (*Balaenoptera acutorostrata*)–rare in the Gulf of Mexico and Atlantic Ocean
- [ ] **Sei whale** (*Balaenoptera borealis*)–rare in the Gulf of Mexico and Atlantic Ocean
- [ ] **Bryde's whale** (*Balaenoptera edeni*)–rare in the Gulf of Mexico and Atlantic Ocean
- [ ] **Humpback whale** (*Megaptera novaeangliae*)–rare in the Gulf of Mexico and Atlantic Ocean E
- [ ] **Right whale** (*Balaena glacialis*)–rare in the Gulf of Mexico and Atlantic Ocean E
- [ ] **Manatee** (*Trichechus manatus*)–rare in rivers and coastal marine environments, statewide E
- [ ] **Wild boar** (*Sus scrofa*)–abundant in most habitats, statewide
- [ ] **White-tailed deer** (*Odocoileus virginianus*)–abundant in most habitats, statewide

AMPHIBIAN AND REPTILE CHECKLIST

Frogs and Toads

☐ **Oak toad** (*Bufo quercicus*)–throughout north Florida, common in pine flatwoods, dry hammocks, and scrub

☐ **Southern toad** (*Bufo terrestris*)–throughout north Florida, abundant in neighborhoods, hammocks, pine flatwoods, freshwater marshes

☐ **Florida cricket frog** (*Acris gryllus dorsalis*)–throughout north Florida, common in freshwater wetlands

☐ **Cope's gray treefrog** (*Hyla chrysoscelis*)–throughout north Florida, common in damp woods, farmlands, parks

☐ **Green treefrog** (*Hyla cinerea*)–throughout north Florida, common in pinelands, freshwater marshes and ponds, neighborhoods

☐ **Southern spring peeper** (*Hyla crucifer bartramiana*)–northeast Florida, common in woodlands near ponds, roadside ditches, shallow ponds

☐ **Pinewoods treefrog** (*Hyla femoralis*)–throughout north Florida, common in pinelands and a variety of other habitats, including neighborhoods

☐ **Barking treefrog** (*Hyla gratiosa*)–throughout north Florida, common in pinelands and pineland depressions

☐ **Squirrel treefrog** (*Hyla squirella*)–throughout north Florida, common in freshwater marshes, ponds, and neighborhoods

☐ **Little grass frog** (*Limnaoedus ocularis*)–throughout north Florida, common in shallow ponds, marshes, savannas, wet prairies

☐ **Southern chorus frog** (*Pseudacris nigrita nigrita*)– throughout north Florida, common in freshwater ponds, marshes, ditches

☐ **Florida chorus frog** (*Pseudacris nigrita verrocosa*)– throughout north Florida, common in freshwater ponds, marshes, ditches

☐ **Ornate chorus frog** (*Pseudacris ornata*)–throughout north Florida, common in freshwater ponds, marshes, and pinelands

☐ **Greenhouse frog** (*Eleutherodactylus planirostris planirostris*) - northeast Florida, common, exotic in virtually all habitats

☐ **Eastern narrowmouth toad** (*Gastrophryne carolinensis*)– through-out north Florida, common burrower found under leaf litter in hammocks

215

- ☐ **Eastern spadefoot toad** (*Scaphiopus holbrookii holbrookii*)– throughout north Florida, common in dry, sandy areas
- ☐ **Florida gopher frog** (*Rana areolata aesopus*)–throughout north Florida, uncommon in gopher tortoise burrows in sandy pinelands
- ☐ **Bullfrog** (*Rana catesbeiana*)–throughout north Florida, common in freshwater ponds
- ☐ **Bronze frog** (*Rana clamitans clamitans*)–throughout north Florida, common in freshwater marshes, swamps, and ponds
- ☐ **Pig frog** (*Rana grylio*)–throughout north Florida, common in shallow lakes, ponds, wet marshes
- ☐ **River frog** (*Rana heckscheri*)–throughout north Florida, uncommon in river swamps and freshwater marshes
- ☐ **Southern leopard frog** (*Rana utricularia*)–throughout north Florida, common in both freshwater and brackish habitats
- ☐ **Carpenter frog** (*Rana virgatipes*)–northeast Florida, uncommon and local in sphagnum bogs

Salamanders
- ☐ **Flatwoods salamander** (*Ambystoma cingulatum*)– throughout north Florida, rare in wet areas of pine flatwoods
- ☐ **Marbled salamander** (*Ambystoma opacum*)–throughout north Florida, locally common under debris and logs in hydric and mesic hammocks
- ☐ **Mole salamander** (*Ambystoma talpoideum*)–throughout north Florida, common under logs and debris in wet places
- ☐ **Eastern tiger salamander** (*Ambystoma tigrinum tigrinum*)– throughout north Florida, rare in mixed woodlands and temporary ponds
- ☐ **Two-toed amphiuma** (*Amphiuma means*)–throughout north Florida, common in freshwater sloughs and marshes
- ☐ **One-toed amphiuma** (*Amphiuma pholeter*)–throughout north Florida, rare and local in freshwater sloughs and seepage streams
- ☐ **Alabama waterdog** (*Necturus alabamensis*)–western panhandle, common in muddy-bottomed, moderately sized streams
- ☐ **Southern dusky salamander** (*Desmognathus auriculatus*)–throughout north Florida, common in ponds, bogs, and streams

☐ **Southern two-lined salamander** (*Eurycea cirrigera*)– throughout north Florida, common underground as well as under rocks, logs, and leaf litter

☐ **Dwarf salamander** (*Eurycea quadridigitata*)–throughout north Florida, common in a variety of wetlands

☐ **Slimy salamander** (*Plethodon glutinosus glutinosus*)–through out north Florida, common in moist, rotting logs and under leaf litter in damp places

☐ **Rusty mud salamander** (*Pseudotriton montanus floridanus*)– throughout north Florida, uncommon under logs in sandy spring runs

☐ **Southern red salamander** (*Pseudotriton ruber vioscai*)– throughout north Florida, common in clear streams of ravines

☐ **Many-lined salamander** (*Stereochilus marginatus*)–throughout north Florida, uncommon in local blackwater streams, ponds, ditches

☐ **Central newt** (*Notophthalmus viridescens louisianensis*)– through-out north Florida, common in shallow ponds and heavily vege-tated, slow-moving streams

☐ **Peninsula newt** (*Notophthalmus viridescens piaropicola*)– north-east Florida, common in the root system of water hyacinths

☐ **Striped newt** (*Notophthalmus perstriatus*)–northeast Florida, rare in a variety of freshwater ponds

☐ **Narrow-striped dwarf siren** (*Pseudobranchus striatus axanthus*)– northeast Florida, common in aquatic vegetation, especially in the roots of water hyacinth

☐ **Gulf hammock dwarf siren** (*Pseudobranchus striatus lustricolus*)– north Florida, rare in aquatic vegetation

☐ **Slender dwarf siren** (*Pseudobranchus striatus spheniscus*)– throughout north Florida, common in aquatic vegetation

☐ **Broad-striped siren** (*Pseudobranchus striatus striatus*)– northeast Florida, common in aquatic vegetation

☐ **Eastern lesser siren** (*Siren intermedia intermedia*)– throughout north Florida, common in aquatic vegetation in ditches, ponds, and cypress heads

☐ **Greater siren** (*Siren lacertina*)–throughout north Florida, common in aquatic vegetation in shallow ponds

Alligators and Crocodiles

☐ **American alligator** (*Alligator mississipiensis*)–throughout north Florida, common in marshes, ponds, lakes, rivers, and a variety other wetland habitats

Turtles

☐ **Loggerhead** (*Caretta caretta caretta*)–Atlantic and Gulf, common

☐ **Atlantic green turtle** (*Chelonia mydas mydas*)–Atlantic and Gulf, uncommon, E

☐ **Atlantic hawksbill** (*Eretmochelys imbricata imbricata*)– Atlantic and Gulf, rare, E

☐ **Atlantic ridley** (*Lepidochelys kempi*)–Atlantic and Gulf, rare, E

☐ **Common snapping turtle** (*Chelydra serpentina*)–northeast Florida, common in nearly all freshwater bodies

☐ **Florida snapping turtle** (*Chelydra serpentina osceola*)–throughout north Florida, common in nearly all freshwater bodies

☐ **Alligator snapping turtle** (*Macroclemys temminckii*)–through-out north Florida, uncommon in slow-moving streams and lakes

☐ **Leatherback turtle** (*Dermochelys coriacea coriacea*)– Atlantic and Gulf, rare, E

☐ **Spotted turtle** (*Clemmys guttata*)–northeast Florida, rare in sphagnum and slow-moving waters, possibly exotic

☐ **Florida chicken turtle** (*Deirochelys reticularia chrysea*)– northeast Florida, common in ponds, marshes, sloughs

☐ **Eastern chicken turtle** (*Deirochelys reticularia reticularia*)–throughout north Florida, common in ponds, marshes, sloughs

☐ **Diamondback terrapin** (*Malaclemys terrapin*)–north Florida, locally common in coastal marshes and estuaries

☐ **Carolina diamondback terrapin** (*Malaclemys terrapin centrata*)–northeast Florida, locally common in coastal marshes and estuaries

☐ **Ornate diamondback terrapin** (*Malaclemys terrapin macrospilota*)–north Florida, locally common in coastal marshes and estuaries

☐ **Florida east coast terrapin** (*Malaclemys terrapin tequesta*)– northeast Florida, locally common in coastal marshes and estuaries

☐ **Suwannee cooter** (*Pseudemys concinna suwanniensis*)– northeast Florida, common in rivers and slow-moving streams

☐ **Florida cooter** (*Pseudemys floridana floridana*)–throughout north Florida in rivers and slow-moving streams

☐ **Peninsula cooter** (*Pseudemys floridana peninsularis*)–northeast Florida, common in rivers and slow-moving streams

☐ **Florida redbelly turtle** (*Pseudemys nelsoni*)–throughout north Florida, common in rivers and slow-moving streams

☐ **Box turtle** (*Terrapene carolina*)–throughout north Florida, common in a variety of habitats including dry woodlands and neighborhoods

☐ **Florida box turtle** (*Terrapene carolina bauri*)–throughout north Florida in mesic hammocks and pine flatwoods

☐ **Eastern box turtle** (*Terrapene carolina carolina*)–northeast Florida, common in mesic hammocks and pine flatwoods

☐ **Gulf coast box turtle** (*Terrapene carolina major*)–throughout north Florida, common in upland hammocks and flatwoods

☐ **Yellowbelly slider** (*Trachemys scripta scripta*)–throughout north Florida, common in rivers

☐ **Striped mud turtle** (*Kinosternon baurii*)–northeast Florida, common, shallow marshes ponds, E

☐ **Mud turtle** (*Kinosternon subrubrum*)–throughout north Florida, common in shallow marshes and ponds

☐ **Florida mud turtle** (*Kinosternon subrubrum steindachneri*)– northeast Florida, common in swamps, ponds, lake edges, saltmarshes

☐ **Eastern mud turtle** (*Kinosternon subrubrum subrubrum*)– throughout north Florida, common in swamps and marshes

☐ **Loggerhead musk turtle** (*Sternotherus minor minor*)– throughout north Florida, common in shallow ponds, streams, spring runs

☐ **Stinkpot** (*Sternotherus odoratus*)–throughout north Florida in lakes, ponds, and streams

☐ **Gopher tortoise** (*Gopherus polyphemus*)–throughout north Florida, dry, sandy, well-drained habitats

☐ **Florida softshell** (*Apalone ferox*)–throughout north Florida, common in lakes, marshes, and ditches

☐ **Gulf coast spiny softshell** (*Apalone spinifera aspera*)– throughout north Florida, common in slow-moving rivers and streams

Worm Lizards

☐ **Florida worm lizard** (*Rhineura floridana*)–northeast Florida, common in dry, sandy habitats

Lizards

☐ **Eastern slender glass lizard** (*Ophisaurus attenuatus longicaudus*)–throughout north Florida, common in grasslands

☐ **Island glass lizard** (*Ophisaurus compressus*)–northeast Florida, uncommon in marshes and pinelands

☐ **Mimic glass lizard** (*Ophisaurus mimicus*)–throughout north Florida, uncommon in hammocks and pinelands

☐ **Eastern glass lizard** (*Ophisaurus ventralis*)–throughout north Florida, common in hammocks and pinelands

☐ **Mediterranean gecko** (*Hemidactylus turcicus*)–northeast Florida, uncommon in urban areas

☐ **Green anole** (*Anolis carolinensis*)–throughout north Florida, common in many habitats, including yards and gardens

☐ **Cuban brown anole** (*Anolis sagrei sagrei*)–northeast Florida, common, exotic and found in many habitats

☐ **Texas horned lizard** (*Phrynosoma cornutum*)–throughout north Florida, uncommon, exotic, found in open, sandy areas

☐ **Southern fence lizard** (*Sceloporus undulatus undulatus*)–throughout north Florida in pine flatwoods, turkey oak hammocks, and dry woodlands

☐ **Florida scrub lizard** (*Sceloporus woodi*)–northeast Florida, common in pine scrub and other fire maintained habitats

☐ **Cedar Key mole skink** (*Eumeces egregius insularis*)–north Florida, uncommon

☐ **Peninsula mole skink** (*Eumeces egregius onocrepis*)–northeast Florida, common in sand scrub

☐ **Northern mole skink** (*Eumeces egregius similis*)–throughout north Florida, common

☐ **Five-lined skink** (*Eumeces fasciatus*)–throughout north Florida, rare around hydric hammocks in rotting logs and trash piles

☐ **Southeastern five-lined skink** (*Eumeces inexpectatus*)– throughout north Florida, common in dry and pineland habitats as well as around suburban homes

☐ **Broadhead skink** (*Eumeces laticeps*)–throughout north Florida, common in mesic hammocks and moist habitats

☐ **Sand skink** (*Neoseps reynoldsi*)–north Florida, uncommon in sand pine scrub, turkey oak woods, and other dry habitats

☐ **Ground skink** (*Scincella lateralis*)–throughout north Florida, common under leaves in almost any habitat

☐ **Six-lined racerunner** (*Cnemidophorus sexlineatus sexlineatus*)– throughout north Florida, common in dry areas, including beach areas

Nonpoisonous Snakes

☐ **Florida scarlet snake** (*Cemophora coccinea connicea*)– northeast Florida, common in pine flatwoods and sandy uplands

☐ **Northern scarlet snake** (*Cemophora coccinea copei*)– throughout north Florida, common in pine flatwoods and sandy uplands

☐ **Southern black racer** (*Coluber constrictor priapus*)– throughout north Florida, common in nearly all habitats

☐ **Southern ringneck snake** (*Diadophis punctatus punctatus*)– throughout north Florida, common in pine flatwoods and other moist, open areas

☐ **Eastern indigo snake** (*Drymarchon corasis couperi*)– throughout north Florida, uncommon in gopher tortoise burrows

☐ **Corn snake** (*Elaphe guttata guttata*)–throughout north Florida, common in nearly all habitats

☐ **Yellow rat snake** (*Elaphe obsoleta quadrivittata*)–northeast Florida, common along woodland edges as well as near building and trash piles

☐ **Gray rat snake** (*Elaphe obsoleta spiloides*)–throughout north Florida, common in woods and near swamps, also in suburban neighborhoods

☐ **Eastern mud snake** (*Farancia abacura abacura*)–throughout north Florida, common in marshes, swamps, bogs, savannas, prairies

☐ **Rainbow snake** (*Farancia erytrogramma*)–northeast Florida, common in swamps, bogs, marshes, spring runs, rivers, clear streams

☐ **Eastern hognose snake** (*Heterodon platyrhinos*)–throughout north Florida, common in dry pinelands and turkey oak woodlands

☐ **Southern hognose snake** (*Heterodon simus*)–throughout north Florida, common in same areas as eastern hognose snake

☐ **Mole kingsnake** (*Lampropeltis calligaster rhombomaculata*)– throughout north Florida, rare, little is known about its habitat

☐ **Eastern kingsnake** (*Lampropeltis getulus getulus*)– throughout north Florida, common near wetlands, along canals, and in trash piles

☐ **Scarlet kingsnake** (*Lampropeltis triangulum elapsoides*)– throughout north Florida, uncommon

☐ **Eastern coachwhip** (*Masticophis flagellum flagellum*)– throughout north Florida, common in dry, sandy areas

☐ **Gulf saltmarsh snake** (*Nerodia clarkii clarkii*)–throughout north Florida, locally common in saltmarshes

☐ **Mangrove saltmarsh snake** (*Nerodia clarkii compressicauda*)– northeast Florida, locally common in mangroves

☐ **Atlantic saltmarsh snake** (*Nerodia clarkii taenita*)–northeast Florida, locally common in saltmarshes

☐ **Redbelly water snake** (*Nerodia erythrogaster erythrogaster*)– throughout north Florida, common along large rivers

☐ **Banded water snake** (*Nerodia fasciata fasciata*)–throughout north Florida, common in many aquatic habitats

☐ **Florida banded water snake** (*Nerodia fasciata pictiventris*)– northeast Florida, common in many aquatic habitats

☐ **Florida green water snake** (*Nerodia floridana*)–throughout north Florida, common in ponds, marshes, roadside ditches

☐ **Brown water snake** (*Nerodia taxispilota*)–throughout north Florida, common in rivers and lakes

☐ **Rough green snake** (*Opheodrys aestivus aestivus*)– throughout north Florida, common in shrubs along the edges of rivers, lakes, and ponds

☐ **Peninsula green snake** (*Opheodrys aestivus carinatus*)– northeast Florida, common in similar habitats to rough green snake

☐ **Florida pine snake** (*Pituophis melanoleucus mugitus*)– throughout north Florida, uncommon in longleaf–turkey oak woods

☐ **Striped crayfish snake** (*Regina alleni*)–northeast Florida, common in swamps, ponds, and lakes

☐ **Glossy crayfish snake** (*Regina rigida rigida*)–throughout north Florida, uncommon, not much is known about its habitat

☐ **Gulf crayfish snake** (*Regina rigida sinicola*)–throughout north Florida, uncommon

☐ **Pine woods snake** (*Rhadinaea flavilata*)–throughout north Florida, rare in flatwoods and cypress heads

☐ **North Florida swamp snake** (*Seminatrix pygaea pygaea*)– throughout north Florida, common in aquatic vegetation of lakes and ponds

☐ **Short-tailed snake** (*Stilosoma extenuatum*)–northeast Florida, rare in longleaf–turkey oak woodlands

☐ **Florida brown snake** (*Storeria dekayi victa*)–northeast Florida, common in many aquatic habitats

☐ **Midland brown snake** (*Storeria dekayi wrightorum*)– throughout north Florida, uncommon

☐ **Florida redbelly snake** (*Storeria occipitomaculata obscura*)– northeast Florida, uncommon in mesic hammocks and moist woods

☐ **Central Florida crowned snake** (*Tantilla relicta neilli*)–northeast Florida, common in sandhills and moist hammocks

☐ **Peninsula crowned snake** (*Tantilla relicta relicta*)–northeast Florida, common in scrub

☐ **Bluestripe ribbon snake** (*Thamnophis sauritus nitae*)– northwest Florida, locally common in aquatic habitats of the Big Bend

☐ **Peninsula ribbon snake** (*Thamnophis sauritus sackenii*)– northeast Florida, common in aquatic habitats

☐ **Bluestrip garter snake** (*Thamnophis sirtalis similis*)–northeast Florida, locally common in a number of habitats

☐ **Eastern garter snake** (*Thamnophis sirtalis sirtalis*)– throughout north Florida, common in many habitats

☐ **Rough earth snake** (*Virginia striatula*)–throughout north Florida, uncommon in pine flatwoods and dry hammocks

☐ **Smooth earth snake** (*Virginia valeriae valeriae*)–throughout north Florida, uncommon in mesic hammocks and moist woods

Poisonous Snakes

☐ **Eastern Coral snake** (*Micrurus fulvius fulvius*)–throughout north Florida, common in many habitats

☐ **Florida cottonmouth** (*Agkistrodon piscivorus conanti*)– throughout north Florida, common in many aquatic habitats

☐ **Eastern diamondback rattlesnake** (*Crotalus adamanteus*)– throughout north Florida, common in pine–palmetto flatwoods and dry woodlands

☐ **Timber (or canebrake) rattlesnake** (*Crotalus horridus*)–northeast Florida, locally common in wet flatwoods and hydric hammocks

☐ **Dusky pygmy rattlesnake** (*Sistrurus miliarius barbouri*)– throughout north Florida, common in many habitats including pinelands and scrub

COMMON, SCIENTIFIC, AND BOTANICAL FAMILY NAMES OF PLANTS MENTIONED IN THE TEXT

Agalinis (*Agalinis* sp.) Scrophulariaceae

Agarista (*Agarista populifolia*) Ericaceae

American basswood (*Tilia americana*) Tiliaceae

American beautyberry (*Callicarpa americana*) Verbenaceae

American beech (*Fagus grandifolia*) Fagaceae

American elm (*Ulmus americana*) Ulmaceae

American holly (*Ilex opaca*) Aquifoliaceae

Angelica (*Angelica* sp.) Umbelliferae

Arrowhead (*Saggitaria* sp.) Alismataceae

Arrowwood (*Viburnum dentatum*) Caprifoliaceae

Ash (*Fraxinus* sp.) Oleaceae

Aster (*Aster* sp.) Compositae

Atamasco lily (*Zephyranthes atamasco*) Amaryllidaceae

Atlantic white cedar (*Chamaecyparis thyoides*) Cupressaceae

Bachelor's buttons (*Polygala nana, P. lutea, P. balduinii*) Polygalaceae

Bald cypress (*Taxodium distichum*) Taxodiaceae

Barbara's buttons (*Marshallia* sp.) Compositae

Beach elder (*Iva imbricata*) Compositae

Beakrush (*Rhynchospora* sp.) Cyperaceae

Beggar-tick (*Bidens* sp.) Compositae

Black cherry (*Prunus serotina*) Rosaceae

Black-eyed susan (*Rudbeckia hirta*) Compositae

Blackgum (*Nyssa biflora*) Nyssaceae
Black mangrove (*Avicennia germinans*) Avicenniaceae
Black needlerush (*Juncus roemerianus*) Juncaceae
Black oak (*Quercus velutina*) Fagaceae
Black root (*Pterocaulon pycnostachyum*) Compositae
Black tupelo (*Nyssa sylvatica*) Nyssaceae
Bladderwort (*Utricularia* sp.) Lentibulariaceae
Blanketflower (*Gaillardia pulchella*) Compositae
Blazing star (*Liatris* sp.) Compositae
Blueberry (*Vaccinium* sp.) Ericaceae
Blue curls (*Trichostema* sp.) Labiatae
Blue flag iris (*Iris virginica*) Iridaceae
Bluejack oak (*Quercus incana*) Fagaceae
Bluff oak (*Quercus austrina*) Fagaceae
Bog buttons (*Lachnocaulon* sp.) Eriocaulaceae
Bracken fern (*Pteridium aquilinum*) Dennstaedtiaceae
Butterwort (*Pinguicula* sp.) Lentibulariaceae
Buttonbush (*Cephalanthus occidentalis*) Rubiaceae
Cabbage palm (*Sabal palmetto*) Palmae
Cane (*Arundinaria gigantea*) Gramineae
Canna lily (*Canna flaccida*) Commelinaceae
Carolina ash (*Fraxinus caroliniana*) Oleaceae
Carolina holly (*Ilex ambigua*) Aquifoliaceae
Carolina laurel cherry (*Prunus caroliniana*) Rosaceae
Carolina silverbell (*Halesia carolina*) Styracaceae
Catesby's lily (see pine lily)
Cattail (*Typha* sp.) Typhaceae
Cedar elm (*Ulmus crassifolia*) Ulmaceae
Chapman oak (*Quercus chapmanii*) Fagaceae
Chestnut oak (*Quercus michauxii*) Fagaceae
Chickasaw plum (*Prunus angustifolia*) Rosaceae
Chinquapin (*Castanea pumila*) Fagaceae
Cinnamon fern (*Osmunda cinnamomea*) Osmundaceae
Climbing butterfly pea (*Centrosema virginianum*) Leguminosae
Climbing hydrangea (*Decumaria barbara*) Saxifragaceae
Coastal plain willow (*Salix caroliniana*) Salicaceae
Colic root (*Aletris* sp.) Liliaceae
Coontie (*Zamia pumila*) Zamiaceae

Coral bean (*Erythrina herbaceae*) Leguminosae
Cork elm (*Ulmus alata*) Ulmaceae
Cornel (*Cornus* sp.) Cornaceae
Cross vine (*Bignonia capreolata*) Bignoniaceae
Cypress (*Taxodium* sp.) Taxodiaceae
Deerberry (*Vaccinium stamineum*) Ericaceae
Deer tongue (*Carphephorus* sp.) Compositae
Devil's walking stick (*Aralia spinosa*) Araliaceae
Diamond leaf oak (*Quercus laurifolia*) Fagaceae
Duck potato (*Sagittaria* sp.) Alismataceae
Duck weed (*Lemna* sp.) Lemnaceae
Eastern hophornbeam (*Ostrya virginiana*) Betulaceae
Eastern redbud (*Cercis canadensis*) Leguminosae
Elderberry (*Sambucus canadensis*) Caprifoliaceae
Elm (*Ulmus* sp.) Ulmaceae
Fetterbush (*Lyonia* sp.) Ericaceae
Fire wheel (see blanketflower)
Flag pawpaw (*Asimina incarna*) Annonaceae
Fleabane (*Erigeron* sp., *Pluchea* sp.) Compositae
Florida dogwood (see flowering dogwood)
Florida maple (*Acer floridana*) Aceraceae
Florida rosemary (*Ceratiola ericoides*) Empetraceae
Flowering dogwood (*Cornus floridana*) Cornaceae
Gallberry (*Ilex glabra*) Aquifoliaceae
Gaura (*Gaura* sp.) Onagraceae
Giant water dropwort (*Oxypolis greenmanii*) Umbelliferae
Glasswort (*Salicornia* sp.) Chenopodiaceae
Goldenrod (*Solidago* sp.) Compositae
Gopher apple (*Licania michauxii*) Chrysobalanaceae
Grass-pink (*Calopogon* sp.) Orchidaceae
Green dragon (*Arisaema dracontium*) Araceae
Green eyes (*Berlandiera* sp.) Compositae
Green haw (*Crateagus viridis*) Rosaceae
Gum bumelia (*Bumelia lanuginosa*) Sapotaceae
Hackberry (*Celtis laevigata*) Ulmaceae
Hat pins (*Eriocaulon* sp.) Eriocaulaceae
Hazel alder (*Alnus serrulata*) Betulaceae
Haw (*Crateagus* sp.) Rosaceae

Hearts-a-bustin'-with-love (*Euonymous americanus*) Celastraceae
Hickory (*Carya* sp.) Juglandaceae
Highbush blueberry (*Vaccinium corymbosum*) Ericaceae
Hooded pitcher plant (*Sarracenia minor*) Sarraceniaceae
Horse sugar (*Symplocos tinctoria*) Symplocaceae
Indian pink (*Spigelia marilandica*) Loganiaceae
Ironwood (*Carpinus caroliniana*) Betulaceae
Jack-in-the-pulpit (*Arisaema triphyllum*) Aracea
Ladies tresses (*Spiranthes* sp.) Orchidaceae
Lantana (*Lantana camara*) Verbenaceae
Laurel oak (*Quercus hemisphaerica*) Fagaceae
Liatris (*Liatris* sp.) Compositae
Little silverbell (see Carolina silverbell)
Live oak (*Quercus virginiana*) Fagaceae
Lizard tail (*Saururus cernuus*) Saururaceae
Lobelia (*Lobelia* sp.) Campanulaceae
Loblolly bay (*Gordonia lasianthus*) Theaceae
Loblolly pine (*Pinus taeda*) Pinaceae
Locust (*Gleditsia* sp.) Leguminosae
Longleaf pine (*Pinus palustris*) Pinaceae
Lowbush blueberry (*Vaccinium darrowii, V. myrsinites*) Ericaceae
Lupine (*Lupinus* sp.) Leguminosae
Manatee grass (*Syringodium filiforme*) Sannichelliaceae
Maple (*Acer* sp.) Aceraceae
Marsh elder (*Iva frutescens*) Compositae
Marsh pennywort (*Hydrocotyle umbellata*) Umbelliferae
Marsh pink (*Sabatia* sp.) Gentianaceae
May haw (*Crataegus aestivalis*) Rosaceae
Meadow beauty (*Rhexia* sp.) Melastomataceae
Milkweed (*Asclepias* sp.) Asclepiadaceae
Minty rosemary (*Conradina canescens*) Labiatae
Mist flower (*Conoclinium coelestinum*) Compositae
Mockernut hickory (*Carya tomentosa*) Juglandaceae
Morning glory (*Ipomoea* sp.) Convolvulaceae
Muscadine (*Vitis rotundifolia*) Vitaceae
Myrtle oak (*Quercus myrtifolia*) Fagaceae
Myrtle-leaved holly (*Ilex myrtifolia*) Aquifoliaceae
Needle palm (*Rhapidophyllum histrix*) Palmae

Needlerush (see black needlerush)
Oak leaf hydrangea (*Hydrangea quercifolia*) Saxifragaceae
Ogeechee tupelo (*Nyssa ogeche*) Nyssaceae
Overcup oak (*Quercus lyrata*) Fagaceae
Panhandle lily (*Lilium iridollae*) Liliaceae
Panic grass (*Panicum* sp.) Gramineae
Parsley haw (*Crataegus marshallii*) Rosaceae
Partridge berry (*Mitchella repens*) Rubiaceae
Passion flower (*Passiflora incarnata*) Passifloraceae
Pawpaw (*Asimina* sp.) Annonaceae
Persimmon (*Diospyros virginiana*) Ebenaceae
Pignut hickory (*Carya glabra*) Juglandaceae
Pine lily (*Lilium catesbaei*) Liliaceae
Pineland hibiscus (*Hibiscus aculeatus*) Malvaceae
Pitcher plant (*Sarracenia* sp.) Sarraceniaceae
Planer tree (*Planera aquatica*) Ulmaceae
Poison ivy (*Toxicodendron radicans*) Anacardiaceae
Poison oak (*Toxicodendron toxicarium*) Anacardiaceae
Poison sumac (*Toxicodendron vernix*) Anacardiaceae
Pond cypress (*Taxodium ascendens*) Taxodiaceae
Pond pine (*Pinus serotina*) Pinaceae
Possum haw holly (*Ilex decidua*) Aquifoliaceae
Prickly ash (*Zanthoxylum clava-herculis*) Rutaceae
Prickly pear cactus (*Opuntia* sp.) Cactaceae
Pyramid magnolia (*Magnolia pyramidata*) Magnoliaceae
Railroad vine (*Ipomoea pes-caprae*) Convolvulaceae
Rain lily (*Zephyranthes atamasco*) Amaryllidaceae
Rattan vine (*Berchemia scandens*) Rhamnaceae
Rattlebox (*Crotolaria* sp.) Leguminosae
Rayless sunflower (*Helianthus debilis*) Compositae
Red bay (*Persea borbonia*) Lauraceae
Red buckeye (*Aesculus pavia*) Hippocastanaceae
Red cedar (*Juniperus virginiana*) Cupressaceae
Red maple (*Acer rubrum*) Aceraceae
Red mulberry (*Morus rubra*) Moraceae
Red root (*Lachnanthes caroliniana*) Haemodoraceae
Resurrection fern (*Polypodium polypodioides*) Polypodiaceae
River birch (*Betula nigra*) Betulaceae

Rhododendron (*Rhododendron* sp.) Ericaceae
Rosebud orchid (*Cleistes divaricata*) Orchidaceae
Roserush (*Lygodesmia aphylla*) Compositae
Ruellia (*Ruellia caroliniensis*) Acanthaceae
Sabal palm (*Sabal palmetto*) Palmae
Sabatia (*Sabatia* sp.) Gentianaceae
Saltbush (*Baccharis halimifolia*) Compositae
Saltgrass (*Distichlis spicata*) Gramineae
Saltmarsh aster (*Aster tenuifolia*) Compositae
Saltwort (*Salicornia bigelovii, S. virginica*) Chenopodiaceae
Sand holly (see Carolina holly)
Sand live oak (*Quercus geminata*) Fagaceae
Sand pine (*Pinus clausa*) Pinaceae
Sand post oak (*Quercus margaretta*) Fagaceae
Sassafras (*Sassafras albidum*) Lauraceae
Saw palmetto (*Serenoa repens*) Palmae
Scrub holly (*Ilex opaca* var. *arenicola*) Aquifoliaceae
Scrub palmetto (*Sabal etonia*) Palmae
Sea lavender (*Limonium carolinianum*) Plumbaginaceae
Sea oats (*Uniola paniculata*) Gramineae
Sea oxeye (*Borrichia frutescens*) Compositae
Sea purslane (*Sesuvium portulacastrum*) Aizoaceae
Seaside elder (*Iva imbricata*) Compositae
Seaside pennywort (*Hydrocotyle bonariensis*) Umbelliferae
Sebastian bush (*Sebastiania fruticosa*) Euphorbiaceae
Shoal grass (*Halodule wrightii*) Zannichelliaceae
Showy crotolaria (*Crotolaria spectibilis*) Leguminosae
Silk bay (*Persea humilis*) Lauraceae
Silverbell (*Halesia* sp.) Styracaceae
Slash pine (*Pinus elliottii*) Pinaceae
Small fruited pawpaw (*Asimina parviflora*) Annonaceae
Smilax (*Smilax* sp.) Smilacaceae
Smooth cordgrass (*Spartina alterniflora*) Gramineae
Sneezeweed (*Helenium* sp.) Compositae
Soapberry (*Sapindus marginatus*) Sapindaceae
Sourwood (*Oxydendron arboreum*) Ericaceae
Southern crabapple (*Malus angustifolia*) Rosaceae
Southern magnolia (*Magnolia grandiflora*) Magnoliaceae

Southern red oak (*Quercus falcata*) Fagaceae

Southern sugar maple (*Acer saccharum*) Aceraceae

Sparkleberry (*Vaccinium arboreum*) Ericaceae

Spatterdock (*Nuphar luteum*) Nymphaeaceae

Spiderwort (*Tradescantia ohiensis*) Commelinaceae

Spring coral root (*Corallorhiza wisteriana*) Orchidaceae

Spruce pine (*Pinus glabra*) Pinaceae

Spurge nettle (*Cnidoscolus stimulosus*) Euphorbiaceae

St. Johns-wort (*Hypericum* sp.) Guttiferae

Staggerbush (*Leucothoe* sp.) Ericaceae

Star anise (see Florida anise)

Stiffcornel dogwood (*Cornus foemina*) Cornaceae

Strawberry bush (*Euonymus americanus*) Celastraceae

Sugarberry (*Celtis laevigata*) Ulmaceae

Sundew (*Drosera* sp.) Droseraceae

Swamp bay (*Persea palustris*) Lauraceae

Swamp candelberry (*Myrica heterophylla*) Myricaceae

Swamp chestnut oak (*Quercus michauxii*) Fagaceae

Swamp coreopsis (*Coreopsis nudata*) Compositae

Swamp cyrilla (*Cyrilla racemiflora*) Cyrillaceae

Swamp privet (*Forestiera acuminata*) Oleaceae

Sweet pepperbush (*Clethra alnifolia*) Clethraceae

Sweetbay (*Magnolia virginiana*) Magnoliaceae

Sweetgum (*Liquidambar styraciflua*) Hamamelidaceae

Sweetleaf (see horse sugar)

Tar-flower (*Befaria racemosa*) Ericaceae

Tape-grass (*Vallisneria americana*) Hydrocharitaceae

Thistle (*Cirsium* sp.) Compositae

Thread dew (*Drosera filiformis*) Droseraceae

Tickseed (*Coreopsis gladiata*) Compositae

Titi (see swamp cyrilla)

Tough bumelia (*Bumelia tenax*) Sapotaceae

Trifoliate orange (*Poncirus trifoliata*) Rutaceae

Trillium (*Trillium* sp.) Trilliaceae

Trout lily (*Erythronium umbilicatum*) Liliaceae

Trumpet creeper (*Campsis radicans*) Bignoniaceae

Turkey oak (*Quercus laevis*) Fagaceae

Turtle grass (*Thalassia testudinum*) Hydrocharitaceae

Twin flower (*Dyschoriste oblongifolia*) Acanthaceae
Verbena (*Verbena brasiliensis*) Verbenaceae
Vine-wicky (*Pieris phillyreifolius*) Ericaceae
Violet (*Viola* sp.) Violaceae
Virginia creeper (*Parthenocissus quinquifolia*) Vitaceae
Virginia willow (*Itea virginica*) Saxifragaceae
Wafer ash (*Ptelea trifoliata*) Rutaceae
Wake robin (*Trillium maculatum*) Trilliaceae
Walter viburnum (*Viburnum obovatum*) Caprifoliaceae
Water hickory (*Carya aquatica*) Juglandaceae
Water oak (*Quercus nigra*) Fagaceae
Water tupelo (*Nyssa aquatica*) Nyssaceae
Wax myrtle (*Myrica cerifera*) Myricaceae
White baneberry (see baneberry)
White water lily (*Nymphaea odorata*) Nymphaeaceae
White-topped pitcher (*Sarracenia leucophylla*) Sarraceniaceae
White-topped sedge (*Dichromena latifolia*) Cyperaceae
Widgeon grass (*Ruppia maritima*) Ruppiaceae
Wild azalea (*Rhododendron canescens*) Ericaceae
Wild coffee (*Psychotria nervosa*) Rubiaceae
Wild grape (*Vitis* sp.) Vitaceae
Wild hibiscus (*Hibiscus* sp.) Malvaceae
Wild olive (*Osmanthus americanus*) Oleaceae
Wild rice (*Zizania aquatica*) Gramineae
Willow (*Salix* sp.) Salicaceae
Winged sumac (*Rhus copallina*) Anacardiaceae
Wiregrass (*Aristida stricta*) Gramineae
Witch hazel (*Hamamelis virginiana*) Hamamelidaceae
Wood nettle (*Laportea canadensis*) Urticaceae
Wood vamp (*Decumaria barbara*) Saxifragaceae
Yaupon holly (*Ilex vomitoria*) Aquifoliaceae
Yellow anise (*Illicium parviflorum*) Illiciaceae
Yellow poplar (*Liriodendron tulipifera*) Magnoliaceae
Yellow-eyed grass (*Xyris* sp.) Xyridaceae
Yellow-fringed orchid (*Habenaria* sp.) Orchidaceae
Yucca (*Yucca* sp.) Agavaceae

REFERENCES AND SUGGESTED READING

Ashton, Ray E., and Patricia Sawyer Ashton. 1981. *Handbook of Reptiles and Amphibians of Florida. Part One: The Snakes.* Miami, FL: Windward Publishing.

Ashton, Ray E., and Patricia Sawyer Ashton. 1985. *Handbook of Reptiles and Amphibians of Florida. Part Two: The Lizards, Turtles & Crocodilians.* Miami, FL: Windward Publishing.

Ashton, Ray E., and Patricia Sawyer Ashton. 1988. *Handbook of Reptiles and Amphibians of Florida. Part Three: The Amphibians.* Miami, FL: Windward Publishing.

Avers, Peter E., and Kenneth C. Bracy. undated. *Soils and Physiography of the Osceola National Forest.* Osceola National Forest.

Boyd, Mark F., Ed. 1956. *Florida Place-Names of Indian Derivation Either Obsolescent or Retained Together with Others of Recent Application.* Special Publication No. 1. Tallahassee, FL: Bureau of Geology, Florida Department of Environmental Protection.

Brown, Larry N. 1987. *A Checklist of Florida's Mammals.* Tallahassee, FL: Nongame Wildlife Program, Florida Game and Fresh Water Fish Commission.

Carter, Elizabeth F., and John L. Pearce. 1985. *A Canoeing and Kayaking Guide to the Streams of Florida. Volume 1, North Central Peninsula and Panhandle.* Hillsborough, NC: Menasha Ridge Press.

Cerulean, Susan, and Ann Morrow. 1993. *Florida Wildlife Viewing Guide.* Helena, MT: Falcon Press Publishing.

Clark, William E., Rufus H. Musgrove, Clarence G. Menke, and Joseph W. Cagle, Jr. 1964. *Water Resources of Alachua, Bradford, Clay, and Union Counties, Florida.* Report of Investigations No. 35. Tallahassee, FL: Bureau of Geology, Florida Department of Environmental Protection.

Cruickshank, Helen G., Ed. 1986. *Bartram in Florida, 1774.* The Florida Federation of Garden Clubs.

Easley, M. Caroline, and Walter S. Judd. 1993. Vascular Flora of Little Talbot Island, Duval County, Florida. *Castanea* 55(3): 162–177.

Florida Natural Areas Inventory. 1990. *Guide to the Natural Communities of Florida.* Tallahassee, FL: Florida Natural Areas Inventory and Florida Department of Natural Resources.

Forested Wetlands of Florida - Their Management and Use. 1976. Gainesville, FL: Center for Wetlands, University of Florida.

Gildersleeve, Nancy B., and Susan K. Gildersleeve, Eds. 1991. *Florida Hiking Trails.* Gainesville, FL: Maupin House.

Godfrey, Robert K. 1988. *Trees, Shrubs, and Woody Vines of Northern Florida and Adjacent Georgia and Alabama.* Athens, GA: University of Georgia Press.

Grow, Gerald. 1987. *Florida Parks: A Guide to Camping in Nature.* Tallahassee, FL: Longleaf Publications.

Kurz, Herman, and Kenneth Wagner. 1957. *Tidal Marshes of the Gulf and Atlantic Coasts of Northern Florida and Charleston, South Carolina.* Florida State University Studies, No. 24. Tallahassee, FL: The Florida State University.

Lane, Ed. 1986. *Karst in Florida.* Special Publication No. 29. Tallahassee, FL: Bureau of Geology, Florida Department of Environmental Protection.

Lane, James A. 1984. *A Birder's Guide to Florida.* Denver, CO: L & P Press.

Mohlenbrock, Robert H. 1976. Woody Plants of the Ocala National Forest, Florida. *Castanea* 41:309–319.

Moler, Paul. 1988. *A Checklist of Florida's Amphibians and Reptiles.* Tallahassee, FL: Nongame Wildlife Program, Florida Game and Fresh Water Fish Commission.

Myers, Ronald L., and John J. Ewel, Eds. 1990. *Ecosystems of Florida.* Orlando, FL: University of Central Florida Press.

Nelson, Gil. 1994. *The Trees of Florida: A Reference and Field Guide.* Sarasota, FL: Pineapple Press.

Patton, Janet Easterday, and Walter S. Judd. 1986. Vascular Flora of Paynes Prairie Basin and Alachua Sink Hammock, Alachua County, Florida. *Castanea* 51(2):88–110.

Puri, Harbans S. and Robert O. Vernon. 1964. *Special Publica-tion No. 5 Revised: Summary of the Geology of Florida and A Guidebook to the Classic Exposures.* Tallahassee, FL: Bureau of Geology, Florida Department of Environmental Protection.

Rosenau, Jack C., Glen L. Faulkner, Charles W. Hendry, Jr., and Robert W. Hull. 1977. *Springs of Florida.* Bulletin 31 (revised). Tallahassee, FL: Bureau of Geology, Florida Department of Environmental Protection.

Sanger, Marjory Bartlett. 1983. *Forest in the Sand.* New York: Atheneum.

Snedaker, Sammuel C., and Ariel E. Lugo. Undated. *Ecology of the Ocala National Forest.* Ocala National Forest.

Soil Conservation Service. 1981. *26 Ecological Communities of Florida.*

Stevenson, Henry M. 1976. *Vertebrates of Florida.* Gainesville, FL: University Presses of Florida.

Stevenson, Henry M. 1988. *Checklist of Florida's Birds.* Talla-hassee, FL: Nongame Wildlife Program, Florida Game and Fresh Water Fish Commission.

Tebeau, Charlton W. 1973. *A History of Florida.* Miami: Univer-sity of Miami Press.

Williams, Kenneth E., David Nicol, and Anthony Randazzo. 1977. *The Geology of the Western Part of Alachua County, Florida.* Report of Investigations No. 85. Tallahassee, FL: Bureau of Geology, Florida Department of Environmental Protection.

OTHER SOURCES OF INFORMATION

DeLorme Mapping Company
P.O. Box 298
Freeport, ME 04032
(207) 865-4171
publishes *Florida Atlas & Gazetteer* (detailed road maps with guide to out-door recreation)

Florida Association of Canoe Liveries & Outfitters
Box 1764
Arcadia, FL 33821
(941) 494-1215
free list of canoe outfitters

Florida Audubon Society
460 Hwy. 436, Suite 200
Casselberry, FL 32707
(407) 260-8300

Florida Board of Tourism
Florida Department of Commerce
126 West Van Buren St.
Tallahassee, FL 32399-2000
(904) 487-1462
free road map of Florida

Florida Department of Environmental Protection
Division of Recreation and Parks
3900 Commonwealth Blvd.
Tallahassee, FL 32399-3000
(904) 487-4784
information on parks, free canoe trail guide, and maps with access points for 36 Florida canoe trails

Florida Game and Fresh Water Fish Commission
620 S. Meridian St.
Tallahassee, FL 32399-1600
(904) 488-4674 for general information
(904) 488-1960 for Florida freshwater fishing handbook

Florida Sierra Club
462 Fernwood Rd.
Key Biscayne, FL 33149
(305) 361-1292

Florida Trail Association, Inc.
P.O. Box 13708
Gainesville, FL 32604
(904) 378-8823
(800) 343-1882 (Florida only)

Florida Wildlife Federation
  2545 Blairstone Pines Dr.
  P.O. Box 6870
  Tallahassee, FL 32314-6870
  (904) 656-7113

Save the Manatee Club
  500 N. Maitland Ave.
  Maitland, FL 32751
  1-800-432-JOIN

St. Johns River Water Management District
  P.O. Box 1429
  Palatka, FL 32178-1429
  (904) 329-4500

The Nature Conservancy
  Florida Field Office
  2699 Lee Rd., Suite 500
  Winter Park, FL 32789
  (407) 628-5887

U.S. Fish & Wildlife Service
  6620 S. Point Dr., South
  Suite 310
  Jacksonville, FL 32216-0912
  (904) 232-2580

U.S. Forest Service
  Woodcrest Office Park
  325 John Knox Rd.
  Building F
  Tallahassee, FL 32303
  (904) 942-9300

INDEX

Listings of wildlife and plant species in this index generally refer to locations with significant information about the cited species. Not all references to plants and animals in the text are included.

239